Abraham Coles

The Light of the World
being the second part of the Life and teachings of Our Lord, in verse

ISBN/EAN: 9783337886141

Printed in Europe, USA, Canada, Australia, Japan

Cover: Foto ©Lupo / pixelio.de

More available books at **www.hansebooks.com**

Abraham Coles

The Light of the World

being the second part of the Life and teachings of Our Lord, in verse

THE

LIGHT OF THE WORLD,

BEING

THE SECOND PART

OF THE

Life and Teachings of our Lord,

IN VERSE.

By ABRAHAM COLES, M.D., LL.D.

AUTHOR OF "DIES IRÆ IN THIRTEEN VERSIONS,"
"THE MICROCOSM AND OTHER POEMS,"
"OLD GEMS IN NEW SETTINGS,"
ETC., ETC.

NEW YORK

D. APPLETON AND COMPANY

1885

ADVERTISER PRINTING HOUSE,
NEWARK, N. J.

CONTENTS.

PAGE

THE PREFACE, - - - - - - - xi.-xxxi.

I. THE KINGDOM OF GOD.—*Christ's discourse with Nicodemus. The New Birth. God's great love. The Son of Man lifted up. Hymn.* (John ii. 23-25 ; iii. 1-21.)   1

II. JOHN'S FINAL TESTIMONY — THE HEAVENLY BRIDEGROOM.—*Everlasting Life in the Son. Hymn.* - - - - - - - (John iii. 22-36.)   14

III. THE DIALOGUE AT JACOB'S WELL.—*The Living Water. True Worship. "This is the Christ, the Saviour of the World." Hymn.* (John iv. 1-42.)   19

IV. RETURN TO GALILEE.—REJECTION AT NAZARETH.— *The nobleman's son healed at Cana. Jesus teaches publicly. Leaves Nazareth and comes to Capernaum. Hymn.* - - - (John iv. 43-54 ; Luke iv. 16-31.)   29

V. ABODE AT CAPERNAUM.—THE APOSTOLATE.— *Call of Peter, Andrew, James and John. Hymn.* - - - - - - - (Matt. iv. 13-22 ; Mark i. 16-20 ; Luke v. 1-11.)   38

VI. HEALER AND SAVIOUR.—*Christ heals a demoniac, Peter's wife's mother, and others. De-*

PAGE.

*scription of diseases. Cures a leper. Proves
His power to forgive sins by making a paralytic walk. Psalm ciii.* - - - - 44
(Mark i. 21—ii. 12 ; Luke iv. 31—v. 26 ; Matt. viii.
2-4 ; ix. 2-8.)

VII. THE NEW DISPENSATION.—THE SABBATH.—
*Call of Levi (Matthew). Why Jesus' disci-
ples do not fast. New wine put into new bottles. He heals the impotent man at the Pool
of Bethesda on the Sabbath. Justifies Himself before the Sanhedrim. His disciples
pluck ears of corn. The Son of Man is Lord
of the Sabbath. Restores a man with a
withered hand. The elders charge blasphemy
and seek to kill Him. Hymn,* - - - 55
(Matt. ix. 9-13 ; xii. 1-21 ; Mark ii. 13-28 ; iii. 1-12 ;
Luke v. 27-32 ; Luke vi. 1-5 ; John v. 1-47.)

VIII. THE SERMON ON THE MOUNT.—*He chooses and
ordains the Twelve. Heals great numbers
come from all parts. Teaches and legislates
with supreme authority. Psalm i.* - - 75
(Matt. v. 1—vii. 29; Mark iii. 13-19; Luke vi. 12-49.)

IX. THE CENTURION.—WIDOW OF NAIN.—IMPRIS-
ONMENT AND DEATH OF JOHN.—*He heals
the Centurion's servant. Raises the Widow
of Nain's son. John in prison sends two of
his disciples to Jesus. Christ's eulogy. Ode.* 98
(Matt. viii. 1, 5-13; xi. 2-19; xiv. 3-12; Mark vi. 17-
29; Luke vii. 1-35.)

X. THE PENITENT WOMAN.—THE UNPARDON-

PAGE.

ABLE SIN.—BEWARE OF COVETOUSNESS.—
*While at meat at the house of Simon, the
Pharisee, a woman, who was a sinner, enters
and anoints his feet. Psalm li. Demons
cast out with a word. Blasphemy against
the Holy Ghost. They seek a sign. The sign
of the prophet Jonah. Who are His mother
and brethren. The rich fool. The spared
fig tree.* - - - - - - - 109

(Luke vii. 36-50; viii. 19-21; xi. 14-36; xii. 13-21;
xiii. 1-9; Matt. xii. 22-50; Mark iii. 19-35.)

XI. WHAT THE KINGDOM OF HEAVEN IS LIKE.—
*The Parable of the Sower, of the Tares, of
the Mustard Seed, of the Leaven, of the Hid
Treasure, of the Pearl, of the Drag-net.
Hymn.* - - - - - - - 128

(Matt. xiii. 1-52; Mark iv. 1-20; Luke viii. 4-15.)

XII. TEMPEST STILLED.—DEMONIAC OF GADARA.—
JAIRUS' DAUGHTER.—A BELIEVING TOUCH.
He heals two blind men and a dumb man. - 135

(Matt. viii. 23-34; Mark iv. 35—v. 43; Luke viii. 22-
56.)

XIII. THE TWELVE SENT OUT.—FIVE THOUSAND
FED. — *Walks on the water. The True
Bread. Hymn.* - - - - - 143

(Matt. ix. 35—x. 39; xiv. 12-36; Mark vi. 7-13; Luke
ix. 1-17; John vi. 1-69.)

XIV. WHAT DEFILES.—SYROPHENICIAN WOMAN.—
SEVEN THOUSAND FED. - - - - 159

(Matt. xv. 1-39; Mark vii. 1—viii. 9.)

CONTENTS.

PAGE.

XV. The Transfiguration.—Demoniac Cured.
—*Duties of Faith, Humility, Forgiveness.
Parable of the Unmerciful Servant.* - - 166
(Matt. xvi. 13-23; xvii. 1-27; xviii. 1-35; Mark ix. 1-
50; Luke ix. 18—x. 20.)

XVI. Jerusalem through Samaria.— *Ten lepers
cleansed. Feast of the Tabernacles. The
woman taken in adultery. True Freedom.
The Good Samaritan. Martha and Mary.
The man born blind healed on the Sabbath.
The Good Shepherd. I and My Father are
one. Hymn.* - - - - - - 176
(Luke ix. 51-56; xvii. 11-19; John vii. 8—x. 42.)

XVII. I am the Resurrection and the Life.—
*Sickness and death of Lazarus. Raised to
life. Theories. Explanation of terms. Hymn.* 194
(John xi. 1-46.)

XVIII. Retires beyond the Jordan.—*Dines with a
chief Pharisee on the Sabbath. On coveting
chief seats at table. Parable of the Great
Supper, of the Lost Sheep, of the Prodigal
Son, of the Unjust Steward, of the Rich
Man and Lazarus, of the Unjust Judge, of
the Pharisee and Publican. Blesses little
children. The Rich Young Man. Danger
of riches. Following Him in the regeneration. Parable of the Laborers in the Vineyard; Unprofitable Servants.* - - - 210
(John xi. 47-54; xii. 1, 17-19; Mark x. 1, 13-31;
Luke xiii. 22, 31—xiv. 24—xvi. 31; Matt. xxi.
1-46; Luke xvii. 7-10.)

PAGE·

XIX. RETURN TO JERUSALEM THROUGH JERICHO.—
*James and John's ambitious request. Blind
Bartimeus. Zaccheus the Publican. Para-
ble of the Ten Pounds. Public entry into
Jerusalem. Second cleansing of the Temple.
Of the Two Sons. Parable of the Wicked
Husbandman.* - - - - - - 231
(Matt. xx. 17-34; xxi. 1-41; Mark x. 32-52; xi. 1—
xii. 9; Luke xviii. 31—xix. 27—xx. 19.)

XX. NEARING THE END.—*Of paying tribute to Cæsar.
The question of the Sadducees, deniers of the
resurrection. The Messiah David's Son and .
Lord The pride and hypocrisy of the Scribes
and Pharisees exposed. Vision of the fate
of Jerusalem. The widow's mite. Leaves
the Temple for the last time. The disciples
admire its stones, etc. He foretells its destruction and that of the City. The duty of
watching. The Parable of the Ten Virgins,
of the Sheep and Goats. Dies Iræ.* - - 245
(Matt. xxii. 15—xxv. 46; Mark xii. 13—xiii. 37; Luke
xx. 20—xxi. 37.)

XXI. THE LAST SUPPER.—FAREWELL WORDS.—*At
a supper given in Bethany at the house of
Simon the leper, Mary anoints His head and
feet. Passover and Memorial Supper. He
washes the disciples' feet. The many mansions. Intercessory Prayer.* - - - 276
(Matt. xxvi. 1-35; Mark xiv. 1-25; Luke xxii. 1-38;
John xii. 1-8, 46; xiii. 1—xvii. 26.)

PAGE.

XXII. The Betrayal, Trial and Sentence.—
Judas' remorse and suicide.   -   -   -   295

(Matt. xxvi. 36—xxvii. 66; Mark xiv. 26—xv. 20;
Luke xxii. 39—xxiii. 24; John xviii. 1—xix. 16.)

XXIII. The Crucifixion and Entombment.—*Hymns.*   317

(Matt. xxvi. 31—xxvii. 66; Mark xv. 20-47; Luke
xxiii. 26-49; John xix. 16-42.)

XXIV. Resurrection and Ascension. — *Touch me
not. I am not yet ascended. Note. Joins
two disciples on their way to Emmaus.
Easter and Ascension Hymns. Pentecost.
Speaking with tongues. Peter's discourse.
Veni, Creator Spiritus.*   -   -   -   -   331

(Matt. xxviii. 1-20; Mark xvi. 1-16; Luke xxiv. 1-51;
John xx. 1—xxi. 25; Acts ii. 1-38.)

PREFACE.

THE EVANGEL,* forming the First Part of *"The Life and Teachings of Our Lord,"* in Verse, barring some anticipations of events, stopped at the threshold of His ministry; and the present Volume—THE LIGHT OF THE WORLD—is a continuation of the same through the entire Four Gospels to the end. Since the publication of that First Part, other Lives of Christ in Prose have appeared; but if it be true as George Herbert supposes,

"A verse may find him who a sermon flies,"

the writer indulges the hope that the novelty of a Complete Life in Verse, including all His Words, conscientiously faithful, and one from which everything fictitious is care-

---

*There has appeared, since the first publication of THE EVANGEL, Mr. Edwin Arnold's interesting (but somewhat misleading) Poem entitled "The Light of Asia, or, the Great Renunciation, being the Life and Teaching of Gautama, Prince of India and Founder of Buddhism." Four hundred and seventy millions of our race, the author estimates, live and die in the tenets of Gautama. Who was Gautama? Did such a person ever exist? If so, What was the purport of his teachings? According to our author, he was born in the seventh century before Christ; other authorities make his birth two centuries later. Gautama was the family name; his individual name was Siddartha; Buddha was titular, meaning "The Enlightened One." He appeared as a Reformer of Brahminism, and an Opposer of Caste. His history is full of fable. Concerning his teaching, the author remarks, there has arisen prodigious controversy among the learned. He states his "own conviction that a third of mankind could never have been brought to believe in blank abstractions, or in Nothingness as the issue and crown of Being." The battle has raged chiefly around the import of three terms

fully excluded—if tolerably executed, may still find acceptance at the hands of some readers. All people are not alike.
Tastes differ. Some people seldom or never read a line of
poetry, good or bad. Another class are so exclusive in
their likings as to deny even the name of poetry to some of
the most admired pieces in the language. They will not
allow, for example, that Goldsmith's "Deserted Village"
has any just claim to be called poetry. They affirm, and
affirm truly, that it contains no expression that might not

viz.: "Nirvana," "Dharma" and "Karma." According to most authorities, Nirvana
means annihilation, the Buddhist's *Summum Bonum ;* for, to be is to be miserable ; all
existence is sorrow. Dharma is law or truth or righteousness. Karma (literally
"doing") expresses the sum of a man's deservings, both his merits and demerits,
which is the only thing that survives when a man dies. The soul and self cease to exist, but this Karma, which is a pure abstraction, a mere word, and not an entity at all,
is, nevertheless, the active cause of a new being ; and transmigration consists in innumerable transfers, not of a soul for that has perished, but of merit and demerit,
until at last all demerit being done away with, Nirvana is reached, which is the end
of births and the final extinction of being. When a bad man dies, the demerit may
be such, as that, passing by the vilest of animal forms, it shall descend to originate a
new existence in one of the 136 Buddhist hells situated in the interior of the earth,
where the shortest term of punishment is ten millions of years ; the longest in-
computable. This is what makes Nirvana so desirable, that all existence even
the highest, that of deva or god, involves the possibility of this degradation.
Never was there a system more intensely pessimistic. Mr. Arnold has given us only
the brighter side—in obedience, as he says, to the laws of poetic art, omitting much·
Beyond some humane and excellent precepts, Buddhism has little to recommend
it. Its highest hope is a horror, and this is attainable only on impossible conditions.
No one may pray, for there is no one to pray to, no Helper. This is Buddhism at its
best ; as it was– not as it is, "sorely overlaid with corruptions," its vitality gone.
Woe to the race, if it had no other Gospel. In view of the disposition exhibited on
the part of some to challenge a comparison between the system of Buddhism and Christianity, to set up Gautama as a rival to Christ, the writer has been led to give to
this Second Part the title of THE LIGHT OF THE WORLD, in contradistinction to that of
the somewhat invidious one, *The Light of Asia,* adopted by Mr. Arnold for his work.

be used in eloquent and descriptive prose. For like reasons they regard Dryden and Pope as clever versifiers, but not as entitled to take rank as poets; so true is it, that bigots are not confined to religion. These devotees of a creed and slaves of a theory scornfully reject what does not conform to their standard. But that narrowness, which refuses to let people be pleased in their own way, is unamiable to say the least.

In view of the impossibility of framing a definition of Poetry, that shall so fix its meaning, as to furnish a just rule for determining in all cases what is Poetry and what is not, it is fortunate, that some security, against the caprice of individual opinion and the tyranny of fashion, can be found in one easily applied test, if not of genuineness, of fitness. It is within everyone's reach, and no one need fear to apply it. Poetry is certainly Verse, even if it be something more. Verse, regarded as a means to an end, which is pleasure—either the pleasure of beauty or utility, one or both—is always, it is safe to say, a legitimate instrument, when it serves these purposes, whether men choose to dignify it with the name of Poetry or not. The mere fact, that Pope's " Essay on Man " has passed through numerous editions, and given pleasure to countless readers during a hundred and fifty years and more, is a sufficient vindication of its metric form, in spite of all that has been said, or can be said, in regard to the unfitness of the subject for poetical treatment. His biographer, Dr. Johnson, says: "Its reception was not uniform: some thought it a very imperfect piece, though not without good lines." To say that it is shallow in its philosophy, and sophistical in its reasoning, and of no moral value, besides being, in no proper sense, Poetry, only strengthens the evidence in favor of the superior effectiveness of Verse; since, in that case, it would be due to the inherent buoyancy of this alone, that a showy piece of pretentious wisdom has been kept afloat so long.

Some go so far as to assert, that Didactic Poetry is a contradiction in terms; and that no poetry can have the function of teaching; which, if it be true, so much the worse for Poetry; for if the name is to be so restricted, as to sever Poetry from all moral and religious uses, then is there relegated to Verse distinctively, a preëminent office of instruction and delight, not attainable to Prose and unfitted for Poetry, making it the nobler of the two. It suffices for the argument, that Verse has been used from time immemorial for setting forth highest things; and found to be an admirable expedient for stimulating attention and awakening interest, less perfectly accomplished by other means. If Pope chooses to trammel himself with the incumbrance of metre and rhyme in a Moral Piece, having found that he could express himself with greater conciseness, force and grace in that way than any other, he surely ought to be allowed to do so, without subjecting himself to the imputation of folly. Doubtless his Essay could have been written in prose. Indeed it was declared at the time that it was so written, and that the poet did little more than translate Bolingbroke's prose into verse. But in prose it is certain that it would have had but few readers.

Hegel is credited with saying, "That metre is the first and only condition absolutely demanded by poetry, yea, even more necessary than figurative, picturesque diction."

Sir Philip Sidney wrote a Defense of Poetry. We are satisfied to limit ourselves to a Defense of Verse. Archbishop Trench in the Introduction to his *Sacred Latin Poetry* elaborates a Defense of Rhyme. He says: "The non-recognition of this, man's craving after, and deep delight in, the rhythmic and periodic—a craving which nature everywhere meets and gratifies and which all truest Art seeks to gratify as well—a seeing nothing in all this but a trick and artifice applied from without, lies at the root of that singular theory concerning the unfitness of poetry to be the vehicle of our highest addresses to God, and most reverent utterances about Him. * * * Everyone who has watched the effect on his own mind of the orderly marching of a regiment, or of the successive breaking of the waves upon the shore, or aught else which is thus *rhythmic and periodic*, knows, that in this, inspiring as it does the sense of order and proportion and purpose, there is ever an elevating and solemnizing power." Young, in his "Essay on Lyric Poetry," accounts for the *pleasure of rhyme* on the principle, that "difficulties overcome give grace and pleasure." He further remarks: "It holds true in the province of writing as of war, the more danger the more honor." To a person engaged in a hazardous undertaking such a thought is certainly encouraging.

Of Lives of Christ in Prose there are many and excellent. The present one in Verse grew out of the conviction that a true non-epical Life in Verse (there being none) was a desideratum; that it was fitting, feasible, and calculated to be useful; that if a Prose Life was lawful, a Life in Verse was equally so; that no objection could be urged against the one, that did not lie against the other; that if a Life in Verse involved a change in diction, so did a Life in Prose involve it; so did every translation out of the original Greek, the most literal as well as the most free, involve it; so did all exegesis and interpretation involve it; the plain conclusion being, that nothing is sacred but the sense; and that to a proper understanding of this even, the employment of verbal and sentential equivalents is often indispensable. As well might one quarrel with his Dictionary, as to make these inevitable changes a ground of offense. Were they less inevitable, they would still be useful, for everybody knows how much light is derived from synonyms —from putting, that is to say, the same truth into new words.

It is surprising, how much real ignorance is to be found among not a few habitual readers of the Bible, so that, if singly asked, 'Understandest thou what thou readest?' they would suddenly be roused to the consciousness, how imperfect was their knowledge of the meaning of words with which they had been familiar from childhood; for nothing is more delusive, than this external familiarity with the mere garb of thought, the language and nothing more. The mind, under the benumbing spell of these incessant repetitions of old words, may have come to perceive vaguely or not at all their import; so that an important point is gained, if, startled by the strangeness of new phraseology, this slumber of the faculties is broken. For nothing profits, unless it is understood.

It may be reckoned among the advantages of the poetical form that it necessitates these explanatory changes. Owing, moreover, to the fact, that the poetic diction is naturally allied to the antique style of the Received Version, and shares its aloofness from everyday speech, a Poetic Life may fairly claim this as weighing in its favor, against the exclusive pretensions of Prose. This matter of literary perspective is not a thing to be slighted. An object can be too close to the eye. A certain remoteness is favorable for right vision. No writer, without necessity, would wish to cut himself off from the benefit to be derived from this source. But in the present case, the haze of distance

b

would not be the only gain, could the writer, when he had
transported himself back to the time when our matchless
English Version was first made, so far catch the spirit of the
age, as to animate and mould his diction into some likeness
of the prevailing form—for, by so doing, he might hope to
appropriate a portion of that favor accorded to the sweetness and charm of that Version so dear to all hearts.

There is a fashion in Verse no less than in dress. The
reigning mode of the fifteenth and sixteenth centuries differed from that of the seventeenth and eighteenth. The
earlier mode was characterized by a greater naturalness,
variety and freedom—"robes loosely flowing," a graceful
negligence, "a wild civility," not unfrequently more be-
witching,

> "Than when art
> Is too precise in every part."

The later mode is chiefly distinguished from this, by having no lines overlapping and running into each other, but
each complete in itself; weighed as well as measured; a
nice adjustment and balancing of parts; a rigid properness
and stateliness, and a strictness of etiquette, requiring you

> "Still to be neat, still to be drest
> As you were going to a feast."

This kind of Verse in long poems is apt to tire from its mo-
notony ; and, owing to its artificial structure, is particularly

unfavorable, in translating, to exactness and fidelity. The
earlier mode was therefore chosen, both because of its con-
temporaneousness and its greater suitableness for his purpose.

Lessing is undoubtedly right in considering, that the
Gospels are immortal masterpieces, which it would be vain
to hope to rival. " Who," he asks, " after the Evangelists
will venture to write the Life of Jesus?" So far from dis-
senting from this view, it is the writer's own ; and therefore
it is, that he has studiously avoided the slightest departure
from those divine originals. He has reverently and faithfully followed them word by word, line by line, verse by
verse, chapter by chapter, each Gospel apart and the four
together. At the same time, he has been glad to avail himself of the labors of those (Robinson in particular) who
have devoted much time and study to the necessary task of
rearranging, blending and harmonizing the statements of
the Inspired Four, without which a complete and consecu-
tive Life were impossible. The Evangelists wrote in Greek.
Of course, the great critic could not have intended to in-
terdict translations; nor would he mean to say that there
should be no new versions. A new version is not a new Life
nor a different one. While no version can have the authority of the Greek Original, still in view of the great excellence of our Protestant Version, its claim to consideration
is hardly inferior. The writer, taking this for a basis, has

sought to preserve unaltered, as far as possible, its abounding felicities of expression; to retain, as it has been itself so successful in retaining, the unstudied simplicities and sincerities of the Sacred Story; to imitate the swift brevities of a record, which finds means to crowd into the narrow compass of a few pages the prodigious fulness of an unparalleled Life and Mission. Aiming at something higher than merely chopping up prose into rhymed couplets, he has labored to combine, with his attempt to weave into a seamless oneness the Fourfold Gospel, an exegetical purpose, making his work interpretative like a Commentary. In the spirit of loyalty to the Greek Original as well as to the English Version he was careful to consult both; and to avail himself of such critical helps as were within his reach, in order that he might get at the right meaning and the exact shade of meaning. In performing a task so delicate and difficult, it would have been unpardonable not to have done so.

Great and good men for many hundred years, having given their lives to the study and explanation of these Divine Writings, it would be strange, if their learned labors had not yielded some fruit worth the gathering. Besides what has come down to us from the past, the modern press is teeming with new publications of the greatest value, all having reference to one great central Figure. The shelves of our libraries groan with the weight of voluminous Com.

mentaries—conspicuous among these is a most painstaking and excellent one (Stier's) consisting of nine large volumes devoted to " The Words of Jesus " alone. The entire field having been found too large for cultivation, it has been divided into sections, one of which is given to "The Miracles of Our Lord," another to " The Parables." etc., forming books of ample size—the last few months having added two more on the Parables to those already existing. During the last decade the Lives of Christ have multiplied as never before, eloquently written and rich in information.

With these sources of knowledge and help open to him, it would seem that he ought to have been well equipped for his undertaking; and that his only difficulty would be the embarrassment arising from abundance. But while he endeavored to glean from all these fields, what was adapted to throw light upon the Sacred Text, he aimed to make all subservient to a textual, not a glossarial, enrichment, and a completer setting forth, elucidation and unfolding of the entire Gospel story in unadorned verse, relying on the intrinsic beauty and grandeur of the theme for awakening interest, making a book, which should be at once a Life and a Commentary, that could be easily read in a few sittings. Any attempt to add to or take from the sacred narrative, except in the way of elucidation, he felt was a kind of impiety. Besides, he saw no occasion for any profane inventions. Nothing was wanting to completeness in respect to plan or material. It has its own beginning, middle and end, and all needful machinery within itself. To seek to refashion it according to heathen models was, therefore, he considered, to place the human above the divine; and was sanctioned neither by religion nor taste.

A writer setting out to produce an Epic Poem of which Christ should be the Hero, his first step, in conformity with all custom, is from the region of Truth into that of Fable. The Muse, to be sure, is now no longer tethered and held down by reality: but while in this there may be some poetical gain, it cannot be denied that this ampler freedom has, in this case particularly, a most serious drawback; for unhappily, the ornaments of fiction tend, as has been repeatedly said, to give to truth itself the appearance of fable. It is difficult for those, not under the dominion of classical prejudice, to become wholly reconciled to the introduction of these heathenisms, or any modification of them, into a Christian Poem. At best, they belong to another age, and deserve to become obsolete. Poetry loses nothing by the rejection of these pedantic fopperies—the cast-off finery of former times; and the substitution of a direct and manly utterance for glittering prettinesses, insincerities and affectations. Even Virgil's,

" Oceanum interea surgens Aurora reliquit—"

is a round-about and pretty way of saying that the sun

rose, but is not necessarily more poetical than the statement of the fact in plain words.

Examples of the Epic, with Christ for the subject, are not wanting. One of the earliest and most famous of these is Vida's "CHRISTIAD, *in Six Books*," written, we are told, in the purest Virgilian Latin, and "first published in the year 1535, with an apologetical advertisement at the close of the work, in which the author excuses the boldness of the attempt by informing the reader, that he was induced to begin and to persevere in his undertaking by the solicitations and munificence of the two pontiffs Leo X. and Clement VII."* Vida was born at Cremona; and it is to his "Christiad" that Milton refers in the fourth line of the fourth verse of his poem on "The Passion:"

> " Loud o'er the rest Cremona's trump doth sound."

It is mentioned as one of the merits of his work that " he avoids the error of mingling the profane fables of the heathen mythology with the mysteries of the Christian Religion," by which, however, is not meant that he dispenses with all fiction. A specimen of the Poem may be seen in the following extract, descriptive of the descent of the Holy Ghost as a dove at the baptism of Jesus:

> " Protinus aurifluo Jordanes gurgite fulsit;
> Et superûm vasto intonuit domus alta fragore.

*Roscoe's Life of Leo X.

Insuper et coeli claro delapsa columba est
Vertice per purum candenti argentea pluma
Terga, sed aurati circum et rutilantibus alis:
Jamque viam late signans super astitit ambos,
Coelestique aura pendens afflavit utrumque.
Vox simul et magni rubra genitoris et aethra
Audita est nati dulcem testantis amorem."

Christiad IV., 214–222.

In German, we have Klopstock's "Messiah, *in Fifteen Books*," which came to be regarded, by many of his own countrymen at least, as an Epic equal to those of Dante, Milton and Tasso. In English, Samuel Wesley, the father of John and Charles, wrote " The Life of Christ, *a Heroic Poem, in Ten Books*," more remarkable, it is thought, for piety and learning than poetic merit; although it did not want admirers among contemporaries.

The only other attempt of this kind known to the writer is "The Christiad, *a Divine Poem*," by Henry Kirk White. It was a work, it seems, that lay very near the poet's heart, and he touchingly laments in a couple of stanzas appended to the unfinished work, written a short time before his death, that he should not live to complete it. His biographer, Southey, while praising the Fragment as evincing great power in its execution, nevertheless objects to it, for the reason already adverted to, that "the mixture of mythology makes the truth itself appear fabulous."

A common cause of failure in this and other undertakings, no doubt, is over-ambition. Did we not know that what

is simple and what is obvious is apt to be despised or over-
looked, we should be at a loss to explain why some poet
qualified for the undertaking, has not long ere this, dis-
carding fiction and the high heroic method, been tempted,
out of the sufficient and matchless materials supplied in the
authentic memorabilia contained in the Four Gospels, to
compose a True Life instead of a partly false one.   It can
hardly be pretended, that the reason for such a Life remaining so long among "things unattempted," is its unfitness
in that naked shape for poetic treatment.   If a noble life
purely human, as Milton imagines, is of itself a true poem,
surely a Life divinely perfect like that of Christ cannot be
less; and the supposition that it stands in need of fictitious
aid to make it beautiful is wholly inadmissable.

The writer is not sure, that it will be accepted as an
apology for his temerity, that, believing in the utility of
such a work, he ventured because there was no one else to
venture.   Having observed that verse lent itself wonderfully to the requirements of brevity and strength, he knew
no reason why it should not be used in unfolding the unspeakable uniqueness of that Divine Personality, manifested
both in the sphere of speech and conduct, with which we
are made familiar in the Gospels.   Painting and Sculpture
have done their best; but neither pencil nor chisel has been
able to produce anything better than a lifeless copy of the
Divine Original.   But portrayed in the pages of the Four
Evangelists, the picture lives :

" Let be, let be ;
What was he that did make it? See, my lord,
Would you not deem it breathed, and that those veins
Did verily bear blood?"

He did not hide from himself the difficulties or dangers of
the undertaking; or his individual unfitness to execute it
worthily. If, as Cowper says, "A just translation of any
ancient poet in rhyme is impossible, since no human in-
genuity can be equal to the task of closing every couplet
with sounds homotonous, expressing at the same time the
full sense and only the sense of the original," how could he
hope to succed in a work, certainly not less difficult, and
infinitely more delicate—owing to the sacredness of the
matter—that of turning the plain prose of the Gospels into
easy rhyme, without injury to the sense or expression? Had
he shared in the opinion that it was impossible, he would,
of course, have abstained from an attempt, which imposed
not only the duty of fidelity to the sense, but such a literal-
ness of rendering and preservation of the precise diction
of the English version, as that the likeness should be per-
ceptible to the ear as well as to the understanding.

As in music, amid the most complex variations, the
original melody is perpetually suggested; so, to meet the
ideal requirement, his poetical reproduction would need in
the reading, to be resonant with the voices and echoes
of the prose original, more or less distinctly heard in every

line. He dare not hope that he has achieved more than a moderate success; but did he suppose that he had failed to do fair justice to the letter and spirit of the sacred narrative, equal to what would be attainable in prose, he would not be justified, he considers, in publishing. It is an experiment which he felt was worth the making just for the once. It has cost him a good deal of time and labor which if thrown away, he cannot help it. It will be his own loss, not that of the critic nor the public.

A single word in regard to another point. The writer considers, that a man's utterances ought to be his own, and not another's. Unless he has something to say, it is his duty to keep silent. The timidity, that limits itself to parrot-like repetitions of what has been said ten thousand times, is of little account. So long as we speak sincerely, we may speak boldly, and the more boldly, because the right of dissent is inherent. A conscientious man would hardly dare to speak at all, if he knew that all he said would be received as unquestionable truth. He is honestly glad that, if he is wrong, everybody is at liberty to show it. The writer, having ventured in some cases to deviate from received interpretations, he congratulates himself that they will carry with them no weight outside of the reasons that accompany them. He firmly believes that the interests of truth have suffered from no one cause more than from the authority of great names.

Upon the general question of the propriety and suitableness of scriptural subjects for poetry, the opinion of
Cowley even in our day is entitled to some weight. He
says: "All the books of the Bible are either already admirable and exalted Poesy, *or are the best materials for it.*"

As bearing on questions which have been much discussed,
touching the authenticity of the Gospels and the reality of
the Divine Life they portray, we append the following remarkable admissions coming from men of the highest genius,
whose value and force are, certainly, enhanced rather than
diminished by the fact, that their authors have generally
been classed with unbelievers. One cannot help honoring
their candor, whatever may be thought of their consistency:

"I esteem the Gospels to be thoroughly genuine, for
there shines from them the reflected splendor of a sublimity
proceeding from the person of Jesus Christ of so divine a
kind, as only the divine could ever have manifested upon
earth."—GOETHE.

"I confess the majesty of the Scriptures astonishes me,
and the holiness of the Gospel speaks to my heart. Behold
the books of philosophy, with all their pomp, how small
they appear beside this! Can it be, that a book at once so
sublime and so simple, is the work of man? Can it be, that
He who forms its history is only a man? What sweetness,
what purity in His manners! What touching grace in His
instructions! What elevation in His maxims! What pro-

found wisdom in His discourses! What presence of mind!
What fineness, what justness in His answers! What empire
over His passions! Where is the man, where is the philosopher, who knows how to act, to suffer and to die without
feebleness and without ostentation? When Plato painted
his imaginary just man, covered with all the opprobrium of
crime, and worthy of all the rewards of virtue, he gave an
exact portrait of Jesus Christ. The resemblance is so
striking and unmistakeable that all the fathers perceived
it. What prejudice, what blindness, to compare the son of
Sophroniscus with the son of Mary! What a distance one
from the other! Socrates, dying without pain, without
ignominy, sustained easily his part to the end. His death
philosophizing tranquilly with his friends, is the sweetest
that could be desired; that of Jesus, expiring in agony
reviled, mocked, cursed by all the people, is the most hor-
rible that could be feared. Socrates, taking the poisoned
cup, blessed him who wept as he presented it to him; Jesus
in the midst of frightful tortures, prayed for his infuriated
executioners. Surely, if the life and death of Socrates
were those of a philosopher, the life and death of Jesus
Christ were those of a God! Shall we say that the Gospel
History is an invention? My friend, it is not so easy to
invent; and the facts concerning Socrates are not so well
attested as those concerning Jesus Christ. Indeed, this
were but to shift the difficulty without destroying it. It

would be more inconceivable, that many men should have united to fabricate this book, than that one man should have furnished the subject of it. The Gospel has characters of truth so grand, so striking, so perfectly inimitable, that the inventor of it would be more astonishing than the hero."—Rousseau.

"I know men; and I tell you that Jesus is not a man. Everything in Him amazes me. His spirit outreaches mine, and His will confounds me. Comparison is impossible between Him and any other being in the world. He is truly a being by Himself. His ideas, and His sentiments; the truth that He announces; His manner of convincing, are all beyond humanity and the natural order of things. His birth and the story of His life; the profoundness of His doctrine, which overturns all difficulties, and is their most complete solution; His Gospel; the singularity of His mysterious being; His appearance; His empire; His progress through all centuries and kingdoms;—all this is to me a prodigy, an unfathomable mystery. I see here nothing of man. Near as I may approach, clearly as I may examine, all remains above my comprehension—great with a greatness that crushes me. It is in vain that I reflect—all remains unaccountable. I defy you to cite another life like that of Christ."—Napoleon.

"Jesus Christ is in the noblest and most perfect sense the realized ideal of humanity."—Herder.

"Whatever may be the surprises of the future, Jesus will never be surpassed. His worship will grow young without ceasing. His legend will call forth tears without end; His sufferings will melt the noblest hearts; all ages will proclaim among the sons of men there is none born greater than Jesus."—RENAN.

"There once trod our earth a single being, who, by His sole moral omnipotence, controlled other ages, and founded an immortality peculiarly His own. He, gently blooming, and tractable to influences from on high, like the sunflower, but in His ardor and power of attracting, a sun, He, still with mildness of aspect, drew alike Himself, nations and ages to the universal and original sun. It is the meek spirit whom we call 'Jesus Christ.' If he was, then there is a Providence—or rather He was it."—JEAN PAUL RICHTER.

"The Life of Christ concerns Him, who being the holiest among the mighty, the mightiest among the holy, lifted up with His pierced hand empires off their hinges, and turned the stream of centuries out of its channel, and still governs the ages."—JEAN PAUL RICHTER.

THE LIGHT OF THE WORLD.

I.

THE KINGDOM OF GOD.

John II. 23-25 ; III. 1-21.

THE Incarnate Word of the Eternal Mind
Unfolds His high credentials to mankind ;
And manifests His glory hour by hour
In gracious acts of Godlike love and power.
At His command all sicknesses depart,
And a new rapture springs up in the heart:
The nerves, no more the avenues of pain,
Thrill with the ecstasy of health again.
With stupid wonder, men behold the sign,
And half believe the miracle divine ;
But, blind to its intent, they do not know
The motive is not thaumaturgic show ;

1

That His main mission is not to make whole   John
ii. —

The mortal body, but th' immortal soul.

With inattentive ears they hear Him tell,

How sinful feet take hold of death and hell:

How God sent down His Son in love and grace

To seek and save a lost and ruined race.

Though to His *teachings* deaf, His *deeds* awoke

Hope of deliverance from the Roman yoke;

And, dallying with the false and vain surmise,

He left for this His throne above the skies—

Seeing the miracles He wrought each day

During the Feast of the Passover,* they

Would Him have owned as the Messiah then,   24

And hailed Him King; but He who knew all men,

---

* The Hebrew year commenced with the first day of Nisan (Abib), "the month of flowers," corresponding nearly to our April, it being the month in which the Exodus took place. As the month was lunar, and its beginning was determined by the new moon at Jerusalem, the point of time necessarily varied. The day appointed for the Passover was the 14th, which made the Feast coincident always with the full moon. The Feast of Unleavened Bread included the Passover, and lasted seven days. It was customary however to apply the name of the Feast of the Passover to the whole period.

We are told (Luke ii: 42), that Jesus when he was twelve years old went up with His parents to the Passover at Jerusalem, but whether in their yearly visits subsequently He accompanied them is left to inference, the Evangelic record being silent as to what occurred during the eighteen years that followed. The present visit was the *first* Passover that He attended after the beginning of His public ministry; the *second* is believed to have been "the Feast" mentioned at John v: 1; the *third* hinted at John vii: 1; the *fourth*, when He was crucified, which would make the term of His ministry three years and more. The Jewish Passover answers to the Christian Easter.

And needed not that any should Him tell John ii. —

What was in man, their motives knowing well,

Committed not Himself to them, whose aim 25

Was foreign to the ends for which He came.

A MAN of rank, a ruler of the Jews, iii. 1.

A Pharisee named Nicodemus,* whose

---

* Nicodemus must have known of John's testimony concerning Jesus, for he was a prominent member of the body that had sent a delegation only a short time before to ask him—then engaged in proclaiming the near approach of the Reign of Heaven —who he was, and specifically, whether he was the Christ or no. John had said that he was not, but that the Christ nevertheless stood unknown in their midst; and then had on the following day pointed Him out in the person of Jesus as the Saviour of the World, speaking of Him as one so divinely exalted, so superior to himself, that he did not count himself worthy to loose the latchet of His shoes. His appearance now in Jerusalem at the feast of the Passover, had enabled the honorable Sanhedrist to judge for himself, and he, having seen with his own eyes the miracles daily performed by Him, was compelled to admit, that in view of such divine attestations and authentications, there could be no doubt whatever that He was come from God.

In the interview which he now sought, while he did not call Him so in express terms, His immediate and easy assumption of the character of the Messiah occasioned him no surprise, that being a thing for which he was prepared. Indeed it is highly probable, that not only was it forseen, but it was in anticipation of a speedy setting up of the Kingdom of God, that he had come to make a proffer of his assistance at its inauguration, not doubting but that the countenance and help of a person of his dignity and importance would be cordially welcomed. What was his amazement, therefore, when Jesus, knowing his thoughts, abruptly, without preface or apology, said to him, "Except a man be born again he cannot see the Kingdom of God!" He was thunderstruck. He could hardly credit his own ears. Literally or metaphorically understood it seemed equally unintelligible and absurd. We do not think he was so stupid or so ignorant as to suppose that the gross natural sense was the only possible sense or the one intended. Oriental every-day speech abounded in the boldest figures, and there is reason to believe that this figure in particular of a New Birth, expressive of an important change and the establishment of a new relation, such as the conversion of a Gentile to Judaism, was a familiar one. Consequently, his materialization of the trope was wilful and perverse, he knowing better, but seeking to make out a *reductio ad*

Divided mind, half convert to the right, John
iii. —

Brought him to Jesus secretly at night—

Ashamed to come by day or else afraid—

Addressed Him courteously, and frankly said :

absurdum, by an expansion on the literal side. The fact is he was far too acute, not to perceive that the words, however construed, whether naturally or spiritually, were confounding and subversive, striking at the foundations of all his most cherished beliefs. What could he say or do with every support swept from under his feet, and he left with nothing to stand on?

That his difficulty was not with the words taken literally, is evident from the fact, that after Jesus' explanation of His meaning, his perplexity and bewilderment continued as before, finding expression in the helpless inquiry, 'How can these things be?' His thoughts would seem to have run in this wise: "Is it so, can it be, that God is no respecter of persons? that Jew and Gentile are placed precisely on the same footing? Shall it avail me nothing that I am of the stock of Israel, a Hebrew of the Hebrews—as touching the law, a Pharisee; as touching the righteousness of the law, blameless? If henceforth there is to be no advantage to the Jew, and no profit in circumcision, what becomes of the promises, and the covenant with our fathers? Has change happened to the Unchangeable?"

His quick apprehension of the stupendous bearing of so leveling and humbling a doctrine does credit to his sagacity. He may not have seized its full significance. It is hardly possible that he should, for in that brief sentence lay a potency which was destined to "lift up empires off their hinges, and turn the stream of centuries into new channels, and govern the ages." It was the beginning of a new epoch; the first assertion of a principle that should revolutionize the world ; the inauguration of a Christian Democracy, the equality of all men before God,—feebly, imperfectly and even falsely apprehended in our own Declaration of Independence, and the Revolutionary watch-words, *Liberté, Egalité, Fraternité*, of infidel France,—but which in its ultimate triumph is pledged to the abolition of all forms of tyranny—the tyranny of thrones, and the worse tyranny of caste—Brahminical and every other—and the establishment on the earth of a true solidarity of Universal Brotherhood.

Certain it is, that in this initial discourse of our Lord there is a most unreserved and ample disclosure of all the distinctive doctrines of Christianity, a marvellous epitome, in fact, of the whole Gospel in its redemptive universality. 'The Teacher come from God' appears at once in the majesty of His character as THE LIGHT OF THE WORLD, and puts in believing hands—

"The golden key
Which opes the palace of eternity."

" Rabbi! Thou art a Teacher come, we know,   John iii. 2.

From God, for this Thy wondrous doings show."

Jesus, discerner of his thoughts, replied :   3

" That which concerns you most I will not hide.

Since I'm a Teacher come from God, hear then

The Faithful and True Witness,[a] the Amen!

Unless reborn[b] no man, whate'er his birth,

Can see the Reign of God upon the earth."[*]

[a] Rev. iii. 14.   [b] 1 Peter i. 23.

[*] Daniel in one place (ii. 44), speaks of an indestructible Kingdom, which the God of Heaven would set up ; in another place (vii. 13, 14), of an universal and everlasting Kingdom, to be given to One like the Son of Man. So the Prophet Micah (iv. 6, 7, predicts a time when Jehovah would reign over the people in Mount Zion forever. Evidently from this Old Testament source comes the title, 'the Kingdom of God,' 'the Kingdom of Heaven,' (the Heavens, *Gr.*) or, 'the Kingdom,' simply—found in the New Testament, having common reference to the predicted Reign of Messiah the Prince (Dan. ix. 25). The Greek word, ἡ βασιλεια, translated 'the kingdom,' means also 'reign.' Strictly speaking the English word, *kingdom*, refers solely to the *place* or region where the sovereignty is exercised, while *reign* has reference to the *time* or duration of it: Hence we say, The *Kingdom* of England and the *Reign* of Queen Elizabeth. While we can properly speak of a Reign as approaching, we can hardly do so of a Kingdom. In view of this admitted two-fold signification of the original, ample justification is afforded for the substitution of Reign for Kingdom, whenever it better suits the context and perspicuity calls for it.

George Campbell's rendering of the clause, "He cannot see the Kingdom of God," is, "He cannot discern the Reign of God"—the thing predicated being man's incapacity, without a spiritual renewal, to perceive the Reign of God, so that even though the Reign had commenced, he would not be able to discover it, because spiritual things are only discerned by the spiritual. If a threat had been intended, no doubt the phrasing would have been future, and we should have had, "He shall not see [share or enjoy] the Kingdom of God." In the fifth verse, where the word "enter" occurs to modify the conception, the Kingdom of God would seem to be the fitter rendering. Seeing, and entering are, no doubt, closely connected, inasmuch as a right idea of the Kingdom must precede the participation and enjoyment of it.

The word ἀνωθεν, translated 'again,' is more literally rendered '*from above,*'

Said Nicodemus: "Thy strange speech unfold— John iii. 4
How can a man be born when he is old?
Can he return into his mother's womb
And be reborn, and a new life assume?"

And Jesus answering said: "Thou as a Jew 5
Canst claim no natural birth-right as thy due.
The Holy Kingdom of which I am King
Is not a secular and earthly thing—[a]
Comes not with observation[b]—no man's eye
Its near and powerful coming can descry—
No hosts are seen with banners high unfurled
In onward march for conquest of the world—
Not of this world, but pure and from above,
A theocratic government of love—
Regeneration of the soul within—
Emancipation from the power of sin,

[a] John xviii. 36.   [b] Luke xvii. 20, 21.

'*from heaven*'; but the first is generally preferred as agreeing best, it is thought, with Nicodemus' words used in reply, "Can he enter a *second* time," etc. This, however, is not conclusive, for if the asseveration had stopped at, "Except a man be born"—the "second time" would be implied in the word 'born,' even if 'again' were not expressed, as any future birth would necessarily be a *second* birth. It is possible that his mind was so filled with the idea of being born, that he lost sight of everything else. Of course, he knew if it took place, it must be a divine act, *i. e.*, 'from above,' and therefore he may not have cared to emphasize that, as his chief difficulty did not lie so much in being born from above as in being born at all.

John
iii. —

Transcending nationality and place,[a]

It knows no limits but the human race.[b]

To Jew no more than Greek[c] is title given

To the exclusive citizenship[d] of heaven.

" Native to no immunities of birth,

My subjects are the good[e] of all the earth,

Of every land the foot of man has trod—

Born not of blood but of the will of God.[f]

For what is born of flesh is flesh ; and what

Is spirit is spiritually begot.

So marvel not at what I said to thee,

Ye* must be born again before that ye

Are qualified to enter that unseen

Kingdom of all the sanctified and clean—

Proud Israel like the rest. The viewless wind

Blows where it will in freedom unconfined ;

Thou hear'st the sound thereof, and feel'st the force,

But canst not tell the secret of its source.

So every one, with Heaven no more at strife,

[a] Matt. xxviii. 19; Mark xvi. 15.   [b] Luke xxiv. 47.   [c] Rom. x. 12.
[d] Gal. iii. 28 ; Phil. iii. 20.   [e] Acts x. 34.   [f] John i. 13.

*Here as elsewhere, in the change from the singular to the plural, the version follows the original—the plural both in the first and second persons having reference probably to his representative character.

In whom the Spirit breathes the breath of life,   John
                                                     iii. —
Knows not, once dead in trespasses and sins,[a]
Whence comes the breath, or how the life begins—
Born of the travail of a holy Grief,
The quickening process of a true Belief—[b]
Of which baptism is the watery sign—
Symbol of cleansing, and a birth divine:
The washing of regeneration,[c] most
Wondrous renewing of the Holy Ghost.
John, My forerunner, has proclaimed the need
Of something more than being Abraham's seed,
Shaken the desert with the warning cry:
'Repent! the righteous Reign of Heaven is nigh.'[d]
Ye must be born of water—not which flows
In earthly channels, this no virtue knows—
But of that water I to men impart,
Which springs to life eternal[e] in the heart.
Born of the Spirit differs not from this:
They must be pure who are the heirs of bliss.
To all who ask[f] by unrespecting Heaven
This universal Gift is freely given."

Said Nicodemus: "How can these things be?"   9

---

[a] Eph. ii. 1; Col. ii. 13.   [b] 1 Peter i. 23; 1 John v. 1.   [c] Titus iii. 5; Eph. v. 26.
[d] Matt. iii. 2.   [e] John iv. 14.   [f] Luke xi. 13.

And Jesus answering said reproachfully : John iii. 10

" Art thou *the* teacher,* specially ordained,

And need'st to have these simple truths explained?

We speak that which we know, and only state 11

What we have seen, and yet ye hesitate.

If I have told you earthly things and near, 12

Plain mundane matters of this lower sphere,

And ye believe not, prejudiced and blind,

And stumble at My word with doubting mind,

How will ye credit Me, when I report

Things of a higher range and heavenly sort,—

The mighty secrets of the Eternal Throne,

Unseen, unheard of, ne'er conceived,ᵃ unknown?

The power to climb to no man has been given, 13

Th' inaccessible and holy heaven :

But in Eternity and Time I dwell,—

The Son of God, and Son of Man as well,—

In both worlds present, nothing from Me hid,

The Father purposed or the Father did.

By pity moved, I have come down to tell

How sinners may escape profoundest hell :

<hr>

ᵃ 1 Cor. ii. 9.

*We are told that the chief officers of the Sanhedrim were a President, Vice-President and ' *the Teacher* ' or Wise Man. Nicodemus is supposed to have been the latter, which accounts for our Lord's use of the definite article found in the original.

" As Moses lifted up for healing sight   John iii. 14

The serpent to the bitten Israelite,

So shall the Son of Man uplifted be,

Made sin that knew no sin,ª for remedy;

That none may perish who on Him believe,   15

But pardon and eternal life receive.

For God so loved the world of man, He gave   16

His sole begotten Son from death to save.

He did not send His Son to judge the race,   17

But on an errand of redeeming grace.

He that believes is judged not for this cause;   18

He that believes not has by righteous laws

Been judged already for transgressions done,

Still more for grace rejected in the Son.   19

This is the judgment, when is come the light,

Men love the darkness and prefer the night,

Because their deeds are evil. Who does ill,   20

He hates the light, avoids the light, and will

Not come thereto, in unacknowledged fear

Lest his iniquity should be made clear.

But he that does the truth, that all may see   21

His works are wrought in God, comes joyfully."

ª 2 Cor. v. 21.

.

H Y M N .

Almighty God! how small
  The accidents of birth;
Thine equal eye looks down on all
  Who dwell upon the earth.

Who dwell upon the earth,
  The Gentile and the Jew,—
All men alike, wherever found,
  Thy Spirit must renew.

Thy Spirit must renew,
  Proud boasts of blood are vain;—
The lips of Truth to all declare,
  'Ye must be born again.'

Ye must be born again,
  There is exception none;
Enlightened eyes alone can see
  The Kingdom of Thy Son.

The Kingdom of Thy Son
  Set up the soul within,
A heavenly rule of purity
  To make an end of sin.

To make an end of sin,
  The work of grace complete,
Inclining evermore the will
  To make obedience sweet.

To make obedience sweet
  On us Thy Spirit shed;
O Holy Ghost, requicken us
  And raise us from the dead!

And raise us from the dead—
  Baptismal grace convey,
And bless the water of the Word
  To wash our sins away.

To wash our sins away
  True penitence impart;
And make us on the Crucified
  Believe with all the heart.

Believe with all the heart
   Thou verily didst give
Thy Son to die upon the cross
   That guilty souls may live.

That guilty souls may live,
   And Christ not die in vain,
May man, once in Thy likeness made,
   Thine image bear again.

Thine image bear again,
   Original and whole,
Enstamped upon his breast and brain,
   And mirrored in his soul.

And mirrored in his soul,
   As in a lakelet lie
The pictured purity and peace
   And glory of the sky.

II.

JOHN'S FINAL TESTIMONY.

JOHN III. 22-36.

LEAVING Jerusalem, His heart aflame,   John iii. 22
Jesus with His disciples elsewhere came
Into Judea, tarried there and taught,
And there baptized, and works of mercy wrought.
For that John also was baptizing, there   23
In Ænon near to Salim, region where
There was much water needful to baptize,
The two baptisms chanced to synchronize —
For John was not imprisoned yet.   Arose   24
Therefore a question on the part of those,   25
Who John's disciples were, about the true
Manner of purification with some Jew.*
And so they said to John:

"Rabbi, decide!   26
He who was with thee on the other side

* The Revised Version adopts the singular.

Of Jordan, and to whom thou, since as then,
Bor'st witness, lo, baptizes, and all men
Come thronging unto Him instead of thee—
He from our fastings sets His followers free."*

Th' unjealous John rebuking answer made—
With frank and noble truthfulness he said:
" A man can naught receive except as given
By the supreme authority of Heaven.
Ye bear me witness, that I witness bore, 23
I am not the Messiah, but before
Him sent, His joyful coming to make known.
He is the Heavenly Bridegroom, He alone; 29
He has the bride ; I am the Bridegroom's friend,
Who, hearing Him, rejoices without end
Because of His dear voice.   This Heaven me willed,
And this my joy therefore is now fulfilled.
He must increase while endless ages run; 30
I must decrease, for now my work is done.

---

* We are told (Mark ii. 18, and Luke v. 33), that the disciples of John *fasted*, and that the disciples of Jesus *did not*. May it not have been, therefore, that John enjoined fasting in connection with his baptism, and that its necessity as a concomitant of baptism formed the subject of dispute with some Jew who had been baptized by Christ's disciples without this fasting accompaniment? In the recently discovered document, "*The Teaching of the Twelve Apostles*," it is there enjoined that "the baptized *fast* for two or three days before baptism "—a practice which may possibly have been borrowed from John. We know the undue importance attached to fasting by the Pharisees ; and the revival of this custom under the Christian Dispensation may be regarded as one of the many evidences of the early working of the Judaic leaven.

He heavenly is, who is of heavenly birth;   John
iii. 31
And earthly he whose origin is earth.
To earthly life but earthly speech is given;
High above all is He who speaks from Heaven.
He testifies what He has seen and heard,   32
And no man takes the warrant of His word.
Who has received His witness, has set to   33
His own believing seal that God is true.
For He, who is God's own Ambassador,   34
Speaks but the words of God, and cannot err
God not by measure does the Spirit dole,
But gives to Him th' immeasurable whole.
The Father loves the Son, and in His hands   35
Has put all peoples, governments and lands.
He that believes on His beloved Son   36
Has everlasting life on earth begun :—
He that believes not, life he shall not see,
But on him rests God's frown unceasingly."

THE HEAVENLY BRIDEGROOM.

The fond youth thinks the maid he loves
  Sums all the beauty of the land ;
But what of Him who shaped her brow,
  And ' the white wonder of her hand '?

The earth and sky no doubt are fair,
  And ravishing to soul and sight :
But fairer He who made them fair,
  And gave us organs of delight.

The violet and the rose are sweet,
  But there 's a sweetness more intense—
His sweetness, who Arabias made
  And odorous hills of frankincense.

When from His orient chamber comes
  The Heavenly Bridegroom—bashful slips
Behind a cloud the risen sun,
  Conscious of a divine eclipse.

2

O Thou, who art the Spouse of souls,
  With curtains of my window drawn,
I watch with weary lids to catch
  The earliest glimpses of Thy dawn.

Dear absent Lord, make swift return!
  My hungry heart faints from delay—
Rise, Sun of Righteousness, now rise,
  And turn my night to happy day!

III.

THE DIALOGUE AT JACOB'S WELL.

JOHN IV. 1-42.

WHEN the Lord knew, His first and fiercest foes,
　　The Pharisees, were plotting to oppose—　John iv. 1
Their minds inflamed with envy, having heard
That Jesus, through His miracles and word,
Was making and baptizing even more
Disciples than was John, their dread before,
(Although baptizing not Himself but His　　2
Disciples)—He, who perfect wisdom is,
Departed from Judea to go back　　3
To Galilee.　As lying in His track,　　4
He needed to pass through Samaria,
So came to Sychar, near which city lay　　5
A plot of ground, old Jacob's present rare
To his son Joseph.　Jacob's Well was there.　　6

Here by the Well's side Jesus found a seat,
Welcome to journeying and weary feet.

The hour was sultry noon. He sat alone,   John
iv.—

Hungry and thirsty, His disciples gone   8

To buy food in the city. While away,

A certain woman of Samaria   7

Came to draw water. Jesus gently said:

" Give Me to drink!"

            The woman answer made: 9

" How is it Thou, a Jew, thus civilly,

Dost ask the favor of a drink of me,

A scorned Samaritan?"* For Jews she knew

With the Samaritans have naught to do.

---

*The Samaritans, as we learn from 2 Kings xvii., were originally Assyrian colonists, made up of five idolatrous nations worshipping different gods, introduced after Israel was led away captive, B. C. 730. From being idolaters they became in course of time extremely zealous for the Mosaic law and ritual. Of the Sacred Writings they acknowledged the Pentateuch alone. Ignoring their heathen origin, they had come to claim descent from Joseph through Ephraim, to which some color was given by probable intermarriages with the native Israelites — a claim, however, which was contemptuously rejected by the Jews, who were accustomed to speak of them as Cuthœans or Cuthites—a part of the original settlers having come from Cuthan, a place in the interior of Persia. The bitter feud, which had existed for centuries, was in full force in the time of Christ. In the mouth of a Jew the very name of a Samaritan was a reproach ; and so, knowing no stronger form of objurgation, the maddened Jews at Jerusalem said to Jesus, " We know Thou art a Samaritan, and hast a devil." To take a mouthful of food which had been touched by a Samaritan was as defiling as eating the flesh of swine. No Samaritan was allowed to become a proselyte. They had been repeatedly anathematized and subjected to every form of excommunication. No bargain made with him was binding. His testimony was not to be taken in a Jewish court. To receive him into one's house would bring down the curse of Heaven.

Jesus was infinitely superior to all this. Not only was His friendliness evinced on this occasion, but afterwards. When He cured the ten lepers, the only one who returned to thank Him was a Samaritan, or to use His own words, " this stranger " (an *obiter dictum*, implying a knowledge of his heathen non-Jewish origin, but mentioned only to emphasize His commendation). Another case in point is the beautiful Parable of the Good Samaritan.

Jesus said kindly : " Hadst thou known the gift _{John iv. 10}
Of God, and Who it is, and what His drift
Who asks, thou wouldst have asked of Him, and He
Would living water have bestowed on thee."

The woman answered: " Sir, deep is the Well,   11
And Thou hast naught to draw with.   Whence then
    tell,
Hast Thou that living water?   Art Thou more   12
Than Jacob was, our father, who of yore
Gave us this Well, and hither used to come
Himself, his sons. and herds, and drink therefrom ?"

And Jesus said, His meaning to make plain :   13
" Who of this water drinks shall thirst again.
But whoso drinks of that which I shall give   14
Shall never thirst : the same shall in him live,
And be a well of water, springing rife
From its deep source unto eternal life."

The woman guessed,while quibbling with the sense,15
The words had mystic meaning and intense,
But answered blindly : " Sir, give me, I pray,
This water that I thirst not, neither may
Come hither more to draw."

He suddenly : John iv. 16
"Go, call thy husband, and come here to Me !"

"I have no husband," blushingly she said, 17
An honest answer seeking to evade.

Jesus replied : "Thou hast said well ; for thou
Hast had five husbands ; he whom thou hast now 18
Is not thy husband.   What thou say'st is true."

Convinced by this, that this mysterious Jew 19
Was come from God ; and being now awake
To know her future welfare was at stake ;
Solicitous to know, if she were wrong
In what she trusted and believed so long
As a Samaritan, she first professed
Her faith in Him, and Jesus thus addressed :
" That Thou a Prophet art I must believe,
And therefore think Thou wilt not me deceive
Our fathers worshipped in this mountain ;* ye 20
Say in Jerusalem should men's worship be."

* Gerizim is a mountain rising 2,500 feet above the level of the sea, and 800 feet above the surrounding plain, from the top of which can be seen the Mediterranean Sea on the West, the snowy heights of Hermon on the North, on the East the wall of the trans-Jordanic mountains, broken by the deep cleft of the Jabbok—a prospect unique in the Holy Land. It was memorable as the place designated by Moses for reading the *blessings*, as the neighboring mountain Ebal was for the *cursing* (Deut.

" Woman, believe Me," Jesus said to her,   John
iv. 21

" An hour is coming when no worshipper,

Touching this mountain or Jerusalem,

Shall deem the Father is confined to them.

The God ye worship is a God half known,*   22

The truth debased with fictions of your own.

Although the Law of Moses ye respect,

The Writings of the Prophets ye reject :

The Oracles of God which ye refuse

Are the divine possession of the Jews;

Whose are the promises, and promised Seed,ª

Life and salvation which from Him proceed.

ª Rom. ix. 4, 5.

xxvii. 12, 13). To the Samaritans it was the most sacred spot on earth. Legend had made it the seat of Paradise, whence all the streams that watered the earth flowed. Adam had been formed from its dust, and had lived on it. It was here he built his first altar. It was the Ararat on which the Ark rested, and where Noah offered sacrifice. It was the Moriah where Abraham made ready to offer up Isaac ; and it was here he met Melchisedek. Here Jacob slept and dreamed of the heavenly ladder. Here Sanballat, the Cuthite, having obtained leave from Alexander the Great, built a rival Temple, which, after it had stood 200 years, was destroyed by Hyrcanus, 129 years before Christ. Thitherward every Samaritan turned his face when he prayed. The Messiah, he believed, would first appear on its summit. No wonder he held it sacred.

It is remarkable that while the Jews no longer offer up bloody sacrifices, the Paschal Lamb has not ceased to be offered on Mount Gerizim down to the present time. What Jerusalem is to the Jew, and Mecca to the Mahometan, Gerizim is to the Samaritan.

* Owing to their rejection of all later revelations made through the Prophets, and the lingering superstitions derived from their heathen origin and intercourse, the worship of the Samaritans was both ignorant and corrupt—they worshipping, like the ancient Athenians and some modern mystics, they knew not what—a God of uncertain or unknown attributes.

But this concerns the passing and the past,   John
iv. —
Things that wax old and were not meant to last.
The hour is coming and is present now,   23
When everywhere, true worshippers shall bow
Knees of pure worship, and earth's common sod
Be one vast Temple* dedicate to God.
For such the Father seeks, who not in show,
But truth and spirit worship Him below.
God is a Spirit, nor can cheated be   24
By the mere mockery of the bended knee.
He not in pomp and postures takes delight,
But humble hearts, believing and contrite."

The woman hints her thought : " I know full well 25
When Christ is come, He will us all things tell."

Jesus replied ; " God has enlightened thee—   26
Thou err'st not, I that speak to thee am He."

While thus conversing, His disciples came,   27
Who saw with wonder not unmixed with blame

In templo vis orare ? in te ora, sed prius esto templum Dei.—AUG.

In temple would'st thou pray?
Thou need'st not go abroad—
Pray in thyself, but previously,
A temple be of God !

Their Master's condescension, doubly strange, _{John}

John
iv. –

Because it was not usual to exchange
Speech with a woman, breaking laws beside,
The birth of Jewish prejudice and pride.
Yet no man said—deep awe might well deter—
" What seekest Thou ? Why speakest Thou with her?"

The excited woman left her water-pot 28
For the Lord's use, His asking not forgot,
And went into the city, all on fire,
Full of the news, and eager with desire,
And said to every one she met: " Come, see 29
A man, who told me my whole history !—
Say, is not this the Christ ?"   And therefore they 30
Went out to Him.

             While these were on the way— 31
A thronging, dense, and waving multitude—
All the disciples prayed Him to take food.
Because just then sweet thoughts His spirit fed,
He felt no appetite for common bread,
So spake refusal: " I have food to eat 32
Ye know not of.   Ask ye who brought me meat?
My meat and joy it is to do the will 34
Of Him who sent Me, and His work fulfill.

Say ye the harvest is four months away?*   John iv. 35

Lift up your eyes, look on the fields, for they

Are white already.   To My scattered seed,

Behold, how quick a harvest doth succeed,

That waits your reaping!   He that reaps   36

Receives good wages in the garnered heaps

Of golden fruit he gathers unto life

Eternal, with celestial glory rife,

His joy and crown[a] forever—so that He

Who sows, and he who reaps shall endlessly

Rejoice together.   For the saying 's true,   37

' One sows, another reaps.'   Lo ! I send you   38

To reap the ripe results of others' toil,

Who ploughed and planted and prepared the soil."

Many of the Samaritans were led   39

To trust because of what the woman said—

' He told me all I ever did '—and some

Later believed when they had to Him come ;   40

---

[a] Phil. iv. 1 ; 1 Thess. ii. 19, 20.

* If this is to be literally understood as referring to the actual harvest, it would make the time somewhere about December ; and would go to show that the Lord's stay in Judea had been about eight months. Noon in Palestine even in December is often, it is said, warm even to sultriness.

And many more, when they had further heard, John iv. 41
Believed on Him because of His own word:
" We know," they said—be sails to bear unfurled— 42
" This is the Christ, THE SAVIOUR OF THE WORLD !"

HYMN.

JOHN IV. 21-23; ACTS XVII. 24-28.

They err who think that God is far—
That I must climb from star to star,
Through mighty intervals of space,
To reach His awful dwelling place.

I put the shoes from off my feet;
I go not forth my God to meet;
For God is everywhere, and here,
Here in this place to make it dear.

Long time I groped and could not find,
For light is darkness to the blind;
How sweet to feel now He is found,
His everlasting arms around!

Upon His bosom thus to rest,
I cannot ask to be more blest.
To know my sins are all forgiven
For Jesus' sake, O this is heaven!

While I love Him, and He loves me,
I care no other heaven to see :
And, if there be some higher bliss,
I am content while I have this.

And there are those beyond the wave,
Whom Christ came down on earth to save :
O let me haste to make it known,
My God and Saviour is their own!

IV.

REJECTION AT NAZARETH.

JOHN IV 43-54; LUKE IV. 16-31.

H IS two days' stay at Sychar ended, He   John
    Departed thence and entered Galilee—   iv. 43
Avoiding Nazareth, because He knew
According to the proverb it was true,   44
A prophet has no honor in his home.
Then when He into Galilee was come,   45
The Galileans—having all things seen
Done at Jerusalem, they having been
Themselves at the Passover feast—received
Him as a Prophet, and on Him believed.
So Jesus came again to Cana where   46
He made the water wine.   A noble there
Of Herod's household, hearing He had come,   47
Asked Him to hasten to Capernaum,
To heal his son,* now at the point of death.
  Then Jesus said, with sad rebuking breath,   48

---

* The definite article before son—in the original " the son of him "—indicates that it was an *only* son.

" Except ye signs and wonders see, ye doubt—   John iv. —
Blessed is he who shall believe without."

The noble made inconsequent reply :   49
" Sir, come down quickly or my child will die."

" The boon thou askest," Jesus said, " I give ;   50
Go thou thy way, thy son shall surely live."

The man believed the word, and, as he went,
The servants met him, for the purpose sent,   51
To tell him his son lived.   When told the hour   52
Of healing tallied with that word of power,
Himself believed and all his house ; for none   53
Doubted a mighty miracle was done.

Divine the power, but with a higher aim
Than to amaze by miracles he came.
" O not for this was I sent forth," He said,   Mark i. 38
"But in your cities to proclaim instead,
The Gospel of the Kingdom.   Then begins   Matt. iv. 17
The Reign of Heaven when you forsake your sins."
He taught in all their synagogues and preached,   Luke iv. 15
Honored of all.   In His own time, He reached
His native Nazareth—thus kindly late,   16
To strip contempt, so quickly changed to hate,
(Offspring of prejudice that shuts its eyes
To worth familiar though it reach the skies)

Of all excuse, when to His well known name   Luke
iv. —

Was joined a wonderful and mighty fame.

As was His custom, on the Sabbath day

He went into the synagogue, and they

Placed in His hands to read the sacred Scroll,   17

Which he forthwith proceeded to unroll,

And in Isaiah lighted on the place,

Where were recorded those sweet words of grace :

· The Spirit of the Lord upon Me rests ;   18

And, by a heavenly unction, Me invests

With power to preach glad tidings to the poor :

To heal the broken-hearted; and assure

Deliverance to the captives ; to restore

Light to the blind ; and limbs, long bruised and sore,

Broken with heavy fetters, to set free :

And sound the gracious Year of Jubilee.'   19

And rolling up the writing as before,   20

He to the servant handed it once more,

And then sat down to teach*—in nothing odd

Observing custom though the Son of God.

All eyes were fastened on Him ; every ear

In the whole synagogue was bent to hear.

* The Rabbis always *sat* when teaching.

"This ancient Scripture," He began to say,   Luke
iv. 21
" Has in your hearing been fulfilled to-day." . . .
The rest is wanting—those dear words of grace,   22
At which each wondered, sitting in his place,
Full of all comfort, mighty to convince,
Worth all that has been said or written since.

Ah, foolish Nazarenes! had ye but known
Your time of visitation, and not thrown
Your golden opportunity away!
While with closed eyelids ye shut out the day,
What wonder that ye stumbled at broad noon,
Rejecting your Messiah, and the boon
Of peace and pardon, life and liberty,
And bliss extending through eternity,
He offered and persuaded you to take!
Ye listened to the gracious words He spake,
Bore witness to their power, and marvelled much,
But all the while your hearts they failed to touch.
Ye should have known Him best, for Him ye knew
Through all those blameless years in which He grew
In favor both with God and man.   Ye saw
In Him exemplified the breadth of law,
The miracle of superhuman grace

Stamped on His conduct, shining in His face. Luke iv. —

Through all the years ye knew Him, testify

If ye e'er heard those pure lips tell a lie.

How durst ye then distrust His solemn word?

How doubt the truth of what ye must have heard?

How leaving Nazareth He straightway went

Where John was warning all men to repent,

Because the heavenly Reign of Christ was nigh,

And was baptized in Jordan?—How the sky

Was rent asunder, what time from above

The Holy Ghost descended as a dove

And lighted on Him, while a Voice Divine

Declared the meaning of the heavenly sign,

Saying, 'Lo, this is My Beloved Son,

Whom herewith I anoint, the Anointed One—

Christ, by the investure of My Spirit's chrism,

And consecrating rite of this baptism!'

   Though it be true, He is, as you aver,

The Son of Mary, and a Carpenter, 22

The hands that work, mechanical and mean,

May in God's sight be honorable and clean.

Than His credentials whose could be more clear?

How foolish then and impious the sneer!

But yet more daring your insulting taunt—

3

" Physician, heal Thyself, else vain Thy vaunt! Luke iv. 23
What we have heard done in Capernaum,
Do also here, now Thou at last hast come!
Give Thy consent, and we will fix a day
To give Thee chance for mountebank display—
To work some miracle, that we may know
Thou canst make God the puppet of a show!
Our claim is greatest, here Thy works repeat,
Else we 're prepared to brand Thee as a cheat!"

" So long as you exclude Me from your heart,"
The Saviour said, " I can no grace impart.
All power to do you good away is swept[a]
While you refuse the Prophet to accept.
I come to your inhospitable door
And ask admittance—what can I do more?
At the low portal, lo, I stand and knock—[b]
I cannot pass unless I break the lock.
Though Heaven is gracious, Heaven is sovereign too.
Ye must not ask as if the least were due.
On proud unthankful greed should God convey
Ten thousand worlds, the gift were thrown away.
God's grace and goodness never were confined

[a] Matt. xiii. 58.   [b] Rev. iii. 20.

To a few bigots, but embraced mankind.   Luke
                                                            iv. —
So He of old, His saving help made known   25
Among the Gentiles, passing by His own.
Be not puffed up!   I, of a truth, you tell,
There many widows were in Israel,
When reigned a famine o'er the land's extent
To none of these yet was Elijah sent,   26
But to a woman of Sarepta, who
A Gentile was: And many lepers too   27
Were living in Elisha's time, but none
Was cleansed save Naäman alone."

They heard thus far, and then would hear no more.[28]
And all was howling rage and wild uproar,
No more a grave assembly but a mob.
The turgid arteries were seen to throb
In their flushed temples; all their eyes shot fire ;
Their frenzied blood was hot with one desire
To kill Him instantly.   They thrust Him out,   · [29]
And drag Him roughly by the nearest route
To the hill's brow, whereon the city stood,
To hurl Him headlong down.   Though Jesus could
Have palsied with all ease each lifted arm,
And thus preserved Himself from threatened harm,

He never exercised His matchless power   Luke
iv. —
To save Himself in danger's darkest hour.

Goodness has majesty and fear and awe

To cow the wretches that defy the law;

The knees of coward Guilt have often shook

At the dissolving terror of a look.

No form of outrage Jesus would resist,

No menace and no malice of the fist,

Till now, when putting on a sterner mien,

He looked the God, and turned His eyes serene

Upon His would-be murderers, who quailed

And falling back let Him pass unassailed.   30

Weep, Nazareth! Thy endless loss deplore!

Thy unprized Lord shall dwell in thee no more;

In all thy habitations is dark night

Now He is gone elsewhere who was thy light.

And Jesus came, not pausing on the road,   31

And in Capernaum fixed His abode.

The voice of Mercy calls aloud,
  But, deaf to all persuasion,
Men, heedless of the offered grace,
  Let slip the one occasion.

Alas! that mortals should not know
  Their time of visitation,
But, madly rushing down to death,
  Reject the great Salvation.

When opportunity is past,
  And time returneth never,
How sad to know, it might have been
  But shall not be forever!

" The figure, veiled and sad, of Judea the Captive, on the Roman coin minted when Titus conquered Palestine, seems the image of a remorse that had wasted opportunity, and of a despair that had cancelled grace."—WILLIAM R. WILLIAMS, D. D.

V.

ABODE AT CAPERNAUM.—APOSTOLATE.

MATT. IV. 18–22; MARK I. 16–20; LUKE V. 1–11.

O THOU to whom such happiness is given!
   Exalted thus above the towers of heaven!
Made now the stated dwelling place of Him,
Whose radiant presence makes the daylight dim!
Thy humblest hovel and thy meanest street
Shine with the lustre of His passing feet.
With frequent coming every lowly door
Is lovely with a light undreamt before.
Hide thy diminished head, Jerusalem!
Rome, wear no more an eclipsed diadem!
Let haughty Cæsar lay his sceptre by
And here before a greater prostrate lie!
Lord of all worlds, He reigns by love alone ;
Makes willing hearts the pillars of His throne ;
Asserts His Godhead by forgiving sin,
And throws His miracles of healing in ;

Before th' omnipotence of heavenly grace
Lo, Satan's empire totters to its base.
Improve, Capernaum, thy honor well,
Lest raised to heaven thou be cast down to hell!

   Since all His mighty merits were designed
To benefit and bless and save mankind ;
His words of wisdom and His works of power
Which crowded every day and every hour,
Were meant for proof, not for Capernaum,
But for all places, in all times to come ;
'Twas needful Heaven some method should contrive,
To keep the memory of these alive—
Provide or find some healthy weft of nerve,
Keen to perceive and faithful to preserve
Each fine pulsation of melodious breath,
The tone and tint of everything He saith,
That nothing may be lost—some honest ear,
With scope of function open, chaste, and clear,
To entertain the sweetness of that Voice,
Which makes th' inhabitants of heaven rejoice,
Discoursing wisdom, soothing hearts that ache
With words of comfort such as man ne'er spake—
Some eye to witness, and some hand to pen

The mighty doings of this Man of men ;
Unconscious skill and artless art to paint
This more than Hero and this more than Saint ;
Careful to let no single trait escape
Of the Eternal God in human shape.

So Jesus pleased to call and to ordain
(Else he had mostly lived and died in vain)
Twelve men to the Apostleship, and sought
The simple and the teachable untaught—
Not lettered Scribe incorrigibly wrong—
As those most fit to go with Him along,
By day and night be with Him and abide,
Eating with Him and sleeping by His side,
Attendant on His footsteps to the end,
To talk with Him as friend would talk with friend,
Sit at His feet, and hear and keep in mind
The sayings of the Oracle enshrined—
Instructed thus, thus qualified to bear
Authentic oral witness everywhere,
While some should by th' imperishable page,
Hand down the published grace from age to age.

Behold Twelve Witnesses, no two the same,
Unlike in mind and person as in name.

While they agree in everything they say
'Tis in a natural and human way—
Like the Evangelists, who speak as Four
In their own manner, and do nothing more.
No matter that the infidel insists
On contradictions in th' Evangelists,
While the Evangel does itself contain
No warring parts, then is th' objection vain—
All beauty and perfection therein lie,
All specks are in the scoffer's evil eye.

The willing winds had borne His matchless fame,
The pure report and wonder of His name,
From o'er the Jordan to the Midland Sea,
And from Judea unto Galilee.
But hitherto, although on every side
Disciples had increased and multiplied,
Jesus, by no authoritative choice,
Had called Him Prophets of the Pen and Voice; *
Till now the time had come to separate
Fit persons wholly to th' Apostolate.

*Rev. Wm. R. Williams, D.D., in his Lecture on John the Baptist aptly designates
him as Prophet of the *Voice* in contradistinction from Prophet of the *Pen*.

As walking by the Lake's delightful shore   Matt. iv. 18
He Simon saw (whom He had named before
Peter) and Andrew, Simon's brother—yet
Plying their trade, about to cast a net
Into the sea, for they were fishers.   He
Gave royal summons : " Come ye after Me,   19
And I will make you, former skill to match,
Fishers of men, immortal souls to catch ! "
And they forsook their nets without delay,   20
And followed Him.   Then He, a little way   21
Proceeding, saw two other brothers, James
And John, the sons of Zebedee,—dear names
Well-known already—mending nets ; and He   22
Called them ; and they, their father Zebedee
Left in the boat, and went, forsaking all,
Swift to obey so powerful a call.
Of His Apostles these elected four
Were first and earliest, soon He added more.

High thanks to Thee we owe, O Christ!
  For Thy dear servants of the pen—
Apostle and Evangelist—
  Whereby Thou art made known to men.

They tell us all Thou saidst and didst;
  And all Thy glorious goodness show;
Make Thee a presence in our midst,
  Acting and speaking here below.

We sit beside Thee at the sea;
  We're made companions of Thy walk;
Our hearts within us burn, while we
  In silence listen to Thy talk.

We learn the lesson of Thy looks,
  And are encouraged to draw near;
More than the lore of all the books,
  Thy welcome whispered in our ear.

When Thy sweet lips forgiveness speak,
  And we can claim Thee as our Friend,
Naught more in heaven or earth we seek,
  Our wants and wishes have an end.

VI.

HEALER AND SAVIOUR.

MARK I. 21-34: LUKE IV. 31-41: Matt. VIII. 14-17.

THEY went into Capernaum. Short rest   Mark i. 21
      Followed long labor, and He woke refreshed.
And on the Sabbath, wrapt in holy thought,
He came into the synagogue, and taught,   22
Not as the Scribes, but with authority—
And they were all astonished. Suddenly,   23
A frenzied shriek was heard, loud, piercing, shrill,
Expressing terror, making hearts stand still—
A demonical, unearthly cry—
And when all turned to learn the reason why,
There stood a maniac. His body shook;
Out of his eyes a demon seemed to look;
His features worked convulsively; his speech
Was less a voice, than an infernal screech
Belonging to another—some foul fiend,
That there mysteriously had introvened,

Mark
i. —

Usurping function, putting powers of soul
And body under devilish control—
Using the passive organs as his own,
Saying with borrowed breath, "Let us alone!   24
For what have we to do with Thee? Comest Thou
Jesus of Nazareth to judge us now?
Drive us not hence with Thy destroying rod—
I know Thee well, Thou Holy One of God!"

Jesus rebuked him, saying, "Hold thy peace!   25
Come out of him!" His power about to cease,
The demon threw him down upon the floor   26
With cries of rage, while wild contortions tore
Each muscle of the frame, and strange grimace
Gave hideous expression to the face.
Then straightway all was peaceful and serene.
How sweet is health! how holy! and how clean!

And they were all amazed at what occurred.   27
What truth of doctrine! majesty of word!
Clothed with divine authority and power,
Unwitnessed, unimagined till this hour—
His high command the unclean spirits hear,   28
And instantly obey with trembling fear.

Leaving the synagogue, the five straightway Mark i. 29
Into the house of Simon went, where lay
Abed the stricken mother of his wife, 30
Sick with a fever dangerous to life.
And they on her behalf to Him appealed— 31
The fever He rebuked and she was healed;
Then rising she with hospitable speed
Prepared them food to satisfy their need. 32

At the cool season of the setting sun,
His hot career through torrid skies now run,
They bring to Him all that are sick, and those
Possessed with demons, and the concourse grows
Till the whole city's gathered at the door. 33
He many heals, and many demons more 34
Casts out, not suffering them to testify,
For that their truth was rancorous as a lie.

Alas! how many are the foes of man,
That lie in wait and his destruction plan.
From the first moment that he draws his breath,
Around him are the instruments of death.
Most fearfully and wonderfully made,
The quick frame trembles of itself afraid,
Lest in each nerve the penalty be felt

Of broken law inevitably dealt,

And the betrayed and suffering organs rise,

And force unwilling groans to reach the skies.

A million shames and guilt of suicide

Attach to such, who thus throw open wide

The doors of penal pain and earthly hells;

But towards these also heavenly pity swells.

While much is due to ignorance and sin,

And lusts that burn incessantly within,

Disease has other causes. No defense

Can make quite safe the child of innocence.

No life is new, original and fresh,

Some latent weakness of the new-born flesh,

Some old ancestral tendency or taint

May make the whole head sick, the whole heart faint—

The germ in former generations sown,

Growing in darkness, suddenly made known

In torments manifold. Lo, thence arise

Dumbness, convulsions, palsies, lunacies—

Perverted function of the brain and nerves,

When will for government no longer serves,

Leaving the temple hallowed and sweet

Open to the abominable feet

Of unclean spirits. Not when doors are barred,

And all the ministers of Health keep guard,
Can these find entrance, nor can longer stay
After that power resumes her broken sway.
But Health though armed is vulnerable still,
Not wholly proof against the darts of ill—
No panoply of most impenetrable steel
Can save the flying unprotected heel.
When stalks the Pestilence, naught can disperse
The dark, unknown, imponderable curse—
Th' unavoidable and needful air
Purveys the poison, and men drink despair.
Dread Epidemics fill the land with woe,
Then o'er the sea to distant regions go.
These pass away, and may not come again,
While chronic plagues, like Leprosy, remain—
Type and superlative of all that 's vile,
Whose neighborhood suffices to defile,
Compelled to warn approaching feet when seen
To stand afar and cry, " Unclean ! unclean !"

   The scaly horror when it first begins
Is often but a spot on fairest skins:
By slow degrees, the multiplying scab
Spreads o'er the whole, and worse succeeds to bad,

Till it becomes to the disgusted sight
A leprous surface hideously white.
The hair falls off; nails loosen; fingers, toes,
Shrivel and rot; teeth disappear; eyes, nose,
Tongue, palate, are consumed; beneath the cope
No remedy, the sepulchre of hope.
This grave of beauty, dreadful to record,
This death in life, so loathsome and abhorred,
Has its own ghastly counterpart within—
The moral death and leprosy of Sin.

O double Saviour from a double death!
Vicarious Sufferer!—as Isaiah saith,
" Himself took our infirmities and bore   Matt.
                                              viii. 17
Our sicknesses "—what could His love do more?
He saved the sinner and He healed the sick—
The blind, the deaf, the dumb, the lunatic,—
At His own cost: the leper white as snow
Released from his hereditary woe,
By virtue which went out of Him—with pain
And vital loss offsetting vital gain—
Payment of penalty, relieving Grace
Obliged to suffer in the sufferer's place.

4

"My Father works," said Jesus, "and I work."   John
v. 17

He paid no heed to Pharisaic quirk,

Still doing good upon the Sabbath day,

In His unparalleled and Godlike way.

Never did hours bear up on loaded wings

So vast a weight and multitude of things:

Enough of mercy in this day appears

For celebration through a thousand years.

MATT. VIII. 2-4 ; MARK I. 35-45 ; LUKE IV. 42-44; V. 12-16.

RISING up early, long before 't was light,   Mark
i. 33

Lengthening the day by cutting short the night,

He went to pray out in a lonely place,

Not for Himself but for the human race.

And Simon followed with the other three,   36

And having found Him, said: "All seek for Thee!"   37

And when they would have stayed Him, He said, "No!

Into the neighboring cities let us go

That I may preach the Kingdom of God there:

To them I also must the Good News bear.

For this end came I forth, for this am sent,

To save from coming wrath and punishment."

As He was entering a certain town,   Luke
v. 12

A leper came to Him, and kneeling down   Mark
i. 40

Besought Him, saying, "If Thou wilt, Thou, Lord, _{Mark} i.—

Canst make me clean." He moved with pity toward 41

The wretched outcast, shrunk not back, averse,

From the contagious foulness of the curse,

But stretching forth His hand, him touched, and said,

"I will. Be clean!" Immediately he shed 4^

The leprous slough, and over his whole frame

The skin all soft and beautiful became.

Jesus charged sternly: "Tell no man, but go, 4 i

And do what Moses has commanded, show 44

Thee to the priest, that he may search for trace

And make the offerings ordered in such case,

For proof to all the cleansing is complete!"

He, disobedient and indiscreet, 45

Blazed it abroad, with the effect to draw

Great crowds about His steps as He foresaw,

Hindering His heavenly work to that degree,

That He could no more enter openly

The cities, but in desert places preached,

Where nevertheless great multitudes Him reached.

MATT IX. 2-8 MARK II. 1-12; LUKE V. 17-26.

RETURNING to Capernaum once more _{Mark ii. 1}

The glad waves sent dear welcome to the shore.

When it was noised He was again at home—   Mark ii. —

And a great number had together come,   2

Who thronged the entrance of the house and street,

While He addressed them loving words and sweet—

Behold a paralytic borne of four   3

Was brought to Him.   Because of the blocked door

Not able to come nigh Him, they the roof   4

Uncovered where He was ; and with this proof

Of their strong trust in the Great Healer, they

Let down the bed whereon the sick man lay.

And when this evidence of faith He saw   5

In bearer and in borne, in tones of awe

As if God spoke, discerning deeper need

Than even that for which they came to plead—

Desire of pardon, hope and fear combined,

With penitence and humbleness of mind—

He to the sick man said: " Be of good cheer,

Thy sins forgiven are !"   And sitting near   6

Were Scribes,who said within themselves, "This man 7

Blasphemes. Why speaks He in this wise? Who can

Forgive men's sins but God alone?"   And He,   8

Their thoughts discerning, said : " Wherefore do ye

Think evil in your hearts?   For of the two,

Whether is it more easy in your view   9

To say, ' Thy sins forgiven are !' or, ' Rise, Mark ii. --

And walk !' But that the Son of Man likewise 10

Has power on earth sins to forgive, thus know—

I say, 'Arise, take up thy bed and go 11

Unto thy house !' " The palsied man straightway 12

Arose, and took up that whereon he lay,

And went to his own house. O'erwhelmed with awe,

All said, " The like of this we never saw.

'T is meet we glorify the God of Heaven,

Who unto men such wondrous power has given."

GRATITUDE.

PSALM CIII. 1-5.

O bless the Lord, my soul!
  Let all within me bless!
Join, all my powers, in psalms of praise
  And hymns of thankfulness!

O bless the Lord, my soul!
  Let memory awake,
And think of all His benefits
  And grateful mention make!

Who all thy sins forgives,
  All thy diseases heals;
Who saved thy life from threatened death,
  And for thee pity feels.

Who gives thee pleasant food,
  And makes an end of pain,
So, like the eagle, is renewed
  Thy faded youth again.

Then bless the Lord, my soul!
  Let all within me bless!
Join, all my powers, in psalms of praise
  And hymns of thankfulness!

VII.

THE NEW DISPENSATION—THE SABBATH.

MATT. IX. 9-13; MARK II. 13-17; LUKE V. 27-32.

H E, wanting space, again the seaside sought,   Mark
ii. 13
And the assembled multitude there taught.

Passing along the shore He saw a man   14

Of priestly lineage, a publican,

Levi, son of Alpheus, better known   Luke
v. 27

As Matthew—scorned and hated of his own

Because of his vocation—sitting there

At the receipt of custom, toll-booth, where

Were Roman toll and tax and tribute paid.

To choose a publican, an outcast Jew,

Would be a scandal well the Saviour knew—

But He, Who could his inner fitness see,

Paused not a moment, saying, " Follow Me ! "

And he arose, obedient to the call,   28

And forthwith followed Him, forsaking all.

After this Levi made Him a great feast   29

In his own house.   The feasters were increased

By publicans and sinners, who sat down   Luke
                                                      v. —
With Him and His disciples—viewed with frown
And murmured disapproval, open sneer,   30
And wrathful whisper hissed into the ear,
By watching Scribes and Pharisees, who came
Only to make malignant search for blame.
" Why eats your Master with these persons vile,"
They say to them, "and thus Himself defile ? "
He, overhearing, said : " They that are whole   31
Need no Divine Physician of the soul,
Only the sick.   I did not come to call   32
Th' already pure, but sinners one and all.
But go and learn what meaning therein lies :
' I will have mercy and not sacrifice.' "

MATT. IX. 14-17: MARK II. 18-22: LUKE V. 33-39.

CERTAIN of John's disciples asked : " For what   33
Do we fast oft and Thy disciples not ? "
                                                       .
And Jesus said : " Of grief is fasting born.   34
Can children of the bridal chamber mourn
While yet the Bridegroom's with them ? Fast will
          they,   35
When He is taken finally away.
No man is so unwise as to attach   36

To an old garment an unshrunken patch, Luke v. —

Formed of new cloth unfulled, which cannot mend,

But only take from it and farther rend.

Neither do men put new wine* into skins 37

Old, yeasty, soaked, and sour, for then begins

At once in the sweet must, intestine strife,

A festering death with mimicry of life.

---

*That by the term "new wine," *must* is meant, can hardly admit of a doubt. In Luther's translation here as elsewhere, "new wine" is invariably rendered *must*. The meaning of *must* as defined by all the Dictionaries is "new wine, wine pressed from the grape but *not fermented*."—IMPERIAL DICTIONARY. The two terms (*i. e.*, new wine and must), are used interchangeably in all the books, and this of itself is conclusive, that wine to be wine need not be fermented. Here, unless by new wine, the unfermented article be understood, the illustration is emptied of all force and propriety. Why does "no man put new wine into old bottles"? Plainly because if new or unfermented wine were put into *old* bottles (bottles previously used), they would be sure to contain some of the *yeasty remains* of their former contents, and so induce fermentation, causing a rending of the bottles, the yeast present having its moral counterpart in the Judaic leaven which later was the means of schism in the Christian Church, for an account of which see Paul's Epistle to the Galatians throughout. New wine is *unleavened* wine. Now if unleavened bread is bread, by parity of reason, unleavened wine is wine. The grape juice and the dough have undergone precisely the same change, for *vinous* fermentation and *panary* fermentation are identical; but while in the one case the alcohol generated is retained, in the other it is driven off entirely by the heat of the oven. It is true, that when wine is spoken of, fermented wine is usually meant, just as in the case of bread, but there is no *usus loquendi*, quite the contrary, which forbids us calling the unleavened varieties, wine and bread.

Webster's Dictionary (last edition, not the earlier ones), makes wine a general term, like cider, defining it as "*the expressed juice of grapes*, usually the fermented juice." Those Dictionaries which confine the word wine to the fermented article alone, supply manifestly an imperfect definition, and are moreover inconsistent with themselves, for turning to the word *Must*, these same Dictionaries (the *Imperial*, for example), give as its meaning, "*new wine*, WINE pressed from the grape but *not* fermented," which is an undeniable example of the use of the word in another sense, the sense contended for. So if we consult the Latin and Greek Lexicons, they all agree in defining the Latin, *Mustum*, and its Greek equivalent, γλευκος, as "new *wine*." For a fuller discussion, see pp. 208-234 of this Work, Part First.

Raging and furious gases therein pent Luke v. —
Boil, hiss, and heave, and struggle to get vent,
Till the distending bottles burst at last,
And the spoiled liquor on the ground is cast.
But when new wine is put in bottles new, 38
Then sealed, no fermentation can ensue—
The vital poise maintained, by nothing swerved,
Contents and bottle are alike preserved.

In John's disciples, as in Pharisee,
The roots had struck of a fond fallacy,
That bodily affliction was an end—
And so they found it hard to comprehend,
That painful fastings, which did not express
Some sacred grief, were vain and profitless.
When men had come to hug the form, mistake
The shadow for the substance, and to make
The number of the fastings the chief test
Of character—accounting them the best
Who fasted oftenest, and every sign
Had grown more meaningless and less divine,—
'T was proof the time for terminating type
And cumbrous ritual was already ripe.
"Lo! I," Jehovah says, "make all things new!"

And Christ is here to make the promise true.   Luke
The old, like an old garment quite outworn
And past all patching, ragged, rent, and torn,
Is cast aside, each fragment and each shred,
So that the new may be all new instead—
A seamless vesture, glorious as the sun,
Immortal looms employed to make it one.

Foolish incongruous mixings are not meet
Of new with old, the fresh with the effete,
The sweet with sour, the living with the dead.
The Heavenly Bridegroom is already wed
To a new bride.   When death has made divorce,
Must He be tied forever to a corse?
A little leaven leavens without end,
Corrupts the pure, and mighty is to rend.
Like specks of rottenness too small to see,
The rot and leaven of the Pharisee,
And later taint of a dead Judaism,
The baneful cause of rupture and of schism.

Christ does not supplement, but supersede—
Both Jew and Gentile are from Moses freed.
He does not mend or piece, but weaves a whole,
And in a clean sweet body pours a soul.

No man, the slave of custom, it is true,
Used to the old, straightway desires the new,
Saying, the old is better.   But while none
Of all the prophets greater is than John,
He is still greater, better taught, more free,
Who knows the perfect law of liberty.

JOHN v. 1-47.

A JEWISH feast was nigh, and Jesus went   John
v. 1
Up to Jerusalem, love motive lent.
Hard by the sheep-gate was a Pool, far famed   2
For healing properties, in Hebrew named
Bethesda, with five porches running round,
Where a great multitude of sick were found—   3
Blind, halt, and withered—waiting for the stir,
Known sometimes in the water to occur—
(For it was said, an angel went down then   4
Into the Pool and troubled it, and when
This happened, whosoever first stepped in
The prize of healing certain was to win).

A man there lay, who thirty-eight long years   5
Had helpless been, and wet his couch with tears
From hope deferred, grown desperate of relief.
Jesus, who knew the term of his long grief,   6

Him pitying asked, " Wouldst thou be whole ? " He

said : John
v. 7

"Always another steps of me ahead."

And forthwith Jesus, without further talk, 8

Commands him : " Rise ! take up thy bed and walk ! "

He rose, took up his bed, and walked straightway. 9

And it so happened 'twas the Sabbath day.

The Jewish elders therefore to him said : 10

" It is not lawful to convey thy bed."

" I do what He who healed me bade me do. 11

What's lawful He should know as well as you."

" Who is the man who bade thee to do so ? " 12

He could not tell them, for he did not know— 13

Jesus, the cure performed, not making stay

Lost in the crowd had passed from sight away.

Him later Jesus in the Temple finds, 14

And what behooves him solemnly reminds :

" Behold thou art made whole, sin thou no more,

Lest something worse befall thee than before ! "

The man departed, and the elders told, 15

'Twas Jesus healed him.   Fiercer than of old 16

Blazed their fanatical and fatal hate.

To murder Him they plot and lie in wait,

For having healed upon the Sabbath day,

And told the cured he should his bed convey,   John v. —

Against the frivolous and foolish rules,

Prescripts and prohibitions* of the schools,

Rabbinical traditions vain and void,

Which the true purpose of the law destroyed.

Not such the holy Sabbath, Heaven decreed,

To meet the physical and moral need

Of all the sons of toil—a double rest,

Rest to the aching back and weary breast;

*An idea of the senseless and burdensome nature of some of these may be got from the following summary taken chiefly from Geikie's Life of Christ. In regard to the tying of knots—To tie or untie a camel-driver's or sailor's knot was unlawful, but a knot which could be untied with one hand was lawful. A shoe or sandal or woman's cap, or a wine or oil skin bag might be tied. A pitcher at a spring might be tied to the body-sash, but not with a cord. It was forbidden to carry food of greater bulk than a dried fig; of honey more than would suffice to anoint a wound ; of paper more than could be put into a phylactery ; of ink beyond what would be needed to form two letters. It was a desecration of the day to kindle or extinguish a fire ; or in sickness to give an emetic, or set a broken bone, or put back a dislocated joint. No healing was permitted except life was in danger. If one was buried under ruins he might be dug out if alive, but not if dead. To wear one kind of sandal was carrying a burden, but not another. One might not alone carry a loaf of bread on the public streets, but two together might. A journey was limited to 2,000 cubits.

The Sabbath began with sunset on Friday, and ended with sunset on Saturday. If it was cloudy the hens going to roost was to be the signal. The beginning and ending were announced in Jerusalem by a trumpet from the Temple ; and so in different towns. From the decline of the sun on Friday to its setting was Sabbath-eve, during which all food must be prepared, all vessels washed, and all lights kindled. No man must go out of his house with a needle or pen lest he should forget to lay them aside before the Sabbath opens. Pockets must be searched to see that nothing is left in them unlawful to carry. The Sabbath was believed to have prevailed in all its strictness from eternity throughout the universe. Even in hell the lost had rest from their torments during its sacred hours.

Sacred to God for worship and for praise—　John v. —
Sacred to man for health and length of days—
For, though a part of the Creator's plan,
Man was not made for it, but it for man—
Was made for man, when man himself was made,
And the foundations of the world were laid.
Since hushed Creation heard the Maker speak
The amen of the cycle of the week,
The mandate springs eternal in the breast,
And draws its sanctions from man's need of rest.
Things that pertain to nature, age, or clime,
Things of it, and not it, may change with time.
The day is as the need—it were not good
To keep the hunger and abolish food.
Meanwhile its Christian freedom is complete,
And all its chaste austerities are sweet.

But, ah! the food that nourishes can make
The deadly venom of the vengeful snake.
Bigots distil from mercy, love, and truth,
The murderous malice of the poisoned tooth,
Turn all to hate, wax hourly worse and worse,
More blind, more deaf, more hardened, more perverse.
Strange, that these men, who sat in Moses' seat,
Did not fall prostrate at His awful feet,

Unable to deny the glorious fact   John v. —
That God was present both in word and act.
More strange, a miracle none could dispute
Should form their only plea to persecute—
That for a work, whose heavenly source was plain,
They should Him cite, and criminally arraign
Before the Sanhedrim, to answer make,
Why He their Sabbath quirk had dared to break.

He threw down challenge in bold words and fit : 17
" My Father works, and does not intermit
His powerful working anywhere in space,
Either in nature, providence, or grace.
And I too work in love, and can attest
Perpetual labor is perpetual rest."

This made the elders more determined still ;   18
Who found therein new pretext Him to kill,
For that, not only He the Sabbath broke,
But in addition blasphemy had spoke—
Calling God ' Father,' arrogating high
Equality with God.   He made reply :   19
" The Son can nothing do but what He sees
The Father do, He duplicates but these.
The Father loves the Son, and to Him shows   20

All things He does and purposes and knows; John
And greater things than healing of the sick v. —
Will show through Him.   As He the dead [a] makes
     quick, 21
The Son too quickens whom He will and when.

  " Nor acts the Father as the Judge of men. 22
Omniscient like Himself, He, judging none,
All judgment has committed to the Son,
That all may honor to the same extent 23
The gracious Sender and the gracious Sent.
Wherefore 't is my prerogative and right
To sins forgive, I judge by inward light.
Who hears My quickening word, and Him believes 24
Who sent Me, everlasting life receives—
Life from above, life spiritual, in room
Of death and condemnation and just doom.
Because this life's unseen, demand ye proof?
The hour is coming and not far aloof, 25
When the entombed and carried on a bier
Shall start to life as they My voice shall hear.
As in the Father life springs unbegun, 26
Life in Himself is given to the Son.

* Deut. xxxii. 39.

5

He's made man's Judge, admire Heaven's gracious
    plan !   John
                                                 v. 27
Because while God He is a Son of man.

  " Marvel ye not at this, the hour is near,   28
When all the buried dead His voice shall hear,
And shall amazed come forth, and all mankind   29
Have their just portions severally assigned.
I can do nothing of Myself alone,   30
Having no will distinctively My own.
Since as I hear I judge, My judgment must,
Clothed with conjoint divinity, be just.

  " If I bear witness of Myself, then you   31
Might justly say, My witness is not true,
As void of proof. But there's Another One,   32
Who bears Me beaming witness like the sun.
Ye sent to John, and he true witness bore—   33
But not from men receive I witness more—   34
Not for Myself do I this reference make,
But that you may be saved, and for your sake—
A burning lamp far shining in the night,   35
Ye for a time were happy in his light.
But proofs of My Messiahship are given   36
Greater than John's, and reaching up to heaven—

" My works, demanding power omnipotent,   John v.
Bear witness that My Father has Me sent.
Though evidenced in Me, ye stand agape,   37
And neither hear His voice nor see His shape.
Because your vain traditions fill the floor,   38
Against the word of God ye shut the door—
Discredit what the Scriptures testify
Of Me, and think they witness to a lie.
Ye search them, for ye think ye have therein   39
Eternal life, without forsaking sin,
But full belief in them refuse to give,   40
And will not come to Me that ye may live.

" I seek not human glory, I desire   41
None of those honors to which you aspire—
For I know you, that ye crave power and pelf,   42
And have not love of God but love of self.
I come, commissioned in My Father's name,   43
And ye with bitter scorn reject My claim.
If comes another, artful to deceive,
All unaccredited, him ye'll receive.
How can one possibly believe, who clings   44
To worldly honors and minds earthly things—
Willing God's favor for their sake to lose?

Think not I'll to the Father you accuse— John v. 45
Moses, in whom ye put your trust, ev'n he
Will you accuse, because he wrote of Me. 46
But seeing Moses' writings ye reject 47
What better for My words can I expect?"

Thus spoke the future Judge of quick and dead,
And all the guilty Court was dumb with dread.
How awful Goodness is! the Truth how-sweet!
Let unborn lips the precious words repeat:

" The Father to the Son all power has given—
His throne established in the height of heaven;
Him raised to sit at His right hand alway,
Above all rule, authority, and sway,
And given Him a name all names[a] above,
And put all things beneath His feet of love.
His dwelling is with men to execute
True judgment and show mercy : to uproot
Satan's dark empire and the reign of death.
The Lord of Life, He quickens with His breath
The dead in trespasses[b] and sins, and lifts
To sit in heavenly places crowned with gifts.

[a] Phil. ii. 9.   [b] Eph. ii. 1-5; Col. ii. 1.

MATT. XII. 1-8 ; MARK II. 23-28 ; LUKE VI. 1-5.

As He returned to Galilee, He went   Matt.
xii. 1

Through cornfields on the Sabbath day.   Intent

Upon the holy work of doing good,

He paid no heed to His own want of food,

But His disciples hungry from long fast,

Plucked a few ears and rubbed them as they passed,

And ate.   And watching Pharisees hard by   2

Said unto Him : "See thy disciples!   Why

Break they the Sabbath, and Thou not forbid ? "

He said :   " Have ye not read what David did   3

When he was hungry, how he scrupled not

With those who were the sharers of his lot,

To go into the House of God, and eat   4

The sacred show-bread, which it was not meet

Nor lawful for himself or any one,

To touch or taste, except the priests alone ?

Or in the law, have ye not read again,   5

The priests by work do not the day profane?

By labor and by rest, by both or each,

The day is holy kept and without breach.

O'er all the motive dominates and sweeps,

The spirit soars, the letter only creeps ;

The Temple needs are not so great, at most,

As man's, the Temple of the Holy Ghost.   Matt.
xii. 6

Of little import is the outward act,

Compared with character and moral fact.

Sabbath and sacrifice in this agree,

They're far less dear to God than charity.

Lord of the Sabbath and the Source of it,   8

The Son of Man is judge of what is fit."

MATT. XII. 9-14; MARK III. 1-6; LUKE VI. 6-11.

DEPARTING thence, he entered on His way   Luke
vi. 6

A synagogue another Sabbath day,

And taught in words they all could understand.

A man was present with a withered hand,

And Scribes and Pharisees made feigned appeal :   7

" Since work is work and it is work to heal,

Is healing lawful wrought on Sabbath days?"

Quite sure by past miraculous displays,

If asked to heal, His love would not refuse,

They watched to see that they might Him accuse.

Knowing their thoughts He gave to him command,   8

Who had the palsied arm and withered hand :

" Rise up and stand forth in the midst!"   And he

Rose up and stood.   And Jesus said : " Let me   9

Ask you.   Is't lawful to do good or ill

On Sabbath days? to save life or to kill?"

They held their peace, not venturing reply.   Mark iii. 4

With an unusual sternness in His eye,

He said: "What man, who having but one sheep,   Matt. xii. 11

Fallen into a dangerous pit and deep,

Would not lay hold of it and lift it out?

Since man is better than a sheep, no doubt,   12

It is most lawful to do good always,

Both on the Sabbath and all other days."

Then looking round with anger mixed with grief   Mark iii. 5

On them so hard of heart, He mandate brief

Spoke to the man: "Stretch forth thy hand!" The will

Flashed power along the nerves, that felt the thrill

Of the returning life, and the disabled hand

Regained its ancient cunning and command.

They, filled with madness, plotted with hot breath   6

With the Herodians His speedy death.

MATT. XII. 15-21 ; MARK III. 7-12.

WITHDRAWN with His disciples to the sea,   7

Vast numbers came to Him from Galilee,

And from Judea and Jerusalem,   8

Peréa, Iduméa, some of them

From Tyre and Sidon and the adjoining coast,

Hearing the things He did, a mighty host.

Though coming crowds around him surged and
    pressed   Mark iii. 8
Leaving Him little or no time for rest,
Of mortal weariness He gave no sign,
Nor paused nor fainted in His work divine.
Howe'er they jostled, pushed on every side,
His holy lips were never heard to chide—
In the fulfilment sweet of what of old   Matt. xii. 17
Was by Isaiah of the Christ foretold:
'Behold My Servant whom I chose! My Sent!   18
My Well-beloved in whom I am content.
Upon Him I My Spirit will bestow,
And judgment to the Gentiles He shall show.
He shall not strive nor cry, no fearful ear   19
His voice haranguing in the streets shall hear,
Urging sedition and fomenting feuds,
Exciting to revolt fierce multitudes.
He without noise shall worldly kingdoms shake,
The bruiséd reed He will in nowise break,   20
And smoking flax He will not quench, but He,
Gentle as kingly, will all patience be,
Till smoke burst forth in clear victorious flame,
And distant Gentiles learn to trust His name.'   21

THE CHRISTIAN SABBATH.

All time, O Lord, is holy time!
   To Thee we wake, to Thee we sleep,
'Mid busiest hours the heavens we climb,
   And a perpetual Sabbath keep.

In Thee we live and move and are,
   From Thy full fountains we are fed ;
Thou makest sun and moon and star
   Meek ministers to yield us bread.

Thy laws relation have to need—
   Water essential is to thirst—
Repeal of water may succeed,
   But want should be abolished first.

While life is toil—most sweet, most kind,
   This boon of leisure and of rest ;
This holy quietude of mind,
   This weekly Sabbath of the breast.

We Sundays keep, and feel no yoke,
  Day of the Lord, the day of days!
When earth's ten thousand altars smoke
  With the sweet incense of Thy praise.

But then, we know, no law sets free
  From that which is above all price—
The sacred claims of charity—
  For Mercy's more than sacrifice.

VIII.

THE SERMON ON THE MOUNT.

MATT. V. I—VII. 29 ; MARK III. 13-19 ; LUKE VI. 12-49.

A ND He went out into a Mountain, where $\quad$ Luke
   He spent the night in solitary prayer, $\quad$ vi. 12

And called to Him, just as the sun arose, $\qquad$ 13

Of His disciples whom He would ; and chose.

With those already gathered to His feet,

As many as would make the Twelve complete—

Ordained them and appointed them to be $\qquad$ Mark iii. 14

Always with Him, to have authority

As His envoys to publish and proclaim

Pardon and peace to sinners in His name,

And heal the sick and demons exorcise, $\qquad$ 15

Under the seal of the attesting skies.

Descending lower down with them, He stood $\quad$ Luke vi. 17

On a raised plain mid a vast multitude,

Composed of His disciples—and all them

Who from Judea, and Jerusalem,

And from the shores of Tyre and Sidon came   Luke
vi. 18
To hear Him and be healed—His blessèd name,
Now on all lips, because there was no case
Too desperate for His relieving grace ;
The virtue that went out of Him was such   19
That men were healed with one believing touch.

All hushed, He sat, and lifting up His eyes   20
On His disciples, taught them in this wise :   Matt
v. 1

Happy the poor in spirit, who   3
            their deep demerit own,
    In them My Kingdom I set up
            with them I share My throne.
Happy are they, who mourn for sin   4
            with smitings on the breast,
    The Comforter shall comfort them
            in ways He knoweth best.
Happy the meek, who patient bear,   5
            unconscious of their worth,
    They shall inherit seats of power,
            and dominate the earth.
Happy who hunger and who thirst   6
            for righteousness complete,
    Their longings shall fulfilments have
            and satisfactions sweet.

Happy the merciful, who know Matt.
v. 7
    to pity and forgive,
They mercy shall obtain at last,
    and evermore shall live.

Happy the pure in heart, whose feet   8
    with holiness are shod,
They shall run up the shining way
    and see the face of God.

Happy the friends of peace, who heal   9
    the wounds by discord given,
The God of Heaven shall hold them dear
    and call them sons of heaven.

Happy are they, who suffer for   10
    adherence to the right,
They shall be kings and priests to God
    in realms of heavenly light.

Happy are ye when men revile   11
    and falsely you accuse,
Be very glad for so of old
    did they the prophets use.

Happy are ye, when for My sake,   12
    men persecute and hate,
Exult! for your reward in heaven
    is made thereby more great.

"Ye are the salt, whose saving power and worth

Arrest corruption and preserve the earth;   Matt.
v. 13

But if the salt its saltness lose, bereft

Of soul and sapience, the remnant left

Is foolish dirt, fit only to be then

Cast out and trodden under foot of men.

Watch, therefore, lest ye fall and lose the grace,

And ye yourselves be cast away as base;

Once lost, no power the savor can restore,

The salt remains unsalted evermore.

Towards them without do ye in wisdom[a] walk,

Seasoned with salt your conduct be and talk.

He who a sinner by his pureness[b] wins

Shall save a soul and hide unnumbered sins.

Devoted be, a sacrifice entire

Salted with salt and purifying fire.[c]

"Ye are the light of this dark world to show   14

The narrow path to erring man below.

Since ye are now, who once in darkness lay,

Light in the Lord and children of the day,[d]

Walk in the light, gainsayers thus confute

By holy arguments of answering fruit!

[a] Col. iv. 5, 6.   [b] James v. 20.   [c] Mark ix. 49.   [d] Eph. v. 8.

A city that is set upon a hill   Matt.
v. —
Cannot be hid, let men do what they will.
Nor do men light a lamp, and put the light   [15]
Under a bushel, but, in open sight
And on a stand, that so it may illume
Each dark and distant corner of the room.
Let your pure light so shine, that all may see,   [16]
In your good works and acts of piety,
Sweet demonstrations of your sonship given,
And glorify your Father Who's in heaven!

   " Think not I'm come to vacate or defeat,   [17]
I'm come not to destroy, but to complete,
Expound and magnify God's perfect law,
And give fulfilment of what prophets saw
Of Gospel promise and predicted grace.
Amen, I say to you that in no case,   [18]
Till earth shall fail, and heaven no more abide,
Shall aught pass from the law, till satisfied
Fulfilled and honored in each sacred jot,
And awful tittle, penstroke, point and dot.
In laws ordained for Israel of old
Were things foreshadowed and events foretold,
That have fulfilments when the time is ripe—

Type in the coming of the antitype,

The shadow in the substance.   Drops the shell

And lo, the kernel it concealed so well.

These, by abolishing fulfilments, end:

But none may blot the writing God has penned,

His permanent sure word : the least command

Is the eternal rescript of His hand.

Because th' authority which clothes the least   19

Of God's commandments cannot be increased,

Who breaks and teaches men to break them, he,

In the New Church and Kingdom of the Free,

Shall be called least ; but who shall do and teach

Them strictly, he shall highest honors reach.

For verily I say to you, unless   20

Yours shall exceed the boasted righteousness

Of Scribes and Pharisees, for you the gate

Of My pure Kingdom shall be all too strait.

   " Ye've heard that it was said by them who made 21

Additions to the law of old a trade—

The ancient glossarists who maimed and clipped

The meaning of the original prescript—

' Thou shalt not kill, and, who shall kill shall be

In danger of the judgment, else is he

Not guilty.'   But I say, ' Thou shalt not hate !'   22

For murders in the heart originate :

The guilt is not confined to outward act—

A murderous temper murder is in fact.

Feelings are judged, by Him who cannot err—

Who hates his brother is a murderer.

Anger that is not moral is forbid ;

Where malice mingles there is murder hid.

The armed assassin, ambushed in the heart,

Shoots unseen arrows at each vital part—

Stabs with mad words, projecting curses fell

With tongue of fire that 's set on fire of hell.

But for the cowardice of heart and hand,

Raca and *fool** were all for which they stand.

Lawless is passion.   Adder in the path

Is not so venomous as waiting wrath.

Like fabled basilisk, its poisoned breath

Is hot and deadly, and its glance is death.

"As love, which neither works nor wishes ill,   22

Alone the law can in its breadth fulfil,

If to the altar thou thy gift dost bring,

And there rememberest there is any thing

Thy brother has against thee, leave behind   24

---

* These terms, especially the latter, are expressive of great contempt and bitterness,
and may be regarded as tantamount to imprecating damnation on another.

6

The gift unoffered, and with friendly mind   Matt.
                                                     v. —
Go first be reconciled to him, then lift
An unshamed head and so present thy gift.

   " Agree with him whom thou hast wronged straight-
       way !   25
Compose thy differences without delay !
Matter of quarrel while thou canst remove,
Lest he, from whom thou keepest back thy love,
Be like a creditor who a debtor meets
And drags him to the judge through all the streets ;
Delivered to the officer at last,
He into prison without hope is cast.
Debtor to love thou shalt be prisoner made   26
Till the last farthing of the debt is paid.
Be warned against the horrors of that state,
The black Gehenna of eternal hate.

   " Ye 've heard it was of old commanded, ' Thou   27
Shalt not commit adultery.'   But now   28
I say, not 'lewd and lavish act of sin '
Alone, but unchaste look alike lets in
Th' adulterous defilement, so that he
Who lusts is guilty of adultery.
Thou shalt be master of thyself, severe   29

Toward every loose desire, nor hold so dear   Matt.
                                                v. —
Th' unmeasured worth of thy right hand or eye,
As a triumphant saintly chastity.
Filled with intense aversions and disgusts
Tread under foot contaminating lusts.
Let no thought enter gross or unrefined
The unpolluted temple of the mind.
Make with thine eyes a covenant, control
These avenues and inlets to the soul.
Of the strange woman[a] and her arts beware,
'T is for thy life, be caught not in her snare.
After her beauty lust not, do not sell
Thy birthright, bargaining it for hell,
Where crawls the worm that ceases not to gnaw
And quenchless flame of violated law.
If thou wouldst not consort with pains and stings,
And all abominable and detested things,
Excise the cancer with unsparing knife,   30
For no adulterer can enter life.

  "And it was said, ' Whoso shall put away   31
His wife, let him in witnessed form convey
A writing of divorce.'   The cause with him
Need be mere weariness or wish or whim.

[a] Prov. vii. 5.

This, for the hardness of your heart once given,   Matt.
xix. 8
Was sufferance rather than the will of Heaven.
From the beginning it was otherwise,
I now pronounce the statute of the Skies: 9
Who shall his wife divorce from board and bed,
Except for lewdness, and another wed;
And he who marries her, not rightly free
Both these and she commit adultery.
What God has joined let none asunder put,   Mark
x. 9
Trampling eternal sanctions under foot.

" Again, ye 've heard in olden time 't was said :   Matt.
v. 33
' Thou shalt not falsely swear, but pay, instead.
All vows expressly made unto the Lord,
For this obligatory makes thy word :—
Oaths that contain not, nor imply God's name,
Are mock oaths, without force and without blame,
Of which ten thousand broken in a day
Stop short of perjury, and nothing weigh.'
The frowns of Heaven on such vain swearing fall.
Therefore I say to you, Swear not at all !   34
Neither by heaven, for it is God's high seat ;
Nor by the earth, the footstool of His feet ;   35
Nor by Jerusalem, of which He is King :

Nor by your head; nor yet by anything.   Matt.
v. 36
Too much protesting* is not wise nor well.
An oath adds nothing to the truth ye tell.
So let your speech be simplest, Yes and No,   37
For from the Evil One additions flow.
The law means this: Thou shalt not falsify!
To bear false witness is to tell a lie.
This is the whole, however men invent
Endless deceits concerning what is meant—
Darken the simple and perplex the plain,
By some unholy juggle of the brain;
Gloze over insincerities of speech,
That crafty men the better may o'erreach.

   "Ye've heard that it was said, 'An eye for eye,   38
A tooth for tooth,' for this is equity.
Equate the wrong by giving blow for blow—
Who showed no mercy, him no mercy show.'
But I enjoin: Resist not evil! learn,   39
If one shall smite thee on one cheek, to turn
To him the other also! If he sue,   40
And take thy cloak, surrender thy coat too!

   * 'T is not the many oaths that make the truth,
   But the plain simple vow that is vowed true.
               —SHAKESPEARE.

And if moreover he shall thee constrain   Matt.
v. 41
To go with him one mile, go with him twain :
Whatever provocation thee assail,
Let not thy patience nor thy meekness fail!
Beware how thou give place to cruel Pride,
Companion of Revenge, the homicide—
The Sin of Self that will no insult brook,
Paying in blood the outrage of a look.

" Ye 've heard 't was said, ' Thy neighbor love, and
        hate   43
Thine enemy.'   But I reiterate   44
The old commandment: Love your enemies,
In word and deed !   Bless them in gentle wise
Who curse! Do good to them that hate!   And pray
For them who persecute! that so ye may   45
Be children of your Father Who 's in heaven,
By whom the dear and high example 's given—
For He on good and bad, on one and all,
Causes His sun to shine, His rain to fall.
For if ye love them only who love you,   46
As publicans do this, what thanks are due?
If ye salute your brethren only, what   47
Do ye the heathen naturally do not?

As is your Heavenly Father, so be ye, Matt.
v. 48
Perfect in love and in benignity!

   " Let not your righteousness be a deceit, vi. 1
A hollow show, and worthless counterfeit,
Done to be seen of men! for in God's sight,
Right done from love of right alone is right—
Base motives render base. Fix your regard
On His approval, as your high reward!
So when thou doest alms, do not proclaim 2
By sound of trumpet everywhere the same,
As do the hypocrites—vain-glorious cheats
Who in the synagogues and in the streets
Publish their charities, that they may gain
Glory of men; 't is all they shall obtain.
When pity prompts, and alms-deeds thee invite, 3
Let not thy left hand know what does the right;
The secret alms thou blushest to make known 4
Thy Father sees, and openly will own.

   " And when thou prayest, let the office be 5
A sacred matter 'twixt thy God and thee!
Be not as are the hypocrites, who pray
In synagogues and streets for self-display—
Whose worship is a mock and an offense—

They have their sought for, worthless recompense.
Enter thy closet, having shut thy door,   ^{Matt.}
Thy Father, Who in secret is, implore!
And He, Who sees in secret, will regard
With favor, and thee openly reward.
But when ye pray, let your weighed words be few! 7
Use not vain babblings as the heathen do,
Who think their gods for their much speaking hear,
So with loud repetitions stun the ear.
Be ye not like to them!   Before ye speak   8
Your Father knows your need, and what ye seek.
After this manner briefly pour your heart,   9
Whether ye pray together or apart :
' Our Father, Who dost make in heaven Thy home,
Thrice hallowed be Thy name! Thy Kingdom come!
Thy will be done—Thy perfect law of love   10
Fulfilled on earth as in the realms above !
Give us this day the bread by which we live !   11
Forgive our debts as we men's debts forgive !   12
Into temptation lead us not, but ever   13
In danger's hour from evil us deliver!
For Thine the Kingdom is, and Power, and Praise, 14
And the Amen, through everlasting days.'
Forgive, and ye shall be (not else) forgiven,—   15
Such is the unalterable law of heaven.

" And when ye fast, let not your fasting be   Matt. vi. 16
An acted piece of sheer hypocrisy—
Vain ostentation, pretence, and parade,
A studied make-believe and masquerade,
With rueful visage and disfigured face,
Hiding gross worldliness, and motives base.
This fast to men, to win men's poor regard,
Has verily from men its sole reward.
As fast from self is more than fast from meat,   17
As sordid looks make not the soul more sweet,
Anoint thy head, and wash thy face, that so
No one the secret of thy fast shalt know,   18
Except thy Father, who will recompense
Thy most sincere and secret penitence !

" Lay not up treasures here with futile zeal,   19
Where moth corrupts, and thieves break through and
            steal ;
But soar aloft on swift and eager wings,   20
To grasp the substance of eternal things !
Provide ye bags that wax not old, secure   Luke xii. 33
A treasure in the heavens that shall endure !
There neither moth consumes nor rust corrodes,
No thieves invade those high and safe abodes :

Set your affections then on things above,　　Matt.
　　　　　　　　　　　　　　　　　　　　vi. —

For where your treasure is will be your love !　　21

　" Lamp of the body is the seeing eye,　　22

Lighted by all the torches of the sky—

If single, clear, and healthy be the sight,

Then is the happy body full of light ;

But if diseased or double be the sense,　　23

Dark in thyself, the dark will be intense—

Like to the utter darkness of the blind,

A double vision and a double mind.

For none can serve two masters with true heart,　　24

Howe'er duplicity may play its part ;

From its allegiance Hate is sure to swerve—

Ye can in no wise God and Mammon serve.

　" Dismiss solicitude and sordid care　　25

About what ye shall eat or drink or wear !

Life 's more than food, the body more than dress,

Who gives the greater will bestow the less.

Behold the birds of heaven, they do not sow　　26

· Nor reap, nor plenty into barns bestow,

And yet your Heavenly Father feeds them—say,

Are ye not of more value much than they ?

Are not five sparrows for two farthings given ?

And yet not one forgotten is of Heaven,
Nor falls unnoticed.   Ye are much more dear
Than many sparrows, therefore do not fear.
So watchful, tender, and minute God's care,
He notes and numbers of your head each hair.
And which of you by dint of anxious thought   27
Can ever add to his fixed stature aught ?
Why are ye troubled about raiment ?   See   28
The lilies of the field, how carelessly
They grow, they toil not, spin not, are at ease—
Yet Solomon was ne'er arrayed like one of these.   29
Wherefore if God so clothe the growing grass   30
Which is to-day, and shall to-morrow pass
Into the oven, will he not clothe and do,
O ye of little faith, as much for you ?
So be not anxious about clothes and food,   31
Which untaught Gentiles seek as their chief good,   32
But seek ye first the glory and success   33
Of God's own Kingdom and His righteousness—
Labor to build on its eternal base
His government of truth and love and grace,
And all these temporal things shall added be
To the possessions of Eternity.

" Be not concerned about to-morrow's fate,   Matt.
vi. 34
For what shall happen be content to wait ;
Meet not the traveling grief that makes delay,
Sufficient is the evil for the day."

" Sit not in judgment on your fellow man ;   vii. 1
God judges righteously, no other can.
Judge not, lest ye condemn yourselves therein,   2
And forfeit needed mercy for your sin!
Measure for measure shall to you be given
By unrespecting and impartial Heaven.
And why art thou so keen and swift to spy   3
And blame the mote that dims thy brother's eye,
But blindly tolerant and dense as night
To the huge beam that darkens thy own sight?
Or how wilt thou assume to purge his sense,
When thine own eyes are full of rank offence?
Bigot and hypocrite, thy beam remove,   5
Then pluck thy brother's mote with hand of love.

" Give not things holy unto dogs—beware   6
Lest currish natures turn on you and tear!
Nor cast your pearls 'fore senseless swine to root
And trample them uncaring under foot!

" Nothing's so free as hospitable Heaven— Matt.
vii. 7
Ask, and all needful grace shall you be given!
Seek, and the gate of Mercy ye shall find!
Knock, and a lofty welcome waits behind!
Who ask receive, who seek they find, who knock   8
To them will God the heaven of heavens unlock.

"For what man of you all, who, if his son   9
Should ask him for a loaf, will give a stone?
Or for a fish, a serpent will bestow?   10
If ye then being evil, always know   11
How to supply your children's hungry needs,
How much more He, whose love all love exceeds,
Your Heavenly Father, shall good gifts impart
To those who ask in singleness of heart!

"Do as ye would that men should do to you,—   12
This is the law, and this the prophets too.

" Enter ye in at the strait gate and low!   13
For wide the gate, and broad the road to woe—
Many there be, who tread that downward path,
Which to destruction leads and waiting wrath.
For narrow is the gate, not letting in   14
The added bulk of unrepented sin ;

And hard the way and difficult to climb Matt.
vii. —
That leads to life and holiness sublime ;
And few there be, who with deep searching eyes
Find out that hidden path and mount the skies.

·

"Be on your guard against false prophets, who   15
Cruel as cunning, heedless souls undo—
Wolves in sheep's clothing—their pretentions try,
Ye by their fruits shall know their claim a lie.   16
Do grapes on thorns, or figs on thistles grow ?
The fruit decides, by it the tree ye know ;   17
As is the fruit, so the producing tree,
Or good or evil, as the case may be ;
If good the tree, so also is the fruit,   18
If evil, evil, each to each must suit.
The tree that brings not forth good fruit, the same   19
Shall be hewn down and cast into the flame.   20

"Not he who mere lip-homage pays to Me,   21
Into My Kingdom shall admitted be ;
But he alone, whose life is in accord ;
Who does God's will, as well as calls Me, Lord.
Many will say to Me in that dread day,   22
When all disguises shall be swept away,
'Lord ! Lord ! do not reject our pious claim !

Have we not prophesied in Thy great name,   Matt.
                                                             vii. —
And cast out demons, many wonders done?'
Then I will all relationship disown,   23
Saying, I know you not, depart from Me,
O, all ye workers of iniquity!

" Therefore, who comes to Me for grace and light, 24
These sayings hears, and does them with his might,
Him will I liken to the prudent man,
Who built a house, and, digging deep, began
By laying its foundations on a rock,
Solid and mighty to resist all shock.
The rain descended, and the floods arose,   25
And the wind blew, and with repeated blows
Smote it, but when the storm was overpast,
Rock-based, unshaken, lo, the house stood fast.
But he who hears My words, and hugs his guilt,   26
Is like unto the foolish man, who built
His house upon the sand.   The winter rain   27
Descending, flooded all the shifting plain;
Fierce blew the wind, loud roared the streams around,
And the house fell quick crashing to the ground."

When Jesus, in the audience of those   28
Assembled, brought His sayings to a close,

All were astonished, for He spake with awe,   Matt.
vii. 29
Not as the Scribes, but as Himself the law—
Proclaiming from that Sinaitic hill,
With all authority, Jehovah's will;
That New Commandment, latest from above,
The deuteronomy summed up in LOVE.

CHARACTER OF A HAPPY MAN.

PSALM I.

Happy the man not led astray,
  Whose feet fly far the fatal snare ;
Who stands not in the sinner's way,
  Who sits not in the scorner's chair.

But in the statutes of the Lord
  Finds evermore a new delight ;
Feeds on the sweetness of His word,
  In meditation day and night.

Like to a tree, that's planted near
  Unfailing streams that feed the root,
On bending boughs 'mong leaves ne'er sere,
  He shows to Heaven immortal fruit.

Whate'er he does shall grow and thrive.
  His joyful soul shall leap and laugh;
Not so th' ungodly; winds shall drive
  Them far away like empty chaff.

They shall not in the judgment stand,
  Nor shall the grace they spurned acquit:
But owned of God, at His right hand,
  The righteous shall exalted sit.

IX.

CENTURION—WIDOW OF NAIN—DEATH OF JOHN.

MATT. VIII. 1, 5–13: LUKE VII. 1–10.

DESCENDING from the Mount, the eager throng
    Follow His footsteps, as He goes along   Luke vii. 1

Towards Capernaum, where elders wait   3

His mighty coming at the city's gate—

Sent forth by a Centurion (one who

Had built a synagogue, though not a Jew,   4

And held most worthy), bearing his request   5

That He would heal his servant, sore distrest

With a dire palsy, ready now to die.   2

Jesus went with them; and, as He drew nigh   6

The house's door, the Roman Captain sent

A second embassy His coming to prevent,

Saying, " Lord, trouble not thyself to come,

It were too great an honor to My home,   7

That thou shouldst enter it, but if thou say

The word, my servant shall be healed straightway.

For I have power committed to my hand,   8

And say to soldiers under my command,   Luke vii.—

Go! and they go: Come! and they come: This do!

And swift compliances at once ensue.

Thy willing vassals are disease and death,

Yielding obedience to Thy sovereign breath."

When Jesus heard He marvelled.   Turning round   9

He to the people said: " I have not found   10

So great faith, no, not in all Israel."

In that same hour the servant was made well,

LUKE vii. 11-17.

ON the next day, divinely prescient,   11

He, journeying swiftly, to a city went

Called Nain.*   Th' attendant multitude scarce kept

Pace with His rapid march.   As on they swept,

Mile after weary mile without a pause,

They wondered greatly what might be the cause

Of His great haste, until as they drew near   12

The city's gate, they saw borne on a bier

A dead man, only son of a poor widow, who

Made loud lament as mourning mothers do.

Much people of the city present were—

And when the Lord her saw He pitied her,   13

* Nain was 25 miles from Capernaum.

And said : " Weep not ! "—then came and touched the
     bier ;   Luke
                                                                 vii. 14

While they that bare stood still in awe and fear,
And said : " Young man, I say to thee, Arise ! "
And, lo ! he that was dead, before all eyes   15
Sat up and spake.   Him, rescued from the grave,
Back to his mother's joyful arms He gave.
A sudden dread and a mysterious awe   16
Came down on all who this great wonder saw ;
And glorifying God, they said, " 'T is plain,
A mighty Prophet has appeared again. :
After long waiting, as in ages past,
His people God has visited at last."

MATT. XIV, 3-12 ; MARK VI. 21-29.

BRIGHT and particular, the Morning Star,
With matchless splendor, prophesies afar
Th' immediate coming of the Orb of Day,
Then with the increasing light it fades away.
So Christ's incomparable Forerunner, John,
Bore brilliant witness, till the Risen Sun,
From the vast firmament in healing streams,
Poured on the world His golden wealth of beams,
To bless the nations, and mankind restore,
And banish ancient night forever more.

John's lofty mission finished, a brief while
Allowed to bask in his great Master's smile—
Rejoicing in the light which made his dim,
And ceasing not to testify of Him—
It on one dark and fatal day befell,   Matt.
                                                        xiv. 3
That Herod Antipas, fit tool of hell,
Him seized and bound and into prison thrust,
To please the haughty partner of his lust,
Herodias, for whom he had defied
All law, and outraged decency beside—
Causing wide scandal, discontent, and strife
By wedding her, his brother Philip's wife.
And so, a Jew, to soften public blame,
He sought from John the sanction of his name;
Who, fearless of the anger of the king,
Said to his face : "'T is not a lawful thing   4
For thee to have her."   He enraged would then   5
Have killed him, but durst not, for that all men
Held John a prophet.   To his foxy eyes,
Later, it seemed not politic nor wise
To put to death one of renown so pure.
Not so his bloody minded paramour.
She—murderous thoughts revolving night and day,
Her thirst for vengeance brooking no delay—

Ceased not to plot with devilish design,   Matt.
xix. —

Till on his birth-night, when inflamed with wine,   6

Keeping high wassail with his guests, it chanced,

Salóme, daughter of Herodias, danced

Before them all, and it pleased Herod so,

That he made drunken promise to bestow   7

On her whate'er she asked, though it should be

Half of his realm.   Urged by her mother, she   8

Said : " Give me here upon a dish the head

Of John the Baptist, other gift instead."

The king was sorry, caught thus in the snare   9

Laid for his feet, but yet he did not dare

Retract his foolish oath,* before them sworn

Who sat at table, dreading secret scorn,

And so he ordered it to be fulfilled,

Ev'n to the letter, as the damsel willed.

With severing stroke, there in his prison cell,   10

On his great neck the axe uplifted fell ;

The bleeding head, just from the body torn,   11

Was to the girl upon a charger borne,

Who it received, and to her mother brought

The gory prize she had so cheaply bought.

* " It is a great sin to swear unto a sin
But greater sin to keep a sinful oath."
—SHAKESPEARE.

When the dread tidings his disciples heard, Matt.
xiv. 12
They took the headless trunk and it interred:
Then went, and Jesus told the horrid tale—
Hearing the news ten thousand cheeks turned pale.

MATT. XI. 2-19 ; LUKE VII. 18-35.

WHILE in the fortress of Machærus pent, xi. 2
Prison and palace, John to Jesus sent
(Told of His works, self-witnessing, divine)
Two of his own disciples with design,
That from Christ's lips they might the truth receive,
And mid adverse appearances believe.
Instructed so, they asked Him : " Art Thou He,
The Christ, the One that Cometh, or do we
Look for another ?"   In that very hour
Jesus cured many by His word of power
Of manifold diseases.   Thereupon
He said to them : " Go ye, report to John, 4
What ye have seen and heard, there answer find.
Yourselves are witnesses, how that the blind 5
Are made to see, the deaf to hear, the dumb
To speak, the lame to walk,—how lepers come
And are made clean, how e'en the dead are reached,
And how the Gospel to the poor is preached.

Happy is he and sure of recompense   Matt.
xi. 6
Who finds in Me nor scandal nor offense !"

Jesus began to speak, when they had gone,   7
Unto the multitude concerning John :
" What went ye in the wilderness to find?
Was it a frail reed rocking in the wind?
But ye went out expecting what to see?   8
One in soft dress apparelled gorgeously ?
Those who live delicately are in king's courts,
And are too dainty for such rude resorts.
Was it to see a prophet ye went out?   9
A prophet and much more beyond a doubt.
For this is he of whom 't is written, ' Lo   10
I send My Messenger, and he shall go
Before Thy face, and shall prepare the way,
What time Thy coming shall no more delay !'
Among them that are born of women, none   11
Of all the prophets greater is than John ;
But not the honor—which to him was given,
As the great Messenger and Mouth of Heaven ;
The Voice and Witness of the speaking Sky
Proclaiming that the Reign of God was nigh—
Equals the greatness of the meanest place

In the established Monarchy of Grace. Matt. xi.
Not height of function, nor related blood,
But holy choice of the eternal good
Gives highest title in that Kingdom blest,
Set up forever in the willing breast.

" John, who at first stood outside and before
The mighty threshold of the palace door,
Was first to enter, and has ever since
Been true and loyal to the Heavenly Prince.
His faithful head, once pillowed on the sod,
Rests on the bosom and the heart of God—
Above all dignity, all height above,
Sharing the privilege of the least that love.*

"From John till now God's Kingdom comes in
        power   12
And might of numbers, growing every hour ;
With holy violence and conquering stress
They storm its gates, and struggle to possess.
For all the prophets prophesied as one,   13
Till high fulfilments were in John begun—
Himself th' Elijah destined to appear—   14
He that hath ears of hearing let him hear :   15

---

* For the grounds of the opinion, that John was *in* and *not outside* the Kingdom of Heaven, see pp. 111, 112 of the Evangel, First Part.

His powerful summons all the people heard,   Luke vii.29
And publicans repented at his word,
Heeded the warning to the nation given,
Being baptized, and justifying Heaven.
Not so the Pharisees and lawyers, they,   30
Rejecting counsel, dared to disobey ;
With towering arrogance God's grace despised,
Refusing to repent and be baptized.

   " With nothing pleased, impossible to suit,   31
Peevish, perverse, and given to dispute,
Malicious, quarrelsome, and prone to strike,
To what then is this generation like?
'T is like to boys who in the market, play   32
Weddings and funerals, and, calling, say
To surly playmates difficult and sour :
' We've used all means to please you in our power;
We piped to you, and yet ye would not dance :
We mourned to you, and ye, with looks askance
In churlish ugliness and sullen spite,
Refused in acted grief your breasts to smite.'
For John the Baptist came, not using food   33
Lawful and innocent, for reasons good—
A Nazarite from birth—and ye proclaim,

He has a devil, jealous of his fame. Luke vii.—

The Son of Man (since not His Kingdom lies 34

In meats and drinks) in general, gracious wise,

Eating and drinking came, unbound by rule,

Severe rigidities of sect or school,

And ye find fault, and slanderously pretend

He is a glutton and a drunkard, friend

Of publicans and sinners.   Ye deride, 35

But Wisdom of her sons is justified."

The Prophet of the Voice!

Made, by Jehovah's choice,

His Messenger to go before His face!

He in the desert bred,

On hermit's diet fed,

A coat of camel's hair his loins embrace.

Hark! hark!   I hear his warning cry:

" Repent! Reform your lives! the Reign of Heaven
    is nigh."

Full loud the thunder rolls

O'er conscience-smitten souls,

And all the land is filled with solemn fears:
To him vast numbers press
Out in the wilderness,
And he baptizes them, baptized before in tears;
But Pharisees and Sadducees drives hence,
Devoid of these wet proofs of honest penitence.

None of the prophets old,
So lofty or so bold!
No form of danger shakes his dauntless breast:
In loneliness sublime,
He dares confront the time,
And speak the truth, and give the world no rest:
No kingly threat can cowardize his breath,
He with majestic step goes forth to meet his death.

Truth may seem stern and proud
To the misjudging crowd;
But Christ's forerunner loving is and mild:
I hear the tender moan
Of Pity in each tone—
A father grieving o'er a wayward child:
Note too, how meanly he himself doth rate,
"Myself am a low nothing, Christ alone is great."

X.

THE PENITENT WOMAN—THE UNPARDONABLE SIN.

LUKE VII. 36-50.

A CERTAIN Pharisee, with coarse design,   Luke vii. 36
  Invited Him one day with him to dine
Ingenious to contrive deliberate slight,
By failure of each customary rite,
Of hospitable welcome.   While at meat,
Reclining with unwashed and dusty feet,
A harlot of the city glided in—   37
Crushed with the shame and burden of her sin,
Full of self-loathing for her life abhorred,
Presuming on the pity of the Lord,
The Friend of Sinners, whose dear lips had spoken
Strange words that morn by which her heart was
       broken:
" Come weary souls with heavy guilt opprest
Come unto Me and I will give you rest!"

  And might she come?   And was not hers a case,
Beyond the reach and remedy of grace?—

A sinner branded with opprobrious names,   _{Luke}
O'erwhelmed with infamies, contempts and shames.   vii.—
Could Heaven so stoop? and was it truly so,
That there was mercy for one sunk so low?

Grateful, and sure His condescension such
He would not shrink from her believing touch,
She with her brought, to show a dumb regard,
An alabaster cruse of precious nard;
And when she saw Him, to all others blind,   38
She softly stole His blessed feet behind,
And wet them with her tears profusely shed,
And wiped them with the tresses of her head,
And kissed them, poured thereon the rich perfume,
The costly fragrance filling all the room.

Meanwhile, much scandalized, the frowning host,   39
Making His sep'rateness his special boast,
With cold, disdainful eyes the scene beheld,
Saw one, a thing for spurning, unrepelled,
Nay welcomed; and, indignant at the sight,
That filled all heaven with pleasure and delight,
He spake within himself, though not unheard
The secret thought that his vain bosom stirred:
" This Man were He a Prophet, would have seen

This woman was a sinner, most unclean."

Luke vii. —

And Jesus fastened on him eyes that read 40
All that was passing in his soul, and said :
" Simon, I have somewhat to say to thee."
Awed by that look of calm divinity,
He spake with due respect: " Master, say on !
I listen "—his self-confidence half gone.
" A creditor two debtors had.   One owed 41
Five hundred pence, for him a heavy load ;
The other fifty.   And when, bankrupt, they 42
Had not wherewith the smallest part to pay,
He generously forgave them both.   Which then,
Tell me, will love him most of these two men ?"

Simon replied : " The chance is more than even, 43
He will love most to whom was most forgiven."

" Thou hast judged rightly," Jesus said, " and here
Is confirmation and example clear.
See'st thou this woman, Simon ?   I, a guest, 44
Entered into thy house at thy request.
Thou gavest Me no water for My feet ;
But she has washed them with the crystal sweet
Of weeping eyes ; and wiped and made them fair
With the abundant tresses of her hair.

Thou gavest Me no kiss; but she has since   Luke
                                                 vii. 45
I came, her love and sorrow to evince,

Ceased not to kiss My feet; nor oil'dst My head :   46

But she has on My feet rich spikenard shed.

Wherefore her sins, though many, are forgiven   47

By the free favor of approving Heaven.

For she loves much, proportioned to the grace

That cancels the demerit of her case.

But thou lov'st little, if thou lov'st at all,

With reason, if the needed grace be small :

Or if thou 'rt pure, and owest naught to Heaven,

Why love at all, with naught to be forgiven ?"

    Jesus then turned, and, her addressing, said :   48

" Thy sins forgiven are, be comforted !"

When they, that sat at meat with Him, began   49

(Blind to the proof that He was God in Man)

To question His authority and right

To sins forgive, He said, from the same height

Of sole prerogative beyond increase :

" Woman, thy faith hath saved thee, go in peace !"   50

    See, O my soul, see pictured in this case

The mind of God and methods of His grace !

The more, if this be Mary Magdalene,

The same* who figured in a former scene, Luke vii. --
When the dear Lord, not measuring her blame,
Cast out seven devils from her tortured frame—
The dread possession having for its cause
Guilty excess and violated laws.
Restored to sanity and self-control,
She melted toward the Power that made her whole.
As now a backward look remembrance cast
O'er all the guilty miserable past,
And her roused conscience, with just terrors tost,
Saw all too plainly that her soul was lost,
Thoughts of God's goodness to repentance led, Rom. ii. 4
And opened all the well-springs of her head.
No longer blind, by a new light within,
She saw th' exceeding sinfulness of sin ; vii. 13
And shuddering saw its ill desert as well,
Dreadful and dark and bottomless as hell ;
Knew that each guilty deed had damning force
To fill eternity with keen remorse.
If but the pure in heart God's face shall see,
What hope was there for one so vile as she ?
  Sincerely penitent, she, ne'ertheless,
Owed it to Heaven her vileness to confess ;

* The tradition that identifies the two is an ancient one, and has been accepted by the painters, but rests on doubtful authority.

8

And felt she could shed voluntary tears,
And make perpetual moan through endless years,
Because that she had sinned and loved not Love.
She wept not that she might God's pity move,
Not to gain favor, but because 't was meet
With streaming eyes to wash the Saviour's feet.
Thus occupied with sorrow and self-blame,
'T was unexpected when the pardon came.
If at the gallows' foot there comes reprieve,
What joy ! but who the rapture can conceive,
When Lips Divine speak peace, and loving breath
Remits the sentence of eternal death?

Much was forgiven, and she lovéd much.
And from that hour was her devotion such,
She lived to Him alone—her whole delight   Luke viii. 2, 3
Adoring ministries from morn till night :
Him giving of her substance, to supply
Shelter and food He was too poor to buy.
Strange sight ! the Bread of Life oft wanting bread ;
Lord of all Worlds, nowhere to lay His head ;
Heir of Eternity, like beggar, He
From woman's hands accepting charity ;
Willing to take what it pleased her to give,

As if dependent on her help to live.
Amazing paradox! the finite set
Above the Infinite to bring God in debt:
Like ocean, grateful to each drop of rain,
As though 't were not his own paid back again.

Her Lord and Saviour saw in her exprest
Soft love and pity, such as filled His breast;
And owned the tears, that for the wretched ran,
As shed for Him, identified with man.
All that she did to soothe another's grief,
He counted ministries for His relief;
The cup of water to the thirsty given,
For His dear sake, a favor done to Heaven.
Ten thousand little acts she valued not,
By Him remembered though by her forgot,
Proofs of a love, that did not what it would
But only that poor something which it could,
Esteeming it unworthy of regard,
Laid yet foundations for undreamt reward.
For God is love, and 'they who in love dwell,
God dwells in them and they in Him as well.
Who shall the " Well-done " of the Master win,
Into His joy at last shall enter in.

DAVID'S PENITENCE.

PSALM LI.

Have mercy, my offended God!
  According to Thy goodness spare!
Let not the judgment of Thy rod
  Sink me still deeper in despair!

O hear, and my transgressions blot!
  Save me from my enormous guilt!
Wash from my soul each leprous spot
  For Thou canst cleanse me if Thou wilt.

My sins are mountainous, they climb
  The heights of air and reach the skies;
The ghastly horror of my crime
  Is night and day before my eyes.

'Gainst Thee this odious deed was done;
  I struck my Maker in the face;—
No wonder blushed th' astonished sun,
  And earth saw shudd'ring the disgrace.

Were not Thy mercies as the sand,
  I do not know, that I would dare

Thus lift to Thee these bloody hands
  In agonizing act of prayer.

Though well I know, there cries to Thee
  The crimson of th' accusing sod,
Hide not Thy face, deliver me
  From my bloodguiltiness, O God!

Burnt offerings and sacrifice
  Didst Thou desire, I would impart—
One only Thou wilt not despise,
  A broken and a contrite heart.

Create in me a heart that's pure!
  Renew, transform, and make me o'er!
Not otherwise can I be sure
  I will not stumble as before.

By Thy free Spirit me uphold,
  For I am weak and sick and sad!
Forgive, and love me as of old,
  And give me back the peace I had!

Then to transgressors I will teach,
  How there are none so far from Thee,
But Thy salvation can them reach,
  For, lo, it did extend to me!

LUKE VIII. 1-3.

DAY after day, from early morn till night, Luke viii. 1

Jesus pursued His labors infinite.

To every city, every village went,

Preaching and healing—mind and body spent,

In minist'ring to crowds that round Him pressed ;

Haggard and worn for want of food and rest.

And certain women, wonderfully restored 2

To health and reason, did not grudge their Lord

Their service nor their substance nor their life—

Mary called Magdalene, Joanna, wife 3

Of Chuza, Herod's steward, aid supplied,

Susanna too, and many more beside.

MATT. XII. 24-50 ; MARK III. 19-35 ; LUKE XI. 14-36 ; VIII. 19-21.

THE Scribes and Pharisees, with new alarm, Mark iii. 22

The people saw won over by the charm

Of His most gracious words and godlike acts ;

Unable to deny th' astounding facts—

Demons ejected by His simple word.

No cabalistic formula was heard, *

* Jewish Cabalists believed that the pronunciation of certain magical words engraved on the seal of Solomon would work marvels. " The mightiest of all agencies was the unutterable name of Jehovah " ; but in addition to the secret name of God or some of the angels, they attributed a magical efficacy to certain mysterious combinations of letters and numbers, and particular texts of Scripture.

A mere, ' Be healed! ' sufficing for the cure.   Mark
                                                         i.i.
Easy, direct, immediate, and sure.

Though visibly, in all, the Godlike towers,

High o'er malefic agencies and powers,

They dare His works bespatter and belie,

And spit their blasphemies against the Sky—

Saying, He is Himself possessed, as well,

And casts out demons by the Prince of Hell;   23

Yea, half persuade, with this invention vain,   21

His friends and family that He 's insane ;

Who seek to apprehend Him on this ground.

He said (His foul maligners to confound),

" No state divided 'gainst itself can stand.   24

The end of Satan's kingdom were at hand,

If he against himself should head revolt,   25

And, leagued with foes, conduct the strange assault.

If I by Satan demons put to rout   Matt.
                                                      xii. 27
By whom then do your children cast them out ?

Be these your judges.   But, if I cast out   28

Demons with God's own finger, then no doubt

God's Kingdom has come nigh to you.   None can   29

Plunder a strong man's house, unless some man

Of greater strength is able him to bind :

Then can he spoil the spoiler to his mind.

Because I stronger am than Satan is,   Matt.
xii. —
I wrest from him the prey he holds as his.
Who is not with Me is to Me adverse—   30
Not simply neutral is, but something worse.
Who gathers not with Me, through envy base,
Scatters abroad and frustrates heavenly grace.

" Wherefore I say to you, All kinds of sin   31
And blasphemy may full forgiveness win,
But blasphemy against the Holy Ghost.
The grace that saves men to the uttermost,
And pardons blasphemy against the Son,   32
Has for this form of sin forgiveness none—
Not in this world nor in the world to come—
Closed is the Court, the Advocate is dumb.

" The fruit decides infallibly the tree—   33
No case admits of higher certainty.
For men do never gather grapes of thorns,   34
Nor figs of thistles.   Therefore, he who scorns
Such final proof, and for some cause denies,
Dupes his own soul and binds it o'er to lies.
He treads the crumbling verge of an abyss,
Who dares discredit evidence like this.

" My works of mercy, wrought by power divine,

Ye to Satanic agency assign.   Matt.
xii. —

Beware, lest sinning thus against the light,

Ye lose the moral faculty of sight;

Commit like Satan the eternal sin,

And be like him infernalized within;

With your own hands the knell of seeing toll,

And so in outer darkness plunge the soul.

" To all who ask, the Holy Spirit 's given,

But, having long and vainly with you striven,

Blunting the keenness of **His** heavenly darts

On the unyielding hardness of your hearts,

Found you opposing evermore the right,

Resisting, grieving, doing .Him despite,

Till diabolic grown in love and hate—

What can He do but leave you to your fate?

Lost irredeemably who thus blaspheme,

Trampling the Godhead of the One Supreme.

" [' False and fair foliaged as the manchineel,'*

Whose every part dire poison doth conceal,

Found in the fruit, and present in the wood],

Entirely evil, how can ye speak good :   35

Your tongue is slander, and your lips are guile;

* Coleridge.

Your breath 'outvenoms all the worms of Nile ' : Matt.
xii.—

True to th' abundance of the heart, always, 36

The blabbing mouth the character betrays;

Hence for each idle word that men let fall 37

They shall account to the Great Judge of all.

"An evil generation seeks a sign, 38

And to its will would sway the Will Divine;

Dissatisfied with proofs already given,

Would dictate new ones to the God of Heaven.

One final sign My mission shall attest, 39

Supreme, unparalleled, unlike the rest—

As Jonah, three days in the belly slept * 40

* It is conceivable that Jonah, while in the fish's belly, was in a state of trance. Cases are on record, where persons were supposed to be dead, and have been perfectly conscious of what was going on around them during the preparations for the funeral. One in point is the well known case of Rev. William Tennent, who died at Freehold, N. J., March 8, 1777. When he had nearly completed his theological course, he became seriously ill, fell into a catalepsy or trance, and remained for several days in a condition of apparent death. His physician perceiving a slight tremor under his left arm, refused to consent to his burial; and although his friends were satisfied he was dead, his funeral was postponed for three days, and subsequently for several hours, efforts being made meanwhile for his resuscitation, which finally occurred just as the physician was giving up in despair. His recovery was slow and painful. He stated, that at the moment of his apparent decease, he found himself surrounded by an unutterable glory, and saw a great multitude apparently in the height of bliss, singing most melodiously; and that when he was about to join the great and happy multitude, some one came to him, looked him full in the face and said : " You must go back." At the shock this intelligence gave him, he opened his eyes, and finding himself in the world fainted. A memoir of him, giving a very full account of his trance was prepared and published by Judge Elias Boudinot.—*New American Cyclopedia.*

Hibernation and *Æstivation*, called by the Germans, *Winterschlaf* (winter sleep)

Of the great fish, miraculously kept— Matt.
xii. —

In dreamy trance, the spirit still awake—

Then to the Lord did supplication make

Out of the heart of hell, what time below

The bottoms of the mountains he did go,

And o'er him all God's waves and billows passed,

And then alive was on the dry land cast—

So shall the Son of Man rest in the gloom,

Three days, of earth's deep heart and teeming womb.

"The Ninevites shall in the Judgment rise

And you condemn ; for they did not despise

The call of Jonah to repent, while here's

A greater Jonah speaking to deaf ears.

The Queen of Sheba shall with wondering mouth

Witness against you, for from the far south

and *Sommerschlaf* (summer sleep), are terms used to denote the torpor or sleep which certain animals fall into and remain during the season of cold or heat. During hibernation (which is by far the most common) the respiration being almost entirely suspended, the maintenance of vitality depends chiefly on the heart. Animals in this state may be placed in Carbonic Acid, or under water for several hours without injury, *though they would die in a very few minutes in their normal state.*

"Long continued suspension of consciousness in man is rare in temperate climates, but is more frequent in India, where some religious ascetics are stated on unimpeachable authority to possess the power of throwing themselves into a state closely resembling hibernation for an indefinite period."—*Encyclopedia Britanica.*

While the facts concerning Jonah's preservation are no doubt to be considered miraculous, it is nevertheless true, that the account given, marvellous as it is, is hardly more so than some seemingly well authenticated modern stories told about the Fakirs.

She came to hear the words of Solomon,   Matt.
xii. —
While here 's the wisdom of a Greater One.

"A sick man for a time shall seem to mend,   43
And deem the foul possession at an end.
But should there be, as many times it haps,
From causes blameable, a sad relapse,
The unclean spirit, multiplied to seven,   44
Again the blood shall permeate and leaven,   45
Making his last state than the first far worse—
So this lapsed generation, more perverse,   46
And more incurable sevenfold has grown,
Than if it ne'er the way of life had known."

A certain woman present cried out: "Blest   Luke
xi. 27
The honored womb that bore Thee, and the breast
That suckled thee!"   He said, "Blest rather they   28
Who hear the word of God, and it obey."

"Thy mother and Thy brethren stand outside,"   Mark
iii. 32
They said, "and wish to see Thee."   He replied: 33
"Who is My mother and My brethren?   Who,   34
But such as God's commandments hear and do?"   35

Another time, when crowds in myriads flocked   Luke
xii. 1
About Him, and approach to Him was blocked

Luke
xii. .

By the compactness of this living wall,
He said to His disciples: " First of all,
Avoid the leaven of the Pharisee,
Which is false seeming and hypocrisy :
In all the veins the dire infection lurks,
Corrupts the blood and sure destruction works.   ²
For nothing 's covered up but shall be shown,
And nothing hid but shall be fully known."

LUKE XII. 13-21 ; XIII. 1-9.

" SPEAK to my brother, Rabbi!" one there cried,   ¹³
" That he th' inheritance with me divide."
And Jesus said: " Man ! why to Me refer?   ¹⁴
For who made Me your judge or arbiter?"
Addressing those around, He said : " Take heed !   ¹⁵
Beware of covetousness, the sin of greed !
For a man's life is of a nature such,
That it depends not on his overmuch."
And then He spake to them this parable :   ¹⁶

" A certain rich man's fertile fields bore well
And plenteously.   And he 'gan on this wise   ¹⁷
To vainly reason and soliloquize :
' What shall I do, since I've no room to store
The produce of my acres any more?

I'll do what thrift me counsels and forewarns :   Luke
xii. 18
I'll pull down present and build greater barns ;
And there will garner all my goods and grain.
Then to my soul say, 'Soul, thou hast much gain   19
Laid up for many years, so take thine ease
Henceforth, eat, drink, thyself enjoy, and please.'
God said to him, ' Thou foolish man, this night   20
A sudden death thee unprepared shall smite ;
Then whose shall be the treasures, which thou hast   21
Heaped for thyself, and naught tow'rd God amass'd ?' "

Some persons told Him, and desired His view,   xiii. 1
Touching the Galileans, Pilate slew,
Lately, at one of the great yearly feasts,
Mingling their blood with blood of slaughtered beasts
Designed for sacrifice : Was theirs the fault ?
Or his who made the murderous assault ?
He said : " From facts like these, ye greatly err,   2
If ye preëminence of guilt infer.
These Galileans sinners were 't is true ;
But think not they were greater ones than you.
Not special was the judgment on them sent ;
For you shall perish unless you repent.   3
Nor think those eighteen men, on whom did fall   4

Siloam's tower, were sinners above all Luke xiii. —
The dwellers in Jerusalem, for you,
Unless that ye repent, shall perish too." 5

He spake this parable: " A certain man, 6
(Be timely warned! repent ye while ye can!)
Had planted in his vineyard a fig tree;
And duly, at the proper season, he
Came seeking fruit; but when he found none there,
He said to the vinedresser in despair, 7
' Lo, these three years I've seeking come, and found
No fruit.   Why longer cumbers it the ground?
Cut th' useless fig tree down.'   He answered, ' Sir, 8
The order still one other year defer,
Till I can dig about it and manure.
Give it this chance to make the matter sure.' " 9

XI.

WHAT THE KINGDOM OF HEAVEN IS LIKE.

MATT. XIII. 1-51; MARK IV. 1-32; LUKE VIII. 4-15.

ENTERING a boat, He sat upon the Sea,   Mark iv. 1

And taught by parable and simile   2

The eager thousands gathered on the shore-

The number growing every moment more.

"Hearken! A husbandman went forth to sow   3

And as he with free hand the seed did strow,   4

Some by the wayside fell, trod under foot,

The birds devoured before it could take root.

Some fell on rocky ground, and sprang up soon,   5

But poorly rooted, withered before noon.   6

'Mong choking thorns some fell; while others found   7

Propitious lodgment in good mellow ground,   8

And multiplied, and brought forth fruit, behold

Thirty and sixty and an hundred fold.

He that has ears to hear it, let him hear!   9

To docile minds the hidden truth is clear.

The willful deaf, their ears to wisdom sealed,   Mark
                                                   iv. --
Shut out the grace unwilling to be healed.
As choice is free, no power can make men choose
The heavenly gift of knowledge they refuse :
But ignorance need never be afraid
To ask of God explanatory aid ;
To seekers, and such only, light is given,
To understand the mysteries of Heaven.
So when alone, asked by the Twelve to tell,   10
The Lord laid open thus the Parable :

" When one, with dull uncomprehending ears,   15
The published Gospel of the Kingdom hears,
Then comes the Wicked One, like evil bird,
And snatches up the unregarded word
On the unloving heart's hard surface strown.
This is the wayside hearer, vainly sown.
He that receives the seed on rocky site,   16
Is one that hears the word with quick delight,
But, in himself not having root, soon falls,   17
When persecution or distress appalls.
He, that among the thorns the seed receives,   18
Is one who hears the word, and half believes ;
But worldly cares, and riches' vain pursuit   19

9

Choking the word, he fails to bring forth fruit.   Mark
                                                      iv. —
That sown upon good ground, it him denotes,   20
Who, having heard the word, himself devotes
To prayerful toil and tillage which ne'er cease,
And bears and brings forth fruit, and makes increase,
Out of the heart's enriched and heaven-blest mould,
Thirty and sixty and a hundred fold.

  Another Parable spake He to show,   Matt.
                                                      xiii.24
" Messiah's Kingdom, set up here below,
Is like a man, that having good seed sown,
While his men slept, his enemy, unknown,   25
Sowed tares among the wheat, and went his way.
When sprang the blade up at a later day   26
And brought forth fruit, appeared the tares likewise.
Then came his servants, filled with great surprise,   27
And told the householder: ' Sir, didst not thou
Sow good seed in thy field? whence came or how
These tares then that we see?'   He answered, 'One   28
Who is an enemy has this thing done.'
The servants say to him : ' Wilt thou we go
And gather up the tares?'   But he said, ' No,   29
Lest ye root up the wheat.   Let them both stand   30
Untouched till harvest; then I will command

The reapers: 'Let it be your first concern, Matt. xiii. —
The tares to gather, and them bind to burn ;
But let the ripe and separated corn
Into my barn in purity be borne.' "

To His disciples, Jesus then declares   36
The meaning of the Parable of tares :
" By Sower of the good seed understand,   37
The Son of Man, the Tiller of the land.
The field is the whole world He came to bless :   38
The good seed are the sons of righteousness,
The children of the Kingdom : but the tares,
Sons of the Evil One, sown unawares   39
By the arch-enemy, the Devil, who
Wakes to beguile and frustrate and undo
The benediction of the wholesome wheat,
With cursing of the poisonous counterfeit :*
The harvest is the end and final stage   40
Of the revolving cycles of the age :
The reapers are the angels—Christ shall send   41
These forth to gather all things that offend,

---

* The plant translated tares is supposed to be identical with the " darnel " (*Lolium temulentum*), a poisonous weed or grass, the grains of which produce vomiting and purging, convulsions, and even death. The darnel, before it comes into ear, is very similar in appearance to wheat.

And them that do iniquity, at last,   Matt.
                                                             xiii. --
Out of His Kingdom, and they them shall cast   42
Into a furnace of devouring fire—
There shall be wailings loud and anguish dire.
Then shall the righteous shine forth every one.   43
In God their Father's Kingdom, like the sun.
    Wake up the sleeping function of the ear!
'T is for your life, consider what ye hear!"

    " Messiah's Kingdom is," He said again,   Mark
                                                             iv. 26
"As if one should into the ground cast grain,
And then should sleep, and night and day should rise, 27
And see it spring and grow in unknown wise.
For of itself the earth, without man's aid,   28
Evolves continuously the sprouting blade,
The ear, the full corn in the ear: the hand
Puts in the sickle then and reaps the land."   29

    He spake another Parable : " Christ's Reign   30
Is like in its beginning to a grain   31
Of mustard seed, a man sowed in his field,
Which is the least of seeds, but holds concealed   32
The greatest of all herbs.   When grown, a shade
By its great branches for the birds is made."

Again He said to them: "The Reign of Heaven
Is like in silent working unto leaven,   Matt.
                                                          xiii. 33
A woman hid in a large batch of meal,
Till every part was made the change to feel."

"'T is like a treasure hidden in a field,   44
Which a man finding, having it concealed,
He goes and sells all that he has, and buys
The field in which the buried treasure lies.

"'T is like a merchantman, who everywhere   45
Roamed, seeking goodly pearls and jewels rare,
And having found one pearl of worth most strange,   46
He sold his all and gave it in exchange.

"'T is like a net, which, cast into the sea,   47
Gathers the good and bad promiscuously:
When it is full and drawn to shore, then they   48
Preserve the good and cast the bad away.
So shall the wicked from the just at last   49
Be severed by the angels, and be cast
Into a furnace of devouring fire,   50
There shall be wailing loud and anguish dire.

   "Have ye these Parables all understood?"   51
"Yea, Lord!" they promptly answered. "Very good.52
See then ye turn them to good use; for each

Instructed Scribe, that's qualified to teach,
Is like a householder who from his store
Brings forth things new and old laid up before."

THE SOWER.

A husbandman went forth to sow :
   And, as with measured step, he swung
An arm of vigor to and fro,
    The seed he flung.

Some by the way-side fell, thence soon
   By birds devoured, not taking root :
On rocky places some, hot noon
    Withered the shoot :

Some among choking thorns : but seed
   That into good ground fell, behold !
Sprung up and brought forth fruit with speed
    An hundred fold.

O Saviour ! lest devouring bird,
   Or shallow soil, or choking thorn,
Frustrate the mercy of Thy word,
    Make sure the corn !

XII.

TEMPEST STILLED—AT GADARA—JAIRUS' DAUGHTER.

MATT. VIII. 18-27 ; MARK IV. 35—V. 20 ; LUKE VIII. 22-25.

NEEDING repose, He said at eventide, Mark
iv. 35
   " Let us go over to the other side ! "
The multitude dismissing, soon afloat, 36
They took their wearied Master in the boat,
Just as He was, and as they sailed, He slept.
And a great storm of wind came down, and swept 37
The Lake, and rolled—the while the night grew dark—
Big angry waves that beat into the bark,
So that it was now full, and sinking fast.
Jesus was in the stern asleep.   Aghast, 38
Come His disciples, and Him roughly shake,
So deep His slumber, crying, " Master, wake !
Carest Thou not we perish ?"   Straightway, He
Arose, rebuked the wind, and to the sea
Said : " Peace, be still ! "   And the wind ceased, and there
           there
Was a great calm, and heaven and earth were fair.

To His awestruck disciples then He saith: Mark iv. 40

" Why were ye fearful, ye of little faith?"

These, filled with wonder, to each other say, 41

" What Man is this whom winds and waves obey?"

Preserved alive by these miraculous means, Mark v. 1

They reach the country of the Gadarenes—

Arriving there as day began to break—

Having passed down the whole length of the Lake:

The boat forced southward, when the wind was strong,

Out of its course had made the passage long.

On a high hill, some distance from the shore,

Looking far down, a thousand feet or more,

Stood Gadara, a semi-heathen town,

Proud of its riches, splendor and renown,

With its long streets, and double colonnade,

Its amphitheatre and marts of trade.

It was no doubt a grand and glorious sight,

Beheld there glittering in the morning light.

The limestone cliffs 'bove which the city lay

Were pierced with natural caves, as at this day—

For dwellings used, or fashioned into rooms,

With niches and appliances for tombs,

The gloomy haunts unholy and defiled

Of savage men and homeless outcasts wild.

As Jesus left the boat, He met a man
Out of the tombs, who towards Him madly ran,
A fierce demoniac, that none could bind 3
Or tame; who oft, when he had been confined,
He chains and fetters had asunder riven, 4
And out into the wilderness been driven. 5
And he would wear no clothes, but, night and day,
Was in the mountains and the tombs alway,
Filling the air with howlings, shrieks, and groans,
And in his frenzy cutting him with stones.
And when he Jesus from afar espied, 6
He ran and worshipped Him, and loudly cried, 7
In tones of terror, " What with Thee have I
To do, Jesus, Thou Son of God Most High? 8
I Thee adjure by God (I know Thy power)
Torment me not before th' appointed hour ! "

And Jesus asked : " What is thy name ?"   He said 9
" Legion, for we are many."   Then they pled 10
Most earnestly, that He would not command
Them to th' abyss, nor drive them from the land.
Now on the neighboring mountain's steep incline, 11
There was seen feeding a great herd of swine :
Begging to enter these, He gave them leave 12

('T was meet th' unclean the unclean should receive).

Then when th' infernal frenzy was transferred,   Mark v. 13

The total number of the swinish herd,

About two thousand, all rushed down the steep

Into the sea and perished in the deep.

And the amazed and frightened swineherds fled,   14

And in the city and the country spread

The wondrous tidings, and they came in mass

To see just what it was had come to pass.

Gathered to Jesus, they the maniac find   15

There sitting, clothed, and now in his right mind.

Then, they, that witnessed it, began to tell,   16

What the possessed and what the swine befell.

   Fear springs up quickly in the guilty heart ;

Because of sin they wish Him to depart.   17

The cure was great, no doubt, and all divine,

But what a loss were the two thousand swine !

The men of Gadara the Saviour weighed,

And found Him wanting by the scales of trade.

They had the power, if not the right to choose :

'T was their one chance to gain life or to lose.

Had they been wise, they would have urged His stay,

And not have turned the Lord of Life away.

When entering the boat, the man restored,   Mark
                                                              v. 18
Healed with a double healing, leave implored
To be with Him, henceforth.   But, He said, " No ! " 19
Back to thy house and to thy friends now go,
And tell them what great things the Lord has done ;
How He had mercy on the outcast one!"
Throughout Decapolis all things he blazed   20
Jesus had done, and all men were amazed.

MATT. IX. 1, 18-35 ; MARK V. 21-43 ; LUKE VIII. 41-56.

THE Lord, meanwhile, across the Lake had come 21
Back to the city of Capernaum.
And a great multitude, advised before,
Awaited Him, and welcomed Him ashore.
Among them one, a ruler of the Jews,   22
Jairus by name, who hearing of the news
Of His arrival, hastened Him to greet.
He, when he saw Him, fell down at His feet,   23
And said to Him, with tears and sobbing breath,
" My only child lies at the point of death.
Come Thou, and lay Thy hands on her, that she
May be made whole and live.   Come instantly ! "

As He went with him—and there went along
A numerous, hurrying, and pressing throng—

A woman (with incurable complaint,   Mark
                                                            v. 25
Of deep defiling ceremonial taint—

A flow of blood, that baffled had the skill

Twelve years of all physicians—still,   26

Not getting better, rather growing worse,

Her living spent, left with an empty purse),

Of Jesus having heard came in the press,   27

And with believing fingers touched His dress,   28

Not doubting healing power there lay concealed;

And, lo, straightway, she felt that she was healed.   29

Knowing that from Him virtue had gone out,

Jesus immediately turned Him about,   30

And said: "Who touched My clothes just now?"

And His disciples said to Him, "See'st thou   31

The crowd all pressing Thee, and dost Thou ask,

Who touched Me?"   When the woman saw no mask   32

Could hide her, she came trembling to His feet,   33

And told how she was healed.   In accents sweet

He said to her: "Thy plague shall henceforth cease.   34

Daughter, thy faith has cured thee, go in peace!"

While He yet spake, word came, "Thy daughter's

    dead,   35

Why trouble thou the Master?"   Jesus said: 36

"Fear not, only believe!"   He suffered none.   Mark
v. 37

Except the parents, Peter, James and John,   38

To enter in with Him.   "Why weep?" He said   39

To weeping friends, "she sleeps, she is not dead—"*

[Not dead beyond recall.   There are two lives,

And life is while organic life survives.]

They laugh His words to scorn.   These sent away, 40

The others entered where the dead girl lay.

Taking her hand, He said: "Damsel, arise!"   41

---

* A person lies dangerously ill. At length the eyes close, the breast ceases to heave and the heart to beat. We say the man is dead, and say truly. So far as *sentient* life is concerned he is dead absolutely, dead beyond recall. But it does not follow that *organic* life is wholly extinct. Nearly all the tissues retain their vital properties to a certain extent for some time afterward. For example, Contractility of the muscular fibre, which is a property of life, continues to manifest itself by contractions more or less violent, under the action of galvanism and other stimuli. The formation of sugar in the liver is a vital function; and the curious fact has been demonstrated that its production had not ceased twenty-four hours after the death of the animal. It might have been literally true, therefore, that the child was both dead and not dead—dead in one sense but not in another.

It would seem more proper to speak of this case, and those other cases of miraculous revival recorded, viz., the son of the widow of Nain and Lazarus—as examples of resuscitation, *i. e.*, of restoration to [mortal] life, rather than of resurrection from the dead, Christ Himself being "the first fruits of them that slept." His case may be regarded as peculiar, inasmuch as there was exemplified in Him both a revival and a true resurrection, meaning thereby, the raising up, or assumption of a spiritual body, incorruptible and immortal. The prophetic words, "Thou wilt not suffer Thy Holy One to see corruption" would seem to indicate that it was intended that *structural* life should not be allowed to become extinct, which might easily have happened without a miracle, considering the brief time that He was in the tomb. It is doubtful whether, even in the case of Lazarus, who had been dead four days, the organic tie was broken. The power of cold in preventing putrefactive changes is wonderfully shown in the well known case of the mammoth of the Siberian Cave, the flesh of which was found sweet and fresh thousands of years after death.

And she, directly, opening her eyes,   Mark
                                                        v. 42
Rose up and walked, for she was twelve years old.
And they were much amazed.   They then were told, 43
To give her something nourishing to eat ;
For life is not sustained except by meat.

   Two blind men waited for His coming out.   Matt.
                                                      ix. 27
As He was passing on His homeward route,
These followed Him, repeating all the way,
"Thou Son of David, pity us, we pray !"
Arrived at home, the blind men entered too.   28
" Believe ye," Jesus said, " I can this do?"
They say, "Yea, Lord !"   He spake, and touched their
              eyes.   29
" As is your faith be it to you likewise."
Straightway their eyes were opened, and He said : 30
" Let no man know it !"   But they disobeyed.   31

   As they went forth a dumb man was brought in, 32
Who with a demon long possessed had been ;
His powerful word the devilish thraldom broke,   33
And the freed tongue loud hallelujahs woke.
Blaspheming Pharisees said : " By, no doubt,   34
The Prince of demons, demons He casts out."

XIII.

TWELVE SENT OUT—FIVE THOUSAND FED—TRUE BREAD.

MATT. IX. 35-38 ; X. 1, 5-39 ; MARK VI. 6-13 ; LUKE IX. 1-6.

AND Jesus went about from place to place,   Matt·
ix. 35

    Employed in arduous ministries of grace :

But when He saw the multitude, and knew,   36

How dark their state, and how distressful too,

Like sheep without a shepherd, all astray,

With no sure hand to guide them in the way—

Moved with compassion, boundless as the sea,

He said to His disciples: " Verily,   37

Abundant is the harvest, but how scant

And few the laborers! To meet this want,

Pray, that the great Lord of the harvest send   38

Into His harvest laborers without end."

And Jesus sent the Twelve, and gave for seal   x. 5

Them power to cast out demons, and to heal :

And charged them, saying : " As by twos ye go,

Go not, this time, among the Gentiles ; no,

Nor any city of Samaria

Enter, but go ye rather to the stray   Matt.
x. 6
And lost sheep of the house of Israel.
And as ye go, proclaim aloud and tell   7
The Reign of Heaven impends.   The sick restore;
The lepers cleanse; make live the dead once more; 8
Cast demons out—not for reward or fee,
Free your receivings, be your givings free.

   Nor, for your journey, do yourselves equip   9
With money in your girdles; nor with scrip;   10
Nor with two coats; nor staves; nor shoes for feet—
Because the workman's worthy of his meat.
Salute no man, nor linger by the way: 11
Into whatever house ye enter, stay   12
Content till ye go thence; and peace implore
Upon the house as ye pass in the door—
Peace on the house, if worthy, shall remain;   13
If not, to you it shall return again.
And whosoever shall you not receive,   14
Nor hear your words, as you the city leave,
The dust shake from your feet—a fiercer doom   15
Than Sodom's or Gomorrah's shall consume.
He that hears you, hears Me; despising you,
He Me despises and My Father too.

" Behold, I send you, as defenceless sheep
Forth in the midst of wolves and perils deep.
Be wise as serpents, harmless be as doves ;
Exceed all hatreds by outnumbering loves.
Be on your guard against malicious men,   17
Who lie in wait to find occasion, then
Stand ready to the Councils to betray—
The Sanhedrim and lesser ones—for they
Will scourge you in the synagogues ; and ye
'Fore kings and governors shall cited be   18
On My account, to testify the true
Against the false of Gentile and of Jew.
Be not solicitous and in suspense   19
About what ye shall say in your defence !
Appropriate speech that hour shall you be given,
For 't is not you that speak but Power from Heaven—20
The Holy Spirit shall your cause defend,
Shall be your Spokesman, Advocate and Friend."

Strange heart of man ! so mad against the truth,
Bloody, unnatural, and void of ruth ;
Hating the light with hatred so intense,
God's saving Word 's a furious offense.
All holy ties, not meant to have an end,
See Bigotry's red hand stretched forth to rend !
10

" Brother shall yield his brother up to death ;   Matt.
                                                          x. 21
Father his child ; and with unfilial breath
Children their parents shall accuse ; and ye,
The special objects of men's hate shall be,   22
For My name's sake.   But whoso shall endure
Down to the end makes his salvation sure !

" If in one city they shall you oppose,   23
Flee to another ; sure, in spite of foes,
The truth shall prosper, and the seed take root
In hearts of not a few, and bring forth fruit.
Ere your round 's finished, make what speed you can,
Already will have come the Son of Man :
In no gross sense His Kingdom will appear,
Being within you, it is now and here.

" Expect hard usage.   A disciple 's not   24
Above his Master.   Learn to bear your lot.
It is enough, if the disciple fare   25
E'en as his Master, and the servant share
The treatment of his Lord.   If they traduce
And Me revile, they 'll not spare you abuse.
Fear not !   Be stout of heart !   Keep nothing back, 26
Though thousand slanders bay along your track !
There 's nothing covered but shall be revealed—

No guilt, no innocence shall lie concealed. Matt. x.

I have no secrets for the favored few, 27

No esoteric teachings meant for you :

That told you in the dark, speak in the light ;

That whispered in your ear, tell from a height.

 " Be not afraid of them who can control 28

The body's life, but cannot kill the soul ;

But fear Him rather, who has power as well

That to destroy, and both cast into hell.

Are not two sparrows for a farthing sold ? 29

Yet not one falls without your Father—told

And numbered are your head's unvalued hairs— 30

Who cares for sparrows much more for you cares. 31

The brave for truth and right with love inflamed, 32

Who Me 'fore men confesses, unashamed,

I 'll him confess, and openly will own

Before My Father seated on His throne.

But whoso shall deny Me before men, 33

Him I'll deny before My Father then.

 " Though peace was sung by angels at My birth, 34

I came not to send peace upon the earth ;

Rather a sword.   For that the peace I bring,

Only from inward purity can spring,

Where this is not, there flows a muddled stream, ^{Matt. x.—}
Foul with all lusts and enmities extreme.
Peace is impossible where hatreds dwell,
Else ye might seek it in the heart of hell.
See Love the smitten cheek turn to the foe !
The very meekness prompts the second blow.
When the fierce vulture tears it from above,
'T were wrong to blame the unoffending dove.
Peace walks with Love in a retired path,
When, forth from ambush, springs the waiting Wrath.
It needs must be, so long as Sin remains
In throned possession of the heart and brain,
There should be fierce antagonisms abroad,
And war against the government of God.

"I come to set at variance and strife   35
A man against the author of his life ;
The daughter 'gainst the mother : among those
Of his own household shall be found his foes.   36
Who father loves and mother more than Me,   37
Unworthy My disciple is to be.
And who that loves a son or daughter more—
Putting mere natural loves My love before,
Preferring these to the transcendent claims
Of Duty under all its various names—

Of true discipleship he gives no sign, Matt. x. -
And is unworthy to be reckoned Mine.

" Who follows Me, he must himself deny: 38
All evil lusts and likings crucify,
Nail them as malefactors to the cross,
And count all sinful gains eternal loss.
Who for My sake shall cowardly refuse 39
To risk his life, his life of life shall lose ;
While he, who freely gives his life away,
Shall find it glorified some future day."

When Jesus of His charge had made an end— xi. 1
Giving it scope, all time to comprehend,
To fortify them against trials near,
And persecutions through their whole career—
The Twelve went forth, and preached men should
　　　repent, Luke ix. 6
And healed and cast out demons as they went.
But the great Master did not, for this cause,
In His undelegated labors pause.

MATT. XIV. 13-36 ; MARK VI. 3-56 ; LUKE IX. 10-17 ; JOHN VI. 15-69.

ONCE more the Apostles were together brought,
And told to Jesus all they did and taught. Mark vi. 31

"Come ye apart," He said with gracious smile,   Mark
                                                        vi. —
" Into a desert place and rest awhile."

For crowds that came and went so thronged His feet,

They had not leisure so much as to eat.

Therefore, by boat they privately withdrew.   32

But many saw them leaving who them knew :   33

So, running round on foot, got there before

Th' unhurrying boat had reached the farther shore.

He going forth—instead of sharp protest   34

Against this rude frustration of His rest—

Seeing the multitude, like sheep without

A shepherd scattered all forlorn about—

Full of sweet pity, with entrancing speech

Things that concerned their peace began to teach.

His voice rang music from the mountain height,

And ears drank in an infinite delight.

So sweet the time, the hours unnoticed passed,

Till the descending sun long shadows cast.

Then His disciples coming to Him say :   35

" This is a desert place, send them away,   36

That they may go somewhere them bread to buy :

For here they've naught to eat, and night is nigh."

The God-man answers: " Give ye them to eat !"   37

They say : " Two hundred pennyworth of meat

Would not suffice to give a taste to each ; Mark vi.
Their needs our means of purchase far outreach."
He asks : " How many loaves have ye ? Go see !"
They, learning, say : " Five, and two fishes." He, 39
When they were brought to Him, at once commands,
That all be made to lie down there in bands 40
On the green grass—disposed in rank and file
By hundreds and by fifties, in short while—
Numb'ring about five thousand. Jesus took 41
The five loaves and two fishes, and with look
Turned heavenward, blessed the loaves, and forthwith
       brake,
And gave to His disciples, charged to make
Free distribution until all were fed ;
With the two fishes following the bread.
When all were filled, then spake th' Almighty Host : 42
" Gather the fragments up that naught be lost !"
They filled (so strangely had the loaves increased) 43
Twelve baskets with the remnants of the feast.

Rose from th' excited throng the whispered hum, John vi.14
" Truly this is the Prophet that should come—
Greater than Moses, who our fathers fed
With manna—multiplying common bread :

Let us by force, if need be, make Him King."   John
                                                       vi. —

When Jesus saw they bent were on this thing,   15
He straightway bade the Twelve to seek the shore,
And to Bethsaida go by boat before,   Matt.
                                                       xiv. 22
While He the multitude should send away.   23
Alone He climbed the mountain there to pray.

The chill of early Spring was in the air,
But Jesus knew what strength was found in prayer;
That weary hearts obtain divinest rest,
When sweetly pillowed on the Father's breast.
Darkness came on, but light from moon* and star
Served to make objects visible afar ;
And·Jesus saw, reclining on the steep,   24
Tempestuous winds the Lake's dark waters sweep,
And saw, some thirty furlongs from the shore,
His worn disciples toiling at the oar,
By baffling winds and waves now wholly spent.
And, in the fourth watch of the night, He went   25
Towards them, walking on the sea.   The sight   26
Filled the amazed disciples with affright.
" It is a spectre !" cried they out for fear.
And Jesus straightway spake: " Be of good cheer !

---

* It being on the eve of the Passover (see John vii.) the moon must have been near
its full.

'T is I, your loving Lord, be not afraid!" Matt.
xiv. —

Impetuous Peter then transported said: 28

" Lord! bid me come to Thee, if it be Thou,

Upon the water." " Come! I thee allow." 29

Leaving the boat, he on the waters stept,

To go to Jesus—fear one moment slept—

When rough winds blew a loud and angrier gust, 30

Buoyant from vanity and not from trust,

His feet began to stagger on the wave,   ·

And sinking fast, he cried out : " Master, save!"

He said, while seizing him with hand stretched out, 31

"O thou of little faith! why didst thou doubt?"

Aboard, winds ceased, or changed to zephyrs bland, 32

And, lo, the bark came instantly to land.

Kneeling they worshipped Him and said, "Thy nod 33

All things obey, Thou art the Son of God!"

When people came next day, and could not find John
vi. 22

Jesus, Who, they supposed, had stayed behind—

Knowing there was no boat, except the one

Which the disciples bore, and them alone—

They thought, as boats had from Tiberias come, 23

He might have crossed back to Capernaum. 24

So passing o'er the Lake they sought Him there,

And drawing nigh addressed Him speeches fair: John vi. 25
" Rabbi, when cam'st Thou hither ? "   Jesus said :   26
" Ye seek Me selfishly for sake of bread.
Work not for food, which perishes each hour,   27
But food which is eternal life and power—
That which the Son of Man will give to you :
For Him has God the Father sealed as true.

 " What works," they asked, " does God claim at our
   hands ? "   28
" This work," He said, " He first of all demands,   29
That ye believe on Him whom He has sent—
By works of God this work is chiefly meant."
They, therefore, said : " If sent from God, what sign 30
Show'st Thou to prove Thy mission is divine ?
What greater work than Moses workest Thou,
That we should Thy superior claims allow ?
Our fathers in the wilderness were fed   31
With ceaseless manna—Moses gave them bread
From heaven to eat, not once, but day by day,
While Thou dost stop at yesterday's display."

 Then Jesus said : " The bread, by Moses given,   32
Was not the true and proper Bread from Heaven ;
But that, My Father gives you, is the true   33

Life-giving Bread of God come down to you, John vi.—

And all the world." Missing the sense, they said:

" Lord, give us now and evermore this bread ! " 34

   Then He: " I am the Bread of Life, therefore, 35

Who comes to Me shall never hunger more,

And who believes on Me shall never thirst.

But, as I told you plainly at the first, 36

Though ye have seen Me, ye do not believe.

All who will come I willingly receive. 37

Ye frustrate not My mission who reject:

'T is as the Father not as ye elect.

I came from heaven to do not Mine own will, 38

But all the Father's pleasure to fulfill.

The will of Him Who sent Me now is this: 39

Of all which He has given Me I should miss

Nothing—that every sorrowing one, 40

Who weeping comes, believing on the Son,

Should perish not, but endless life obtain,

And I at last should raise him up again."

   Accustomed long, their worldliness and pride 41

Under some cloak of sanctity to hide,

They murmured He descent from Heaven should
      claim,

Knowing they said His origin and name.   John vi. 42

Aware, the secret of their discontent

Was that He to their schemes refused consent,

Jesus then said : "Cease cavil ! 'T is Love's law,   43

None comes to Me except the Father draw.   44

Whether ye come, or whether ye depart,

'T is all the same unless ye bring your heart.

'T is in the prophets written and foretold,   45

'And they shall all be taught of God.'   The old

Is soon to cease.   I come to build the new,

And end all types by offering up the true.

He, Who by prophets once His will made known,

Has in these last days spoken by His Son.

No one has seen the Father, only He   46

Who is from God.   Who hears Him, comes to Me.   47

I am the Living Bread, the Heavenly Food,   48

And He that eats My flesh and drinks My Blood   49

Has life eternal.   He in Me abides,   50

And I in him in flowing crimson tides."   51

Said many of His disciples, when they heard,   60

"'T is a hard saying and a staggering word."

And Jesus said to them : " Does this offend ?   61

What if ye see the Son of Man ascend   62

Up where He was before?　He'll still refresh　John
vi.—

Like food—the spirit quickens, not the flesh,　　'ʒ

Which profits nothing.　Lo! the words I speak

Are spirit and are life.　The truth there seek.

'T is not gross feeding and digesting meats—

He that believes appropriates and eats."

Many, who His disciples were before,　　6)

From this went back, and walked with Him no more.

He to the Twelve: "Go ye away also?"　　67

And Peter said: "To whom, Lord, shall we go?　　68

Thou hast the blessèd words, and Thou alone,

Of life eternal.　We believe and own　　6)

Thou the Messiah art, th' Anointed One,

And of the Living God th' undoubted Son."

MORNING HYMN.

Before the lark had left his nest,
   And at heaven's gate poured forth his lay,
My wakeful soul was up and drest,
   And had gone up to meet the Day :
On wings of love and strong desire upborne,
Saluted the Original of Morn.

Light of the World! when Thou dost rise
   On the horizon of my heart,
How quickly every sorrow flies,
   And shadows of the night depart!
Thy rays so tempered to the thirsty sight,
It drinks unharmed the deluge of delight.

Come, my Desire! my spirit's Need!
   My Morning Manna! Heavenly Bread!
Incarnate Love! on Thee I feed,
   By Thy humanity am fed,
And, changed from glory unto glory, grow
To bear Thy blesséd image here below.

XIV.

WHAT DEFILES—SEVEN THOUSAND FED.

MATT. XV. 1-20; MARK VII. 1-23.

SENT from Jerusalem, came Pharisees   _{Matt.
xv. 1}
  And Scribes to watch Him.   And, when these
Saw some of His disciples eat with hands   2
Unwashed, 'gainst the traditions and commands
Delivered of the elders, they found fault,
Saying: " Whence comes this scandalous revolt
Of Thy disciples, daring to transgress
Ancient traditions in their sacredness?"
And Jesus said: " Ye hypocrites!   Most true   7
Is that Isaiah prophesied of you :
· This people with their lips Me homage pay,
But their unloving hearts are far away.'
In vain they worship Me, howbeit, when
They teach for doctrine the commands of men !
You charge transgression. How dare you transgress 3
God's dread commandment, solemn and express,
By your traditions, frivolous and vain,

Annulling duties positive and plain? Matt.
xv. —

' Honor thy father and thy mother too,' 4

Moses has said, ' pay filial reverence due ;

And whosoever curses with vile breath

Father or mother shall be put to death !'

But ye maintain, if one averse, shall say 5

Or to his father or his mother : ' Nay !

That which I have by which I might thee aid,

Is 'Dedicated,' then his debt is paid— 6

Making the word of God, through this respect

To your traditions, all of none effect."

    Calling He spake to those on either hand : 10

" Hearken to Me each one and understand.

Not things which go into the mouth defile ; 11

But that which issues from the mouth is vile.

Whoso has ears to hear it, let him hear.

The meaning to the pure in heart is clear."

    Said His disciples : " Know, Thou didst displease 12

Greatly, by what Thou saidst, the Pharisees."

He said : " My Father will each plant uproot 13

Not of His planting, and of evil fruit.

Let them alone—blind leaders of the blind. 14

A fall into the ditch they both will find."

When from the people Jesus had withdrawn, Matt. xv. 15
And with the Twelve into the house had gone—
Themselves in doubt—they begged the Lord to tell
The meaning of the spoken Parable.

   " Are ye so void of understanding too?   16
Perceive ye not, 't is not what enters you   17
Defiles? The mouth receives the welcome food,
And clean digestions sift out all the good.
But what comes from the mouth, comes from the heart,
And these pollute the man in every part.   18
For from within the human heart proceed   19
Adulteries, fornications, murders, greed,
Thefts, wantonness, deceit, an evil eye,
Pride, malice, foolishness, and blasphemy.
These are the things which render a man vile—   20
To eat with unwashed hands does not defile.

MATT. XV. 21-38; MARK VII. 24-37; VIII. 1-9.

To hide Himself awhile from public view, Matt. xv.—
Jesus arose, and to the coast withdrew   21
Of Tyre and Sidon. Entering a house there
He could not keep concealed with all His care,
For, lo, a certain woman, born a Greek,   22
A Syrophenician, made haste to seek
The Mighty Healer out. She, at His feet   25
11

Falling, with cries Him ceased not to entreat   Matt.
xv. —

To help her daughter, grievously possessed

Now with a demon.   He her faith to test,   26

Said to her : " Let the children first be fed.

It is not good to take the children's bread

And cast it to the dogs."   "Though this be meet,   27

Yet, Lord, the dogs the children's crumbs may eat

Which from the master's table fall."   He saith,   28

All sternness gone : "O woman, great thy faith !

For this word, go thy way ! faith hath such power,

Thy daughter is made whole from this same hour."

And He departing not long after this,   Mark
vii. 31

Passed through the precincts of Decapolis.

Returning to the Sea of Galilee,

Like as before He caused the blind to see ;   Matt.
xv. 30

The deaf to hear ; the dumb moreo'er to talk ;

Cured the deformed,* and made the cripple walk.

His healing power, though limitless and swift,

That moral profit might attend the gift,

Conditioned was on a receiving mind,

---

* The primary and proper meaning of κυλλός is *crooked*.   The term would apply to a large class of deformities both of the trunk and the limbs.   One of the epithets of Vulcan, who was born lame, was κυλλόποδιων=crook-footed [club-footed ?].   So far as we know Christ never created a lost member ; and so " maimed " is probably an incorrect rendering here, although the right one Matt. xviii. 8.

And so to no one method was confined. Matt.
xv. —

Sometimes He chose, removed by miles of space,

To make the air the channel of His grace;

Sometimes He smeared blind eyes with moistened
     clay

In aid of faith, and then poured in the day.

  They brought to Him a man both deaf and dumb: Mark
vii.32

No sound of words could ever to him come,

And so by signs alone, addressed to sight,

Could he be made to understand aright.

His fingers, wet with spittle, He applied   33

Then to his ears, and touched his tongue, and sighed

As He looked up to heaven, then broke the chain, 34

Saying, " Be opened ! " and the man spake plain.   35

And they the God of Israel praised aloud.

Again He sought a refuge from the crowd.

  Once more the Lord of Nature, and our Lord, viii. 1

Vouchsafes to spread His hospitable board

To meet the needs of a vast multitude

Hungry from being three days without food.

When He purveys 't is on a scale immense ;

All forces troop to His omnipotence ;

The powers of nature haste at His command

To pour the fulness of the sea and land ;   1

While all the mighty angels of the sky   Mark viii. —

Upon His errands ready are to fly.

How awful is He! how august! how great!

But then how human! how compassionate!   2

  With tenderness unspeakable, He says   Mark vii.—

To His disciples : " During three full days,

These, fasting, Me have ceased not to attend.

Some came from far, and I will not them send   3

Away, lest they faint on the road, unfed."

They say: " Whence can we get supply of bread,   4

Here in the distant wilderness ? "   " Tell Me,"

The Master saith, " how many loaves have ye?"   5

They say : " Seven and a few small fishes."   When

The multitude had all sat down, He, then

Took the seven loaves and giving thanks, them broke—

Each fragment multiplying as He spoke

In His creating hands to more and more—

Then gave to His disciples, who them bore

To all the wondering people.   Having blessed   7

The fishes, these were given with the rest.

When all had eaten, and were satisfied,   8

They gathered up seven baskets full beside.

There were who ate four thousand men about,   9

Women and children in the count left out.

XV.

TRANSFIGURATION—DEMONIAC CURED—DUTIES.

MATT. XVI. 13-20; MARK VIII. 27-30; LUKE IX. 18-21.

JESUS, with mighty labors overtasked,   Matt·
    While on a journey, His disciples asked   xvi. 13
"Who do men say I am?" They answered, "John   13
The Baptist; some Elijah; others one   14
Of the old Prophets, risen from the dead."
"But who say ye I am?" the Master said.   15
Peter replied: "Thou art the Christ of God."*   •
He charged them not to publish it abroad.   20

    Jesus from this time forth began to show   21
To His disciples, how that He must go
Up to Jerusalem, and that while there
Much cruel treatment must be made to bear—
False accusations, mockings, scourgings, blows,
From elders, chief priests, scribes, His murderous foes,
And be rejected of them, and then slain;
And after three days' burial rise again.

* See The Evangel, pp. 177-81.

He spake this openly. And Peter took

His Lord aside, and 'gan Him to rebuke :

" Be this far from Thee, Lord !   This shall not be !"

But, turning, He to Peter said : " Get thee   23

Behind Me, Satan, thou art an offense—

Not savoring things of God but things of sense."

MATT. XVII. 1-13 ; MARK IX. 2-13 ; LUKE IX. 28-36.

AFTER six days of loving labors done,   Luke
ix. 28

Jesus apart took Peter, James, and John

To a high mountain-top, and while in prayer   29

He was transfigured in their presence there.

His face was as the sun, intensely bright ;

And all His raiment glittering and white.

And with Him talking, lo, two men were seen.   30

Of glorious aspect and majestic mien,

E'en Moses and Elijah, who then spake   31

Of His decease, which should atonement make,

To take place at Jerusalem ere long.

Their eyes, fatigued and dazed with light too strong, 32

Grew heavy—Peter's and the rest—with sleep.

But when they woke from slumber brief and deep,

They saw His glory and the men.   As they   33

Were parting from Him, to prolong their stay,

Peter said, " Master! it is good for us
All to be here—Heaven's pomp around us thus—
Let us three tabernacles make, to be
For Moses and Elijah and for Thee"—
Not knowing what to say or what he said,
For they were in a maze and sore afraid.

While he thus spake, from out a covering cloud   34
There came a Voice, divinely sweet and loud,   35
Which said, " Lo, this is My Beloved Son,
Hear Him!"   It ceased, and He was found alone.   36
They kept it close, as Jesus to them said,
Till after He had risen from the dead.
In doubt what rising from the dead should mean,
They yet spake naught of those things they had seen.

MATT. XVII. 14-21; MARK IX. 14-29; LUKE IX. 37-43.

NEXT day, when they were come down from the hill. 37
He saw great multitudes assembled still;
And the disciples, who remained below,
Disputing with the Scribes, that sought to throw
Shame on late failure.   When the people saw   15
The Master coming, they were struck with awe,
And ran forth to salute Him.   He, the Scribes   16
Addressing, asked the reason of their gibes.

Then kneeling came to Him a certain one,   Mark
                                              ix. 17
Who said : " Master, have pity on my son,
For he 's a lunatic.   All unawares,   18
The demon takes him, throws him down and tears,
The while he foams and grinds his teeth ; at length,
He lies exhausted, drained of all his strength.
And I to Thy disciples spake, but they,
Trying to cast him out, failed in the essay."

" O generation, faithless and perverse !   19
How long shall I be with you, and rehearse
The same old lesson ?   How long suffer you ?
Bring thy son hither !"   When he came in view,   20
Straightway the spirit tare him—with mad bound
He, falling, rolled there, foaming, on the ground.
He asked his father : " How long may it be,   21
Since this him first befell ?"   " Since infancy,"
He said : " It has him often in the past   22
Into the fire, into the water cast,
Him to destroy.   But if Thou canst do aught,
Pity and help and let a cure be wrought."
" All things are possible, if thou canst believe—   23
A little faith can mightiest things achieve."

The father said, with pleading tones of grief,   24
" Lord I believe ; help Thou my unbelief !"

Then Jesus spake once more the word of power. Mark ix. 25

And the possession ceased from that same hour. 26

And the disciples asked Him privately : 28

" Wherefore could we not cast him out?"   And He

Said unto them : " The reason was in brief Matt. xvii. 20

Th' exceeding greatness of your unbelief.

For, I declare, if you, in very deed,

Have faith but as a grain of mustard seed,

Ye to this mountain, stablished on its base,

Might boldly say, ' Remove to yonder place !'

And it should pass.   Yea, all things ye could do.

And naught should be impossible to you."

Who rightly trusts, with him divinely draws,

The Cause of causes, and the Law of laws.

Nothing 's too difficult beneath the skies,

For God's vicegerent, be it fit and wise—

Not that Omnipotence must bend to him,

And be the tool of vanity and whim.

A harder task than demons to expel

Is sin to slay, and balk the powers of hell.

Of all achievements, this is first and best,

To triumph o'er the tyrants of the breast.

Not without prayer and fasting can take place Matt. xvii 21

These mightier miracles of healing grace.

FAITH.

The world is full of pain ;
　　Fierce sickness binds it fast;
And none can break the chain,
　　That sin has round it cast :
Philosophy essays,
　　And Science goes about
In many bootless ways,
　　To cast the demon out:
They magnify th' unchanging reign of law,
And preach the gospel of the tooth and claw.*

Ne'er wizard wove a spell
　　That could the fiend eject ;
But Faith the miracle
　　Can easily effect :
What not the law could do,
　　Through weakness of the flesh,
This strong is to renew,
　　And nature mould afresh :
Can bring down Heaven to exorcise my grief—
" Lord, I believe, help Thou my unbelief ! "

* To men that "bite and devour one another," the Agnostic assurance, that what they do is but the normal and necessary outcome of the predatory instinct which they possess in common with all beasts of prey, may be comforting, but can hardly be deemed reformatory. If the primitive man was all beast in his origin and development, it is difficult to see, why he is more to blame than lions and tigers in obeying the promptings of his nature. Infidel science prides itself on its microscope and telescope, but finds no use for moral and spiritual lenses by which God is discovered and the infinite sweep of moral law is discerned.

MATT. XVII. 24- 7 MARK IX. 30.

COME to Capernaum where He abode, Matt.
xvii. 24

Collectors said to Peter on the road :

" Does not your Master temple-tribute pay ? "

Peter without just warrant answered, " Yea ! " 25

Entering the house, ere he had time to speak,

Jesus said : " Simon, I thy answer seek.

What thinkest thou ?   Of whom do kings of earth

Tribute exact ?   Of sons of royal birth,

Or strangers ? "   Peter said, "Of strangers."   "See, 26

Then," Jesus said, "the sons by right are free.

But to avoid offense, go to the Lake, 27

Throw line, and the first fish that's hooked, that take ;

Opening its mouth thou shalt a stater* see,

Take it and give it them for Me and thee."

Opposed to the infinitudes of chance,

How all surveying His omniscient glance !

Ten thousand proofs are here to end dispute

That He of Godhead lacks no attribute.

MATT. XVIII. 1-35 ; MARK IX. 33-50 ; LUKE IX. 46-50.

WHILE in the house, He asked the Twelve one day,

" What was it ye debated by the way ? " Mark
ix. 33

They held their peace, for they had had debate. 34

* A stater was a Greek silver coin, equal to four drachmas or 72 cents.

Who of themselves might hope to be most great. _{Mark}
Later they asked, that answer might be given,
Who should be greatest in the Reign of Heaven? Matt. xviii.1
He said : " If any man seek first to be,
Let him be last in all humility.
He who contends for precedence and place,
Forfeits all standing in the Realm of Grace."
Taking a child,* He held it up to view,   2
And said to them : " In truth I say to you,   3
Except ye be converted, and be freed
From vain ambitions and from worldly greed,
E'en as this child, ye—shut out by your sin--
Into My Kingdom cannot enter in.
The low is high, the greater is the less,   4
The mean is but inverted nobleness.
Take heed how ye despise My little ones,   10
Who have the rights and privileges of sons.
In heaven their angels, ministers of grace,
Behold perpetually My Father's face.
For I am come to save that which is lost   11
At every sacrifice and any cost."

* "Was it Peter's child?" Peter was so childlike a man, some have fancied that the child of one so childlike might properly serve as a typical example of genuine childlikeness. All children are not childlike.

"Lord!" Peter asked, "my duty to fulfill
How oft must I forgive a brother? Till
Seven times?" "I say not seven," He replied,
" But seventy times seven and more beside.
Therefore My Kingdom answers to a king,
Who with his servants sought a reckoning,
One, who ten thousand talents owed, was brought:
But, forasmuch as he to pay had naught,
His lord, to get back some of his lost gold,
Commanded him, and all his to be sold.
He, falling down before him, pled,* and prayed :
" Have patience with me and thou shalt be paid."
He moved with pity, having him unbound,
Forgave the debt. The same went out, and found
One of his fellow servants, who him owed
One hundred pence. He fiercely toward him strode,
And took him by the throat, and loudly said :
" Pay what thou owest me!" He, kneeling, pled,
" Have patience with me and I will thee pay."
But he refused to wait, and went straightway,
And into prison ruthlessly him threw,
Till he should pay the utmost that was due.

*" Against her *pled*."—SPENCER. "She *pled* her cause."—C. KINGSLEY.

The other servants, witnessing these acts,   Matt.
xviii. 31

Were grieved, and went and told their lord the facts;

Who said, when he had been before him set,   32

"Thou wicked servant! I forgave thy debt

At thy desire.   Shouldst thou not ruth have known, 33

When so much pity had to thee been shown?"

The lord was wroth, and put him to the rack,   34

And held him bound till he should pay all back.

If ye forgive, My Father will you too,   35

But if ye do not, neither will He you."

LUKE X. 1, 17-20.

THE Lord appointed other Seventy, sent   Luke
X. 1

Them out by twos—as the Apostles went

Awhile before—into each town and place,

Whither the Lord would come—with gifts of grace,

And signs of power, that all might understand,

The Reign of the Messiah was at hand.

"Master!" a certain Scribe said eagerly,   Luke
ix. 57

"Where'er Thou goest I will follow Thee!"

He said: "To follow Me, art thou aware,   58

Is loss, contempt, and poverty to bear?

Foxes have holes, and birds of heaven their nest,

But I 've no home, nor where My head to rest."

" Follow thou Me!" He to another said.
But he replied : " My father is just dead ;
To go and bury him me first allow."
" Do what 's more urgent !" Jesus said. " Go thou 60
And preach the Reign of God! Thy first is t' obey,
And not to frame excuses for delay,
Let the dead bury, if need be, the dead—
To save the living be thy work instead."

Another prayed : " Let me first bid farewell   61
To those at home."   He answered : " I thee tell,   62
Who, their hands putting to the plough, look back,
They for God's Kingdom needful fitness lack."

Those sent, returning, with glad voice exclaim : x. 17
" Ev'n demons, Lord, are subject through Thy name."

" I Satan saw as lightning fall from heaven :
O'er all the enemy you power is given.   19
Yet joy not spirits at your bidding fly,   20
But that your names recorded are on high."

XVI.

JERUSALEM VIA SAMARIA,

LUKE IX. 51-56; XVII. 12-18.

THE time for His assumption* nigh fulfilled,   Luke
ix. 51
Henceforth, with steadfast heart and mind, He
   willed
To go up to Jerusalem once more:
And so, He messengers sent on before,   52
Who, having come, as lying in the way,
Into a village of Samaria,
Made ready for Him.   When He came to them,   53
Because His face was towards Jerusalem,
The men would not receive Him.   Filled with ire,   54
Spake James and John: "Lord! wilt Thou that we fire
Call down from heaven, and all these consume,
As did Elijah, by a righteous doom?"
Jesus rebuked them, and mild answer gave: 55
" I came not to destroy men's lives but save."   56
And they went to another village.   Then,   Luke
xvii. 12
As they were entering it, they met ten men,

* Otherwise His " taking up " or return to His Father.

That lepers were, who at a distance stood, Luke xvii. —
And with shrill voice cried loudly as they could : 13
" Master, have mercy on us!" He said : " Go, 14
And to the priests present yourselves, and show
That ye are clean !" And as they went, each one
Was cleansed : but of the total number, none
Returned save only a Samaritan ; 15
Who, finding he was healed, turned back, and ran
And fell at Jesus' feet, and kissed the sod, 16
Giving Him thanks, and glorifying God.
He said : " Were not ten cleansed? Where are the
    nine ? 17
Could they of gratitude afford no sign—
Leaving this stranger the exception sole ? 18
Arise !" He said, " thy faith has made thee whole."

JOHN VII. 8-52 ; VIII. 1-12, 28, 36, 56-59.

JESUS delayed His coming to the Feast, John vii. 8
Feast of the Tabernacles, last not least
Of the great Festivals—each happy day
Of all the sacred seven made glad and gay
With boughs of myrtle, olive, pine, and palm,
Formed into booths, or waved, with chanted psalm
And sound of trumpets, timbrels, horns and flutes,

12

In celebration of ingathered fruits.   John
                                                     vii. --
On the third day the Jews found Him they sought, 14
Now come.   He to the Temple went and taught ;
And all who heard Him wondering comment made 15
Upon th' amazing wisdom He displayed,
Not having letters learned.   He said : "Not mine 16
My doctrine is, not human but divine.
I am God's mouth.   Whoso God's will shall do,   17
He shall discern between the false and true.
Th' obedient only has the seeing mind ;
Who hates the truth is blindest of the blind.
Who speaks not of himself, he truly speaks.   18
He is of God who God's sole glory seeks.

    "I know that murder in your hearts is hid—   19
And is not murder in your law forbid ?
Why do ye seek to kill Me ?   Can ye tell ?   20
Is it because I wrought a miracle   21
Of healing ere now on the Sabbath day ?   22
And is My life the forfeit I must pay ?"

    As many of the people had been won   31
To say : "What greater things could Christ have
              done ?"—
The Pharisees conceived the danger prest,   32
And so sent officers to Him arrest.   40

But half convinced themselves by what they heard, ^{John vii. 44}

These would have taken Him, but were deterred, 45

Saying (when asked, Why have ye not Him brought?)

" Sure never man like this man spake or taught!" 46

Enraged they said : " Are ye likewise deceived ? 47

Who of the rulers have on Him believed ? 48

As for the people, who know not the law, 49

They 're cursed fit ravin for the devil's maw."

Said Nicodemus (he that came by night 50

Being one of the Council), " Is it right 51

Under our law to judge a man unheard?"

They said : " Art thou of Galilee ?   The Word 52

Search through and through—look where you will,
          and see

If any prophet springs from Galilee ?"

He to the Mount of Olives went at night, viii. 1

But to the Temple came at morning light. 2

Such was His daily wont.   All through the Feast

His holy toil for others never ceased.

As there He sat and all the people taught,

The Scribes and Pharisees a woman brought, 3

And set her in the midst—her face aflame,

A piteous spectacle of guilty shame.

They say to Him: "Teacher! this woman here   John
                                                   viii. 4
Was taken in adultery—her guilt is clear.
Such Moses in the law bids us to stone—   5
What sayest Thou of her?"   Their malice known,   6
Jesus stooped down, and with His finger wrote
Upon the ground, not seeming to take note.
Continuing to ask, He raised His head,   7
And with a look that searched their souls, He said :
" Let him among you all, who 's without sin,
Cast the first stone at her, and so begin
(If law and penalty are both so plain)
To execute the sentence ye ordain."

    Again He forward leaned and wrote; and they   8
All, one by one, slunk silently away,   9
Till with the woman He was left alone.
And lifting up Himself when they had gone,   10
He said, "Where are they, woman?   Did no one
Assume to sentence thee?"   She said, "Lord! none."11
And Jesus said : " Neither do I.   Therefore
Go thou thy way, and henceforth sin no more ! "

    JESUS, our Sun, spake, saying: " I the Light   12
Am of the world—I give new powers of sight.
Who follows Me no more shall darkling grope,

But have the light of life and joy of hope. john viii.

When ye have lifted up the Son of Man, 28

Then shall ye know that I am He, and can

Do naught alone. The Sender's with the Sent— 29

I do not singly act—two wills are blent,

Making one will. The Father smiling sees

I always do those things that will Him please."

Many, when He pronounced these words, believed. 30

" If ye hold fast to that ye have received," 31

He said, " My true disciples then are ye—

Knowing the Truth, the Truth will make you free." 32

They answered: "We be Abr'am's seed, and were 33

Never in bondage yet, as we aver:

How sayest Thou, 'Ye'll be made free?'" He gave 34

Swift answer: " Whoso sins, he is the slave

Of sin, not free till he from sin is freed— 35

He, whom the Son makes free, is free indeed. 36

Your father Abraham rejoiced My day 56

To see, and seeing it was glad." They say: 57

" Thou art not fifty yet, and Abraham

Hast Thou seen?" " Yes, ere Abr'am was I am." 58

They took up stones intending Him to slay, 59

But Jesus hid, and passed unseen away.

" MASTER ! " a lawyer said, inviting strife,   Luke
                                                      X. 25
" What shall I do to gain eternal life ?"

He said : " What says the law ? the path's well trod."26

He answered : " Thou shalt love the Lord thy God 27

With all thy heart and soul and strength and mind,

And love thy neighbor as thyself." " I find."   28

He said, " thou answerest right.   This do and live."

Willing to justify himself, and give   29

Excuse for his short-comings, he began :

" Who is my neighbor ? "   Jesus said : " A man   30

Went from Jerusalem to Jericho,

And fell 'mong thieves, who stripped, and gashed him

          so,

He seemed half dead, then left him where he lay.

It chanced, a certain priest came down that way,   31

And, when he saw him, hastened by amazed.

Likewise a Levite passing, stopped, and gazed   32

A moment curiously, then did the same.

But a Samaritan, a stranger, came   33

There where he was ; and, seeing his sad plight,

He, filled with pity, hastened to alight,

And went to him with merciful design,   34

Bound up his wounds, and poured in oil and wine,

Set him on his own beast, and brought with care Luke
x.
Him to an inn, and stayed and nursed him there.
Next day when leaving, giving to the host 35
Two pence,* he said : 'Take care of him, the cost
I will repay thee when I come again.'
Which of these three, I ask thee to explain, 36
Was neighbor to the man, himself a Jew ?"
" He who showed mercy." "Go thou and thus do !"37

He came to Bethany, a village near 38
Jerusalem, place memorable and dear,
As the abode of those whom Jesus loved,
And whose affection He had often proved.
O glad was Martha, Mary, Lazarus, 39
To have their roof once more distinguished thus !
How shall their love and worship be exprest
Tow'rd their great Friend, who deigns to be their
        Guest ?
What will best please Him ?   Is it for a meal
(It is to Martha that we make appeal)
He condescends to enter your low door ?
Plain wholesome food He asks and nothing more.
The Lord of Life, in whom all creatures live,

* Dr. S. Davidson, quoted by Geikie, estimates the purchasing value of two denarii
(pence) to have been equal to from six to seven shillings sterling.

From thee wants little, and has much to give.   Luke
x.—
He in His hands the bread of life doth bear—
What for thy many dishes does He care?
Little avails thy running to and fro ;
There is a better way thy love to show.
If thou wouldst please Him, lend thy heart and ear.
He'll spare one dish to give thee chance to hear.
Rest from thy worry : one brief moment stay.
Nor deem the time thus spent is thrown away.

But Martha—flurried, hot with haste and heat— 40
Beholding Mary at the Saviour's feet,
Hearing His words of wisdom, love and grace,
A mighty pleasure beaming from her face,
Fearing to lose a word He had to say,
The more because He had not long to stay—
Words of complaint and blame 'gainst her advanced,
Distracted speech, that at the Master glanced,
Her whirling thoughts unable Him to spare,
Saying thus wildly : " Lord ! dost Thou not care
My sister has me left to serve alone?
Bid her to share the burden on me thrown !"
And Jesus answered : " Martha, Martha, thou, 41
Witness thy fretful speech and clouded brow,
Careful and troubled art, full of unrest,

Concerning many things to please thy Guest: Luke x.

But one is needful—Mary's chosen part, 42

To sit and give her hospitable heart,

And learn of Me. Let her therefore remain !

Her place beside Me she shall still retain."

JOHN IX. 1-41; X. 1-42.

As JESUS passed along the public way, John ix. 1

He saw a man whose eyes ne'er knew the day,

Quite blind from birth, reduced to beg his bread.

And the disciples to their Master said : 2

" Whence comes this heavy judgment? for whose sin,

His or his parents'?" Jesus said : " Therein 3

Lies not the cause ; on them no blame doth rest ;

But that God's work should be made manifest.

Judge naught before the time, but humbly wait :

God in the end His ways will vindicate :

As in this case, whereby th' occasion 's given,

To show the pity and the grace of Heaven.

I must, while it is day, the hours are few, 4

Finish the work here given Me to do,

And on the earth My Father glorify :

The day is passing, and the night is nigh.

While I am in the world, lo, I the Light 5

Am of the world, and to the blind am sight."

Having said this, He spittle mixed with earth.   John ix. 6
And smeared his eyes who had been blind from birth,
And told him: " Go, wash in Siloam's spring!"   7
He went, and came back seeing.   Wondering
Neighbors, who him had seen when blind, began   8
To ask each other, " Is not this the man
Who sat and begged?"   Made certain it was he,   9
They questioned him: " How is it thou dost see?"   10
" A man called Jesus smeared my eyes with clay,   11
And said, ' Wash in Siloam's Pool!'   Straightway
I saw."   They to the Pharisees him brought   13
('T was on the Sabbath day the cure was wrought),   14
Who asked him how it was?   He answered: " He   15
Put clay upon my eyes; I washed and see."
Some of their number said: " This man is not   16
From God, for He the Sabbath day would blot."
While others said: " How can a sinner do
Such miracles?"   And thence a schism grew.
They asked the man who had been blind again: 17
" What dost thou say He is?"   He said: " 'T is plain
He is a prophet."   But the Jews denied   18
He had been blind, till they had called, and plied
With questions both his parents: " Do ye say   19
This is your son, born blind?"   They answered:
          " Yea!   20

That he 's our son, and was born blind is so : John ix. —

But how it is he sees we do not know. 21

He is of age, ask him !"—observing heed 22

Not to offend the Jews, who had agreed,

Who owned Him Christ, should be (so great their rage)

Cast out—so said, ' Ask him, he is of age.' 23

A second time they called the man born blind. 24

And said to him : " Give God the praise ! We find

This Man 's a sinner." " Whether He be so 25

Or not," he answered, "this one thing I know,

That whereas I was blind I now do see."

They said again : " What did He do to thee ?" 26

" I 've told already, and ye did not hear— 27

Will ye be His disciples ?" Void of fear,

No more he minced his words, but spake out bold,

From their nude malice stripping every fold.

They then reviled him, saying scornfully : 28

" So thou art His disciple. Not so we :

Moses' disciples we are. God, we know, 29

Did speak to Moses a long time ago—

As for this Man we know not whence He is."

" How strange ! since power to give me sight is His, 30

Ye know not whence He is ! God does not hear 31

Sinners, but those who worship Him and fear.

Not since the world began can ye once find,   John
                                                                ix. 32
That any man gave sight to one born blind.

Were not this man from God He could do naught—33

I dare to tell you plainly my own thought."

" Dost thou presume, born child of sin and hell,   34

Us to instruct?" they said.   They him expel.

   Jesus had heard that they had cast him out,   35

And having met him, going on His route,

He said to him, as by His side he trod,

" Dost thou believe upon the Son of God?"

" Who is He, Lord, that so I may believe?   36

My heart thou hast made ready to receive."

" Not only hast thou seen Him, but 't is He   37

Who at this present moment talks with thee."

" Lord! I believe "—and fell down at His feet.   38

   And Jesus said: " Lo! I, for judgment meet,   39

Am come into the world of lost mankind ;

That who see not, may see, who see be blind."

Some Pharisees, applying this remark,   40

Said: " Are we blind, and dwell we in the dark?"

" Were ye without the means or power to see,   41

Blind in this sense, ye then from sin were free.

But since ye boast the keenness of your sight,

And close your eyes because ye hate the light.   John
ix. —
Your sin remains.   To test your love or hate
I come, the touchstone of your moral state.
What help is there, if wilful and perverse,
Ye shall the blessing turn into a curse?

  " Mark the similitude I now begin :   x. 1
Whoso into the sheepfold enters in,
Not by the door of fitness and of right,
But climbs the wall by stealth and in the night,
He is a thief and robber.   Evermore   2
The shepherd enters only by the door.
To him the porter opes without delay,
And all the sheep his well known voice obey :
He calls his sheep by name and leads them out—
Walking before, they follow him about ;   4
But while they 'll follow him from love and choice,
They 'll flee a stranger, knowing not his voice."   5

    When they had heard, and did not comprehend,
Jesus spake further then to the same end :   6
" I am the Door, the true Door of the sheep :   7
All rival claimants are impostors deep—   8
I am the Door and Keeper of the door ;   9
Who by Me pass shall safe be evermore ;

They shall go in and out and pasture find,   John X. .

Secure from wolves and thieves of bloody mind.

I am the Food and Feeder of the flock: 10

I all My fulness will to them unlock :

I come to give them life, life more and more,

Life higher, better, and in ampler store.

I the Good Shepherd am.   My love so deep,   11

I give My life to save th' imperiled sheep.

Not so the hireling.   When the wolf draws nigh,   12

He of his safety thinks and hastes to fly—   13

Because a hireling, little does he care,

So leaves the wolf to scatter and to tear.

I the Good Shepherd am : By many a sign   14

I know My sheep, and I am known of mine ;

Ev'n as the Father knoweth Me, and I   15

The Father know ,* and for My sheep I die.

And other sheep I have not of this fold ;   16

These I must bring and to My likeness mould,

That one flock and one Shepherd there may be.

Therefore it is My Father loveth Me,   17

Because of My free will My life I give,

To be resumed, that they with Me may live.

---

* Although the old reading is retained in the Revised Version, there is no doubt but this is the true rendering, as it makes the sense clear and preserves the parallel, which the other obscures or destroys.

The power to take on My permission stands; John x.
My life's not wrenched from weak unwilling hands:[18]
I have the power—men's malice all in vain—
To lay it down and take it up again.

During the Feast of Dedication,* held [22]
In winter at Jerusalem, compelled,
By stress of wet or cold, somewhere to go
For shelter, Jesus sought the Portico [23]
Of Solomon. As He was walking there, [24]
The Jews, His footsteps watching everywhere,
Surrounded Him and said: "How long dost Thou
Intend to make us doubt? Say plainly now,
If Thou be the Messiah?" He said: "Why [25]
Repeat vain words? My works they testify
Of Me wrought in My Father's name. But ye [26]
Cling to your stubborn incredulity,
Because ye are not of My sheep: for they, [27]
Hearing My voice, Me follow and obey.
I give them life eternal. Firm they stand: [28]
No man shall hurt or pluck them from My hand.

---

* This festival was instituted to commemorate the purging of the Temple, and the rebuilding of the altar, after Judas Maccabeus had driven out the Syrians, B. C. 164. It lasted eight days. To observe it, it was not obligatory to go up to Jerusalem. It occurred near the end of December, some weeks after the autumnal Feast of Tabernacles. It is not probable that Christ had returned to Galilee during the interval.

My Father, who them gave Me, greater is   John
                                                 X. 29
Than all, and none can pluck them out of His
Sure hand, which is the hand too of the Son—
I and My Father are in all things one."   30
The Jews again took stones up Him to stone.   31

　　Jesus said, " Many good works have I shown   32
You from My Father.　Now for which of those
Works do ye stone Me?"　They reply oppose: 33
" 'T is not for a good work, but blasphemy—
That man, Thou makest Thyself God."　Said He: 34
" Is it not written in your law of some
To whom the word of God of old had come,
' I said ye 're gods?'　If then the law thus spake.   35
Styling them gods, and naught can blot or shake
The pure authority of scripture speech,
Wherefore charge ye with blasphemy, and breach 36
Of law, Him whom the Father sanctified,
And sent into the world awhile to bide,
For calling Him His Son?　If I, indeed,   37
Do not My Father's works then are ye freed—
Believe Me not.　But if I do, believe,   38
If not My words, My works which can't deceive;
That ye may know the Father is in Me
And I in Him in glorious unity."

Him therefore to arrest they tried anew ;   John
x. 39
But He escaped them ; and again withdrew   40
Beyond the Jordan where John first baptized.
Many resorted to Him : They (advised   42
That all things John, who wrought no miracle,
Had said of Him as greater, were said well)
Spectators of the works that He achieved—
Hearing the words He spake—on Him believed.

"The Truth shall make you free."

Awake, my soul, from guilty slumber !
   Arise, thy warfare now begin !
Shake off whatever doth encumber,
   And break the fetters of thy sin !
   And break the fetters of thy sin !

Sweet Liberty ! divine in beauty,
   Dear radiant Daughter of the Skies !
Whose other names are Love and Duty,
   Restore Earth's long lost Paradise !
   Restore Earth's long lost Paradise !

XVII.

I AM THE RESURRECTION AND THE LIFE.

JOHN XI. 1-46.

WHEN Lazarus of Bethany was not well,   John xi. 1

His anxious sisters sent, the Lord to tell   3

How that His friend was sick. And, when He heard, 4

He spake a comforting and hopeful word :

" The issue of this sickness is not death—

Departure of th' unreturning breath—

But for God's glory meant, that so thereby

God may His Son declare and glorify."

' T was not because He did not love them well,   5

That He continued in that place to dwell   6

Yet two days longer, but for reasons wise—

Then said to His disciples : " Let us rise,   7

And go again into Judea."   Filled   8

With deep concern, that so their Lord had willed,

They said : " Master ! the Jews but very late

Would Thee have stoned, and still they lie in wait,

And go'st thou thither that they Thee may slay ? "

He said: "Are there not twelve hours in the day?
Who in the light of day and duty walks, John xi. 9
Walks sure: because he sees the sun, he balks
The murderous malice that in darkness hides—
Men stumble when no light within them guides." 10
Then added: "Our friend Lazarus doth sleep; 11
I go to wake him from his slumber deep."
"Lord! if he sleep he will recover." Said 12
The Lord then plainly: "Lazarus is dead. 14
On your account I'm glad I was not there,
That so ye may believe: we 'll thence repair."
Said Thomas to the rest with a deep sigh: 15
"Let us all go that with Him we may die."

When Jesus now to Bethany had come, 16
Four days had Lazarus been in the tomb. 17
Jews from Jerusalem, two miles away, 18
Visits of sympathy had come to pay, 19
With others, gathered in large numbers there,
In funeral rites their mournful part to bear.

One having run the joyful news to broach 20
To mourning Martha of the Lord's approach,
She flew to meet Him. Mary sat at home,
Unconscious of the fact that He had come.

Martha exclaimed, as she to Him drew near .   John
                                               xi. 21
"My brother had not died hadst Thou been here.
And even now, I know, whate'er it be,   22
That Thou shall ask of God, He 'll give it Thee."
"Thy brother, be thou sure, shall rise again."   23

"Yea," Martha said, "I know, as we maintain,   24
That he will in the resurrection rise
At the Last Day ; but far that comfort lies;
While near and now 's the anguish of the knife."

"I *am* the Resurrection and the Life,   25
The *present* Conqueror of hell and death—
I bring back life and the surrendered breath.
He that believes on Me I hold him fast,   26
And though he die, his life shall death outlast.
Of all that live, whoso believes on Me
Shall never die, but live eternally.
Believest thou all this?"   She said : "Yea, Lord !   27
I do believe and have believed Thy word,
And that Thou art the Christ, the Son of God."

    Having said this, she hurriedly retrod   28
The way back to the house, in Mary's ear
To whisper secretly : "The Master 's here,
And calls for thee."   She instantly withdrew,   29

And went to Him outside the village, threw John xi. 30

Herself down at His feet, and weeping cried : 32

" Hadst thou been here my brother had not died."

When Jesus saw her weeping, and the Jews 33

Weeping (who followed her, when at the news

She stole away in silence, fearing they,

Unfriendly to her Lord, might Him betray)

He groaned in spirit, and asked shudderingly,

" Where have ye laid him ?"   They said : " Come and

      see !" 34

And Jesus wept.   As silent tear-drops rolled 35

Down His wan cheeks, the Jews remarked, " Behold ! 36

How much He loved him." But some reasoned, "Why

Did He, who gave blind sight, let this man die ?" 37

Groaning again came Jesus to the grave, 38

Which hollowed out the hill-side formed a cave

Closed with a stone. " Remove the stone !" He said. 39

But Martha interposed : " Lord ! four days dead

He by this time must smell."   " Did I not say, 40

Believing, thou shouldst witness a display

Of the great power of God?"   They it remove. 41

Jesus said, lifting up His eyes above,

" Father, I thank Thee that Thou heardest Me !

Always My filial prayers ascend to Thee   John
xi. 42

I never ask but I at once receive;

I said it only that men might believe."

After these words with a loud voice He said: 43

   Lazarus, come forth!"   At once, he who was dead 44

Came forth, his hands and feet with fillets bound,

And all about his face a napkin wound.

Then Jesus said: " Unbind and let him go !"

Many believed.   Some let the elders know.   46

NOTE.—Some explanation of the terms used in the following Verses seems proper. *Psyche* (Greek) occurs over a hundred times in the New Testament. In about half the cases it is rendered *life*, and in the other half *soul;* while the adjective formed from it, *psychikos*, occurs six times, in four of which it is rendered *natural. Pneuma*, with its derivatives, occurs more than four hundred times, and is rendered uniformly *spirit*, except in those cases where Holy *Ghost* is used instead of Holy Spirit. Trichotomists are those who hold to a threefold division of the nature of man, in accordance with 1 Th. v. 23, which speaks of *spirit* (pneuma), *soul* (psyche) and *body* (soma) as constituting the whole person to be preserved blameless. The dichotomous view (which by the way is the current one and gives a distinct coloring to all the creeds) makes man to consist of two parts, viz.: body and soul. The pneuma or spirit, when it is distinguished from the soul, is regarded as the highest principle in man's nature, being that which distinguishes him from the brute creation, allies him to God, and forms the true ground of his immortality. Strictly speaking it was the pneuma or the spiritual part of man, rather than the intellectual, that fell—that is, suffered degradation and dethronement, with spiritual darkness and death as the result. Regeneration is, therefore, the requickening of the dead or dormant, fallen pneuma; and its reinstatement as the supreme regulative faculty in man, dominating all below. Standing for the godlike, it is rich in all divine capabilities, and so it would be strange, if it were destitute of the power to clothe itself, that being one of the most necessary of all powers. Being in its own nature immortal, it needs an immortal body, and will have it, because it needs it, and when it needs it. Potentially present in the germ al-

O GRAVE, WHERE IS THY VICTORY?

Four days had Lazarus been dead: John xi. 20
  When Martha heard the Lord was near,
She flew to meet Him: " Oh," she said,
  " He had not died hadst Thou been here."
Her eyes in tears, fast flowing, swam;
  Her restless heart was full of strife;
She heard him say, unsoothed, " I AM   25
  THE RESURRECTION AND THE LIFE."

Though speaking in the present tense,
  The comfort of His words was hid:
In some far-off and frigid sense,
  In the same way her fathers did,
She held the dead would rise again   John xi. 24
  At the Last Day; but must she wait
Ten thousand years, and not complain,
  In hope of meeting at that date?

ready, it is the pushing and growing force of the indwelling pneuma that shapes the pneumatical body, and makes it its own. Entombed for the moment in mortal flesh, its resurrection is imminent. Like the butterfly from its rent cocoon, the embodied psyche-pneuma will spring forth, winged and wonderful, and ascend to the highest heavens. Identity always lies in the personal consciousness of the Ego. It is simply Myself, and not an affair of atoms at all.

He said, ' I *am*,' not I shall be.*   John
xi. 23

   The doctrine was divinely new—

A most consoling certainty,

   Not apprehended by the Jew :

The resurrection of the dead,

   He taught was not a dim event,

Re-knitting of a broken thread,

   But near and now and imminent.

* It often happens, that what the Scriptures leave obscure or undefined, men in their attempts to explain darken the more. As nobody was found equal to the task of piecing out the uncompleted lines of Virgil's *Sic vos non vobis*, we distrust the competency of human wisdom to supply the deficiencies of divine authorship. This is applicable to creeds, for there is in the best and most venerated of them a human element which reflects simply the knowledge of the time. Advancing science, while it antiquates so much of these as is human, leaves the divine untouched in all its primitive freshness. The real conflict is not between the inspired text but its interpretation. Creeds have their uses, but Christ says, "Come to Me!" In that case, we have truth at first hand. We drink at the uncorrupted source. We are put into original relation with the Great Teacher Himself. Surely we can know far better by direct tasting that sugar is sweet than by report ; but it is a common fault of the learned and the unlearned alike, that they rely on the say-so of men who had no better means of knowing than themselves, if as good.

Much of our ignorance is of ourselves. Our eyes are full of dust. Prejudice blinds us. It was so, we know, with the apostles. We are amazed at their stupidity. Where, we are tempted to ask, were their ears ? Their Master spoke plainly enough, but they did not listen. He said to Martha, "I am the Resurrection and the Life. Whoever believeth on Me shall never die. Believest thou this?" She did not penetrate His meaning, nor try to. She had glibly expressed her belief in the resurrection as she understood it ; but whether the saying of the Master was in accordance with that old belief she did not stop to inquire. It is wonderful how contented we are in our ignorance. Our Lord's question is addressed, no doubt, to us as much as to Martha ; and we, like her, not seeing perhaps how a present resurrection, which *seems* to be asserted, harmonizes with a resurrection which we have been taught to believe lies in the far future, we pass by the remarkable declaration as something enigmatical or too profound for us.

Believers in the Resurrection may be conveniently divided into three classes. *First*.

Because Immortal Love reigns here, John xvii. 24

   Present and powerful to save,

It were unreasonable to fear Col. iii. 3

   An interregnum in the grave :

Th' imperishable forms of those,

   With tears committed to the ground,

Evoked at death, triumphant rose, Rev. vii. 15

   And now the throne of God surround.

Those who hold that the self-same body will be raised up at the Last Day, meaning thereby all the material particles which happen to compose it at the moment of death. According to the poet Young, however, as set forth in his poem on "The Last Day," members previously lost will be supplied :

> " Now monuments prove faithful to their trust,
> And render back their long committed dust.
> Now charnels rattle ; scattered limbs and all
> The various bones, obsequious to the call,
> Self-moved advance ; the neck perhaps to meet
> The distant head, the distant legs the feet :
> Dreadful to view, see through the dusky sky
> Fragments of bodies in confusion fly,
> To distant regions journeying, there to claim
> Deserted members and complete the frame."

Second. Those who entertain the view thus expressed in the Epitaph ascribed to Milton :

> " These Ashes, which do here remain,
> A vital tincture still retain ;
> A seminal form within the deeps
> Of this little chaos sleeps ; * * *
> This plant thus calcined into dust
> In its Ashes rest it must,
> Until sweet Psyche shall inspire
> A softening and prolific fire,
> And in her fostering arms enfold
> This heavy and this earthly mould."

For form is different from dust,

And 'tis for form alone we care;

Our earthly bodies perish must,

The soul of form no longer there.

The old, that was in weakness sown,   1 Cor. xv. 43

Is made the pattern of the new,   49

But, fashioned like the Saviour's own,   Phil. iii. 21

Stands forth idealized to view.

Third. Those who hold, that while we are justified in assuming that "a seminal form" exists, it is to be looked for not in the ashes of the urn nor the dust of the grave, but in the depths of the immortal spirit itself, forming an essential part of it, being, in fact, the life within the life, possessing genetic aptitudes, whereby, under a divine quickening, a spiritual or pneumatical body emerges. This—constituting what is called the resurrection from the dead—differs from Christ's resurrection chiefly in this particular, that in His case, there was first a revivification of the natural body of flesh and blood, without its seeing corruption; and a spiritualizing or glorification of it afterwards, before His ascension. The advocates of this view conceive that it alone suits the analogy pointed at by Paul in regard to the buried seed—the likeness being properly between the living seed and the living man, not the dead body. "Dead things," as Locke observes, "are not sown; seeds are sown being alive." It is the living acorn that contains the oak; the dead acorn, like the dead body, is empty and contains nothing. It is the psyche, the tree's life, resident in the acorn, to which it owes all its glorious possibilities. It is this, which making use of its environments, builds up this lordliest of vegetable forms. Strictly speaking, life springs only from life, never from death. The seed seems to die, but does not. It descends to ascend. It clothes itself; it puts on beauty and glory; multiplies itself an hundred fold, and is thus made fit to minister to the necessities of man; to nourish and build up the brain—and so become ancillary to thought and love and worship.

Compared with the magnificent potentialities of the human germ those of the seed and acorn are poor and weak. Here too, it is the indwelling psyche, infinitely enriched however by special endowments, which in its marvelous workings under God, crowds into the period of a few brief months the accomplishments of mighty milleniums; repeating, so to speak, the miracles of creation from the beginning; passing up step by step from the lowest to the highest; through numerous imitative metamorphoses, culminating in the perfected form of the child born into the world. From earliest times

That which is natural is first :   1 Cor.
xv. 46.

The body-builder, Psyche, moulds,

Till on the raptured sight there burst

The hidden forms the germ enfolds.

It makes each organ play a part,

Giving what suits the body here—

Were there no blood there were no heart—

It fits the earthly to its sphere.

until now, much use has been made, in the way of illustration, of the conversion of the caterpillar into the butterfly, but the mighty transformations which have already taken place at the time of birth, leaves this poor example a thousand leagues behind. But change and ascent do not stop at birth. The infant ripens into a Newton. When man is at his best and highest, death comes. Believers of this third class regard it as incredible, that at this supreme point there should be any pause or backward step in the march of development. They hold that death rightly viewed, so far from being catastrophic and final, is grandly climacteric ; is not a plunge downwards but a step upwards ; a mystic transition and birth into a higher life ; that it is not more in accordance with Christian hope, than it is with reason, that new forces should now come into play and a new body be formed to take the place of the old one ; that at once, without any yawning interval, under a divine and gracious quickening, this corruptible should put on incorruption, and this mortal should put on immortality, and that death should be swallowed up of life.

All this is exactly in accordance with the assurance of Paul, who said he knew that when the earthly house of this tabernacle was dissolved he had a building of God, a house not made with hands eternal in the heavens ; justifying his exultant expectation that, admitted to the vision of Jesus in His glorified body and seeing Him as He is, he should be like Him ; that, having borne the image of the earthy, he should bear henceforth the image of the heavenly ; and be prepared to praise Him, from the first, for a finished and complete redemption, including that of his body—having attained to the resurrection from the dead which had been the object of so much struggle and endeavor during his natural life upon the earth. As the apostle points out, that is not first which is spiritual (pneumatical) but that which is natural (pyschical) ; afterwards that which is spiritual (pneumatical). As the psyche begets and raises up the pyschical or natural body, by a like formative energy, it is thought, the pneuma begets and raises up the pneumatical or spiritual body, resemblant but different.

In further confirmation of this view, they cite the above declaration of our Lord to

Spirits, when severed from decay,   1 Cor.
xv. 50

Need other organs.   How shall then

They be re-wedded to their clay,

Without becoming mortal men ?

Can Psyche build and Pneuma not?

Pneuma, the nobler of the two,

A glorious body; without blot,

Christ-like, angelical, and new,

Martha: " I am the Resurrection and the Life", made purposely, it would seem, to correct an erroneous impression which Martha entertained, in accordance with the prevalent Jewish belief, that the resurrection was a remote event, too remote to be available for present comfort under bereavement. Prior to Christ's coming, the few brief hints of the Inspired Scriptures on the subject of the Resurrection, had been formulated by the Rabbins into a creed. As Christ came to bring life and immortality to life, it would be a disparagement of His mission to suppose that all His teachings, in regard to the what and the how and the when of the Resurrection, had been antici-pated by these men, leaving Him nothing to reveal ; and so, if in His utterance on this occasion there should be found something new and different from the accepted Phari-saic doctrine, it would be no more than what might be expected. Christ's teachings and the Pharisees' run, we know, counter to each other. They materialized ; He spiritualized. They externalized the Kingdom of God and were looking forward to it. He spoke of it, as both coming and having come. "It cometh not," He said, "with observation, but is within you." He emphasizes the *now*. All is *now*. I am the Resurrection and the Life *now*; the Judgment is *now*. The hour cometh, and *now* is, when the dead shall hear the voice of the Son of God, and they that hear shall live. He that believeth on the Son *is* not judged. He that believeth not *is* judged already. Every day, so to speak, is therefore Doomsday ; but the day of death is, in a special sense, to every individual, the Last Day, and the Coming of the Lord in the clouds of heaven, and the Day of Judgment.   One hundred thousand souls are ushered into the presence of the Supreme Judge every twenty-four hours ; four thousand every hour, night and day, sufficient, one might think, to warrant a continued session. Thus one day is hardly more solemn than another. All days are solemn. "Every meanest moment rests on eternity."

It is admitted, that the language employed in describing the Last Judgment and the End of the World is bold and full of material imagery ; but hardly more so than that applied to the destruction of Jerusalem. All Christ's teachings are full of simili-

Shall rear—a house not made with hands,   2 Cor.
v. 1

A God-devised and mystic dome,

Eternal in the heavenly lands,

    To be the spirit's final home.

The seed is quickened when it dies,   1 Cor.
xv. 36

    Puts on the new, sloughs off the old :   37

The slumbering Pneuma wakes, likewise,   44

    Its mighty marvels to unfold.

tudes. He taught in parables and prophesied in symbols. The apocalypse of the future is given in inspired tableaux—scenic representations, types and adumbrations of awful realities, true in substance if not in form.

It is unfortunate that this view—not this view either but something like it—is made repugnant to many minds by its accidental association with Gnostic and other heresies. It is certainly free from some of the difficulties which attach to both the other two, and has many things to recommend it. In regard to the first, although apparently favored by the Creeds, it is safe to say that it is based on false notions of identity, and is sanctioned by neither reason nor Scripture. Dust is not identity. Had Augustine—who held that all the matter which ever entered into the organism however dispersed here, would be made complete in quantity and quality in the resurrection, even to the hairs cut off and the paring of the nails—known as much of Physiology as every tyro now knows, he must have seen how untenable was such a view. For what are the facts of the case? It is certain that our bodies are never two hours together wholly the same. The body of to-day is not the body of yesterday. "We die daily." Let Augustine's conjecture be judged of by the light of the following extract, taken from Dalton's work on Human Physiology : " It has been ascertained by careful weighing that rather more than *seven pounds are absorbed and discharged daily* by the healthy human subject ; and for a man having the average weight of 140 pounds, a quantity of material equal to the weight of the whole body is thus passed through the system in twenty days "—tantamount to more than a ton in a year. Augustine died at 75. Accepting his view as correct, the size and weight of his own resurrection body would need to be enormous. Thomas Aquinas held the more moderate view, that only the particles which entered into the composition of the body at death would be raised ; but we know, that a sharp sickness—aided perhaps by medicine and a copious blood-letting just before death—can reduce the weight of the body several pounds ; and it would devolve on the Angelical Doctor to give some good reason why the particles that remain should be more sacred and worthy of being raised than those taken away. Tertulian absurdly enough supposed, that the teeth were purposely made indestructi-

To be reborn, the Pneuma must   John iii. 3

   Be quickened by the Spirit's breath;   6

And 't is the Christian's settled trust,

   The Lord of life is Lord of death :   Rev. i. 18

That when he dies, the holy force

   Works normally to beauteous ends,

In orderly and healthy course,

   And always to perfection tends.

ble, that they might serve as the nucleus of the new body at the resurrection.   A Jewish tradition, on the other hand, assigned this honor to a part of the *os coccygis.*

It is presumed that the insuperable difficulties attendant upon this doctrine of literal identity, led to the adoption of the second view, advocated by Drew in his able treatise, viz., that there is an indestructible germ somewhere in our present body, which is to be developed in the future. This—which is, if we mistake not, the belief now most common—agrees, as we have seen, with the third view in assuming the existence of a resident germinal principle by means of which the new spiritual body or organism is to be evolved, but differs in supposing that this descends with the dead body, and lies perdue in the grave until the end of the world, when it is first quickened. If the natural body is to be succeeded by a spiritual body, it would be in accordance with all analogy that provision should have been made in the original constitution of our nature for the metamorphosis, and so it can hardly be doubted that the genetic or active cause of such transformation has a lodgment somewhere in the human economy ; and the question arises in that case, which is most likely to be its seat, the dead body or the living spirit. Could we find good scriptural grounds for believing that it goes with the spirit, then we should have no difficulty in understanding how the embodiment which takes place should be immediate, and how "the just" would have no need to wait to be "made perfect."

The difficulty of harmonizing this view with various texts of Scripture may not, perhaps, be so great as it seems. We do not think it the least of its recommendations, that it does away with the inferential necessity of an intermediate state, with its inexplicable anomalies, contradictions, and twilight underground associations—its Paradise being, as many conceive it, little better than a weird betweenity, a kind of half prison, a place of exile and long waiting. What the state of the soul is without the body, Isaac Taylor, in his Physical Theory of Another Life, tries to imagine and tell us ; and we confess, the conclusions which he reaches are by no means exhilarating. He argues, that as mind is dependent upon corporiety, its powers for the time are in a state of suspension. The intermediate period, being the chrysalis period of the soul, is,

To raise me up at my last day, John vi. 39

Were more than to resuscitate 40

This mortal tenement of clay,

Making me live to die more late :

Give me, O Christ! a nature new ;

Mix Thy sweet life with mine, True Bread! 52

That so I may attain unto Philip. iii. 10

The resurrection from the dead. 11

he infers, marked by the destitution of all the instruments of active life, corporeal and mental. This state of inaction is probably, he thinks, also a state of subterranean seclusion, involving perhaps an unconsciousness of the passage of time.

This picture, it must be conceded, is a far less cheering one than that given in the Westminster Confession, which distinctly affirms, that "the souls of the righteous, immediately after death, being made perfect in holiness, are received into the *highest* heaven," etc. Now, as nothing can be higher than the "highest," there is clearly no room left for anything "intermediate ;" but not content with this implied denial of an intermediate state, the Confession goes on to say expressly, "Besides these two places [*i. e.*, heaven and hell] the Scripture acknowledgeth none." It is silent as to the disembodied soul's mode of existence, but seems to take it for granted, that it has organs perfectly adapted to its exalted condition. Paul speaks of being absent from the body, but present with the Lord ; which might be thought to imply, that he believed in the possibility of the existence of the soul apart from the body ; but, on the other hand, one would be led to think, from the importance which he attached everywhere to the resurrection, that he regarded corporiety—spiritual corporiety—in a sense necessary.

Profoundly impressed with the greatness of the mystery which shrouds the subject, the writer feels that no attitude towards it becomes him but one of reverent inquiry : therefore he desires it to be understood, that the view, set forth in the accompanying Verses, is propounded rather than asserted. He thinks it echoes the hope if not the belief of multitudes. If true and justified by Scripture, it cannot be deemed otherwise than desirable that it should be divorced from the error or the folly with which it may happen to be associated. For who would not like to be scripturally certified, that death was no more than the putting off of one garment and the putting on of another? That as soon as the soul is unclothed, it is clothed upon with the vestments of eternity? It is easy to start objections, and raise difficulties against any view. On a subject involved in so much uncertainty, the writer considers it is lawful to differ.

In a swift moment Thou didst turn
  The water into living wine—   John
                                               ii. 8
The twinkling of an eye, I learn,   1 Cor.
                                              xv. 52
  Suffices for the Power Divine:
Rather than souls leave naked, Thou   2 Cor.
                                               v. 3
  Wouldst clothe them by immediate act;
But there's no need, if law doth now
  Potentiality make fact.

In captive thrall should death retain
  Part of ourselves, the spirit's mate,
We should in heaven with yearning pain   Rom.
                                              viii. 23
  Redemption of our body wait;
And ask, What means this long divorce
  Our exiled half still 'neath the sod?
And spur the ages in their course,
  To consummate us sons of God.   19

Dear risen Lord! does Paul still groan,
  Not clothed upon as he had hoped?
To all but to Thyself alone
  Are the grave's prison-doors unoped?
Dost Thou in heaven a body wear?
  And dost Thou make Thy saints to wait,
Leaving their souls unclothed and bare,
  In nameless embryonic state?

What are those many mansions,* Thou   John xiv. 2

     Didst say Thou wentest to prepare?

Dwell not they all within them now,

     Each housed in his own palace fair?

It cannot be they suffer lack—

     When Love to them all things has given—   Rom. viii. 2

And are now sighing to come back

     To supplement defect in heaven.

* The writer is aware, that such an interpretation, of what Stier calls, "this super-abundant mysterious declaration "—*i. e.*, "In my Father's house are many mansions," etc.—would be novel; but, he is not sure, but that it is as defensible as any that has been hitherto suggested. The objection, that the "many mansions" are spoken of as *already* existing, would apply equally to Paul's affirmation: "We *have* a house [referring clearly, it would seem from the connection, to the spiritual body] not made with hands eternal in the heavens." Jesus speaks in the next verse: "I go to prepare a place for you"; and yet the place is elsewhere spoken of (Matt. xxv. 34) as "prepared for you from the foundation of the world." So we read of "The Lamb slain from the foundation of the world." What is fixed in the divine purpose is considered as already existing. In regard to the many mansions, there is no need, that we should figure them as dwelling-places, empty and expectant, actually existing in heaven; but as potential habitations, preparing and to be prepared for an eternal residence. Admitting, that the spiritual bodies of the redeemed are meant thereby it is not difficult to understand, how that His going before, would have reference to His sending the Holy Ghost with his quickening, upbuilding and shaping influences, guiding and directing the pneuma at last in the way heretofore indicated, so as to give to every sanctified personality at or after death his "own body"; whence it would come to pass that the number of mansions would correspond to the number of the saved; and each house with its inhabitant would be distinctive and peculiar—differing, it may be, as stars differ from one another in glory. The coming again, promised in the same connection, nearly all agree, refers to Christ's coming at death. The Swedenborgian figment, that by many mansions are meant stellar worlds to which souls are distributed, finds no basis in Scripture, nor, we may add, in common sense; and to minimize the meaning to the dimensions of so poor a thought, as that there is room (space) enough in heaven for all believers, is we think, to do injustice both to the speaker and the occasion.

14.

XVIII.

RETIRES BEYOND THE JORDAN.

JOHN XI. 47-54; LUKE XIII. 22—XV. 31; XVIII. 1-14.

CHIEF priests and elders hastened to convoke   John xi. 47

    The Sanhedrim; and, full of cunning, spoke

(Under a show of patriotic zeal,

And pure affection for the public weal,

Hiding the venom of their private hate)

Of great and imminent danger to the State.

" What are we doing?   Nothing that's of use,

While He goes on the people to seduce

By many miracles and wonders great

And a portentous one of recent date.

If we let Him alone, ere long all men   48

Will think He is the Christ; the Romans then

Will come and take away from us, we fear,

Our place and nation."   Caiaphas, that year   49

Being the high priest, said: " Ye nothing know,

Else ye would see, to save from overthrow

The fabric of the Jewish Church and State,

The present is no time to hesitate :

And how, in any case, that this one man

Should for the people die, is better than

That the whole nation perish." Naught he cared,

For truth and innocence howe'er declared—

But herein spake unconscious prophesy,

That Jesus for the nation then should die ;

Nor for that nation only, but likewise,

For all the nations under the whole skies ;

And that He should assemble from abroad

Into one Church the scattered sons of God.

They from that day concerted how they might

Put Him to death. To be from public sight

Removed, away from danger of arrest,

He left Jerusalem, and judged it best

To go to a small town called Ephraim—

And His disciples tarried there with Him.

Quitting at length the place of His retreat

Again He crossed the Jordan, and with feet

That felt fatigue, but felt it to contemn,

Teaching and journeying towards Jerusalem,

He passed through towns and villages that lay

In Herod Antipas' domain. One day,

Marginal references:

John xi.—

50

51

52

53

54

Mark x. 1

Luke xiii.22

31

Came certain of the Pharisees to Him,   Luke
                                                               xiii. —
Saying, with curling lip and visage grim:
" Get Thee away, at once, for Herod means
To kill Thee." Naught from Him their malice
        screens—   32
So He, knowing informers them to be,
Said : " Go, and tell that fox, that I cast out
Demons, and cures perform along My route
To-day, likewise to-morrow : the third day   33
My course completed, I will go away.
I ne'ertheless till then shall walk about,
Because a prophet cannot perish out
Of doomed Jerusalem.   Jerusalem !   34
That kill'st the prophets, and that stonest them
Who 're sent to thee, how oft I, safe from harms,
Thy children would have gathered in My arms,
E'en as the hen, when hawks are hovering,
Gathers her brood beneath her shelt'ring wing,
But ye would not—blind, fierce, and obstinate—
Now is your house left waste and desolate.   35

  As at a ruler's house He sat at meat,   xiv. 1
Guests were ambitious of the highest seat.   7
Observing which, this Parable He spake :

" When to a wedding thou art bidden, take Luke xiv. 8

Not vainly the chief seat at table, lest

There enter a more honorable guest,

And the host come to thee, and say aloud: 9

'Yield this man room!' And thou, who wert so
       proud,

Be forced with shame to take the lowest place.

But when invited, to avoid disgrace, 10

Go to the lowest seat, that in the end

The host may tell thee, 'Go up higher, friend!'

Then thou'lt have honor in the sight of all—

For self descends to rise, and climbs to fall." 11

He said, likewise, to him who was His host: 12

" When thou a dinner or a supper dost

Provide, ask not thy friends, nor brothers, nor

Thy kinsmen, nor thy wealthy neighbors, for

These haply may thee ask in turn, and thence

Thou may'st receive a selfish recompense.

But ask the poor, the maimed, the lame, the blind, 13

And thou a heavenly recompense shalt find." 14

One of the guests, this hearing, warmly said: 15

" How bless'd in God's Kingdom to eat bread!"

Then Jesus said to him : " A certain man 16

Made a great supper, on a scale and plan
Royal and rich, inviting many. So   17
At supper time, he sent to let them know
All things were ready. But, with one consent,   18
They all, preoccupied, excuses sent.
One said : 'I've bought a field which I must see—
Have me excused.' Another, for that he   19
Had bought five yoke of oxen, and must go
To prove them, prayed to be excused also.
A third said : ' I just married am—therefore   20
I cannot come.' These several answers bore   21
The servant to his waiting Master, who,
Incensed, said to his servants : ' Go into
The city's streets and lanes, make search and find,
And bring in here the poor, maimed, lame and blind.'
The servants said : ' According to thy will,   22
This has been done, and there 's room vacant still.'
Once more the Master said : ' Go out again,   23
Into the highways and the hedges, and constrain
Enough my house to fill, and save from waste :
For not one bidden shall my supper taste.' "   24

Now a great multitude, from far and near,   xv. 1
Of publicans and sinners came to hear :
Drawn far more strongly, than with cords and hooks,

By the attraction of His loving looks, Luke
xv.—
And winning sweetness of His friendly speech,
And condescension that to them could reach.
Treated as beings of inferior birth,
Vile outcasts and offscourings of the earth,
When now One rose to tell them, though defiled,
Their Father God still loves His wand'ring child,
What wonder, that the strange and welcome news
Should through their hearts an unknown joy diffuse:
When at this friendliness some took offense, 2
He spake these Parables in His defense : 3

"What man, the owner of a hundred sheep, 4
If one, through failure with the flock to keep,
Be lost, doth not the others leave behind
There in the wold, and go the lost to find?
And, having found it, doth not lay it there 5
On his glad shoulders, and it homeward bear,
And say to friends and neighbors gathered round: 6
' Rejoice with me for I the lost have found '?
So a diviner joy from Heaven doth flow 7
Out towards one sinner that repents below,
Than ninety-nine self-righteous persons, who
Need no repentance or suppose they do."

" What woman with ten drachmas, losing one, Luke
xv. 8
Lights not a lamp to aid th' excluded sun ;
Sweeps not the house, and searches not all round,
Until she find it?   And, when it is found,   9
Doth not her neighbors summon, and accost :
· Rejoice with me, I've found the piece I lost '?

" A father had two sons.   The younger said,   11
· Father ! of thy estate be my share paid.'   12
And he allotted to each son his share.
The younger son began then to prepare   13
For his departure—gathered all and sold—
Turning the fixed into convenient gold,
And journeyed to a country far away,
And there in endless riot night and day,
Wasted his substance.   And, when all was spent,   14
A famine there arose of wide extent ;
And he began to be in want.   So deep   15
His need, he lent himself the swine to keep :
But no man gave him aught, till he was led   16
To crave the husks on which the hogs were fed.
Come to himself, the thought sprang into view,   17
· How many hirelings has my father, who
Have more bread than suffices, while I here
Perish with hunger, ending mad career.

I will arise and to my father go,   Luke xv. 18

And I will say unto him: Father! lo,

I 've sinned, have greatly sinned, 'gainst Heaven and
     thee,

And therefore am not worthy more to be   19

Counted a son.   Make me, I am content,

One of thy hirelings.'   He arose and went.   20

Him when the father afar off descried,

Moved with compassion, he to meet him hied,

And fell upon his neck, and kissed him much,

The love and longing in his heart were such.

  " With tears fast flowing, pierced with new distress,

He should have ever grieved such tenderness,   21

The son said, ' Father! I have sinned 'gainst light,

Before the face of Heaven and in thy sight.

And am not worthy to be called thy son.'

  " But said the father to the servants, ' Run,   22

Bring hither the best robe—rags are unmeet—

A ring put on his hand, shoes on his feet,

And bring the fatted calf and quickly slay,   23

And let us feast, and merry be to-day,

For this my son was dead (let joy abound)   24

And lives again: was lost, and, lo, is found.'

  " The elder son was absent in the field,   25

So what had happened was from him concealed.

Returning home, he heard, as he drew nigh,   Luke
                                                  xv.—
Music and dancing ; and, till he knew why,
He would not enter, but remained without.
Asking a servant what 't was all about,   26
The servant said to him : 'Thy brother 's come—   27
Thy father gives this festive welcome home.
Has killed the fatted calf, made mirth abound.
Because he has received him safe and sound.'
When asked to enter, he refused with heat :   28
Therefore the father came out to entreat.

     " He said : ' Lo, I thee many years have served,   29
And have from none of thy commandments swerved :
And yet thou never gavest me a kid,
My friends to pleasure; but no sooner did   30
This spendthrift son return, who has ere now
Squandered on prostitutes thy means, than thou
Killedst for him the fatted calf.' ' Nay, son,'   31
The father said, ' grieve not at what is done.
Thou'rt ever with me, and all mine is thine.
Be not so foolish then as to repine.
'T was meet, that we a festive joy should spread.   32
For this, thy brother, was aforetime dead,
And is alive again—lost in the wold,
Is found at last and brought into the fold.' "

THE LOST FOUND.

I sing the Shepherd of the sheep :
   Who, for the love He bore the fold,
Did wade through sorrows dark and deep,
   And freely give His life of old.

I sing the love, so strange, so sweet,
   That sought the lost until it found—
With aching heart, and bleeding feet,
   And flowing tears that wet the ground.

I sing the goodness of our God,
   The patient pity and the grace,
That left no dreadful path untrod
   To seek and save the human race.

Great Shepherd of the nations ! Thou,
   Bishop of souls, go forth to find
Thy scattered flock ! O gather now
   The straying millions of mankind !

He said to His disciples : " Hear ye too :   Luke xvi. 1
A certain rich man had a steward, who,
Accused of wasting his estate, was thrust   2
Out of his stewardship for breach of trust.
As sad he mused, a shrewd thought upward flamed :   3
· I cannot dig, to beg I am ashamed
But there 's a way by which, when here I leave,   4
Some of my master's friends will me receive.'

" He called to him the debtors of his lord,   5
And spake to each the same sly cunning word :
· How much,' he asked, the first, ' is it thou ow'st ?
· A hundred baths of oil,' he answered. ' Dost   6
Thou wish 't were less ? Take back thy script, and now
Write one for fifty.' ' How much owest thou ?'   7
He asked another, who replied : ' Of wheat
A hundred homers.' ' The amount 's too great—
Take back thy script, and write one for four-score.'
Clever the scheme, a thing to chuckle o'er.   8
His lord admired the fitness of the plan
To win the favor of his fellow man.
For children of this world, in their affairs,
Are wiser than the sons of light in theirs.

Luke
xvi. - .

" Not worshipped as a god, but held a tool
To work the pleasure of the hands that rule,
Yourselves can carry on by Mammon even
A gainful commerce with the ports of heaven :
Deceitful riches can procure you friends,
When used as righteous means to righteous ends ;
Can gain the friendship of the powers above,
By alms of mercy and by bribes of love.
So use your money, that when earth ye leave,
They into everlasting homes may you receive.

" He that is faithful in a little (such   10
The general law) is faithful too in much.
He that unrighteous is in matters small,
Unrighteous is in great things and in all.
If in low monetary trusts untrue,   11
Who will commit true riches unto you?
If in another's, ye have weakness shown,   12
Who will believe you equal to your own ?
Ye cannot faithful and unfaithful be,   13
Be friends of God and serve His enemy.

Lovers of money, when the Pharisees   14
Heard Him declare these things, they, ill at ease,
Began to jeer, and sneer at Him, and scoff.

He said to them: "Ye may with men pass off   Luke xvi. 15
Yourselves for righteous, but God knows your hearts,
And all the lustings of your inward parts.
Self is your God, for self ye spend or hoard;
But what 's admired of men, of God 's abhorred.
While ye can sit as princes, what care ye
Your brother pines in want and misery?

  "There was a man exceeding rich, who clad   19
In purple and fine linen, daily had
Whate'er could minister gluttonous delight:
While at his gate there lay, a piteous sight.   20
A beggar full of sores, named Lazarus,
Desiring naught of the vast overplus
Whereon to feed but sweepings of the floors: 21
And the dogs came and licked his undressed sores.
The beggar dying, he was borne away   22
To Abraham's bosom.   On another day,
The rich man also died, and with parade
And haughty pomp was to the tomb conveyed.
And he, in hades, lifting up his eyes,   23
Being in torments, Abraham descries
Afar with Lazarus upon his breast,
Free from his sores, most happy and at rest.

Himself a beggar now—from depths of grief   Luke xvi. –

He hurls a mighty cry for some relief,   24

Across the distance, reaching Abraham's ear :

· Have pity, father Abraham, and here

Send Lazarus to dip his finger's tip

In water, thus to cool my tongue and lip,

For I'm tormented in this flame.'   But he   25

Said, ' Son, remember choice was given thee,

And thou didst have the things which thy heart would,

All bodily delights and earthly good ;

And Lazarus had his evil things below—

But now while he 's in joy thou art in woe.

A gulf impassable, moreo'er, is fixed   26

Of separation us and thee betwixt.'

The other said : ' Then, father, send I pray   27

Him to my father's house, that so he may

Warn my five brethren lest they here too come—   28

The grave 's now silent and the dead are dumb.'

But Abraham replied : ' Already they   2)

Have Moses and the Prophets.'   Said he : ' Nay,   30

O father, but if from the dead one went

And warned them, they, in that case, would repent.'

· Not so.   If them they hear not,' Abraham said,   31

They would not hear though one rose from the dead.' "

That he might confidence to men impart Luke xviii. 1
To persevere in prayer, and not lose heart,
He spake this Parable. "There was," He said,
"A certain judge, of God nor man afraid,
Venal, unjust, not caring for the right,
To all but his own ease indifferent quite,
A selfish sybarite devoid of shame.
To him a widow of that city came, 3
Saying, 'Uphold, I pray, my righteous cause,
And vindicate the justice of the laws.'
He would not for a while, but afterward, 4
He said within himself, 'Though I regard
Not right, lest I be battered* with her prayers, 5
I'll righteous judgment give in her affairs.'
Hear what the unjust judge was moved to do. 6
And will not God redress His chosen, who 7
Cry day and night to Him! I tell you, Yea, 8
And that with speed, though there seem long delay.
When comes the Son of Man shall He find dearth
And scarcity of faith upon the earth?"

He spake this Parable to those, who thought
They were the righteous, and all others naught:

* The literal meaning of the original Greek is "to make black and blue under the eyes by blows."

" Two men up to the Temple went one day-- Luke xviii. 10

A Pharisee and Publican—to pray.

Standing apart the Pharisee began 11

His brag : ' O God, I thank Thee I'm a man,

Not as the rest of men, I proudly trust,

Extortioners, adulterers, unjust,

Or as this Publican. I, each week, lo ! 12

Fast twice. I tithes of all I have bestow.'

Meanwhile the Publican with heavy sighs, 13

Standing afar, afraid to lift his eyes,

Smote on his breast, and cried : ' I am undone !

Be merciful to me, the sinful one.'

This man went justified, I say to you, 14

Down to his house the rather of the two.

For who exalts himself shall humbled be,

The road to honor is humility."

MATT. XIX 13-30; MARK X. 13-31; LUKE XVIII. 15-30.

THEN they brought babes to Him, that he might

    lay Matt. xix. 13

His dear caressing hands on them and pray :

And the disciples censured them for it.

And Jesus said : " The little ones permit 14

To come to Me, and do not them prevent—

15

Essential is the childlike element,   Matt.
                                                       .xix. —
Trustful and clinging, finding food and rest,
Warmth and protection on the mother's breast—
Of such God's Kingdom is.   Be not beguiled!   Mark
                                                       x. 15
Who enters it must enter as a child."
Taking them in His arms He them caressed,   16
And laid His loving hands on them and blessed.

  A ruler came to Him, while on His way,   17
And kneeling said : "Good Master! tell, I pray,
What shall I do eternal life to win?"
He said : " The good is one who has no sin ;   18
Why callest thou Me good?   Dost thou Me know ?
None 's good but God, who 's absolutely so.
Thou knowest the Commandments ; keep each one! "19
He said, " From my youth up, I this have done :   20
What lack I that I may be perfected?"
Then Jesus looked on him with love, and said :   21
" Wouldst thou be perfect, and forever live,
Go, sell, and to the poor thy substance give ;
And come, take up thy cross, and follow Me,
Mid persecution, shame and poverty.
For My sake, thou must count all things as loss,
Thy reputation and thy riches dross :

For these thou 'lt forfeit, and 't were therefore wise
To sit down first, and weigh the sacrifice.
Like one who thinks, ere he begins a tower,   Luke xiv.28
Whether to finish it be in his power.
Or like a king, ere he to battle goes,   31
Considers well the number of his foes."

At this he went away with heavy heart,   Mark x. 22
With his possessions not content to part.

Then Jesus His disciples thus addressed: 23
" How difficult it is for those possessed
Of wealth to enter in at the strait gate !
So prone are men its worth to overrate—
To trust in riches, and more highly prize   24
The earthly good than treasures in the skies.
'T were easier for a camel to pass through   25
A needle's eye, than that hard thing to do."
They said, astonished, " Who then can be saved?" 26
" What is not possible with men depraved,   27
Is possible with God through offered grace."   Matt. xix. 27

Peter began to say with foolish face :
" Lo! we've forsaken all and followed Thee—
What shall we have therefore ?" " Be sure, that ye—28

Who Me have followed (O the grace of it !)   Matt.
                                      xix. —

In the regeneration,* when shall sit

The Son of Man upon His glorious throne,

Subduing hearts by might of Truth alone—

Shall be My sovereign mouth, and shall declare

My royal will, and what My judgments are.

Your words inspired shall be the end of strife,

The rule of faith and guiding law of life,

Until the renovation is complete,

And the whole world comes bowing to My feet.

None have house, parents, brethren, children, wife   29

Left for My sake, who shall not, in this life,

Receive an hundred fold, and, in the age

To come, eternal life—but not as wage.

MATT. xx. 1-16.

" FOR in the government of its affairs,   xx.1

Messiah's Kingdom a resemblance bears,

Unto a householder, who had desire

Into his vineyard laborers to hire,

---

* The regeneration of the race is the regeneration of individual souls, and this we believe is ever going on. The Son of Man is surely now sitting on the throne of His glory, being to the right hand of God exalted, and having a name above every name. So the Apostles (certainly ever since the day of Pentecost) have been sitting on their thrones, with their authority so universally acknowledged down to our time, that from their judgments there is no appeal. Here surely is ample fulfilment. Compared with this, the glory of actual thrones, crowns and sceptres is vulgar and poor.

So went out early, and agreed to pay,

To those employed, a penny each a day.

He, going at the end of three hours space, 3

Saw others idle in the market place,

And said to them : ' Into my vineyard go, 4

And what is right I will on you bestow.'

He, at the sixth hour, and the ninth, went out, 5

And did the same.   Again he found, about 6

Th' eleventh hour, more standing, and said : ' Why

Stand idle all the day ? '   They made reply : 7

' Because no man has hired us.'   He said then,

' Go ye also into the vineyard.'   When

Night came, the owner to the steward said : 8

' Call laborers, and let their hire be paid.

Be there a penny to each one disbursed,

Beginning from the last unto the first. 9

When those hired first, received the penny due, 10

They murmured and found fault, and said : 'We who 11

Have borne the heat and burden of the day, 12

Working twelve hours, receive but equal pay

With those who've wrought but one.'

He one addressed

More turbulent and noisy than the rest :

' Friend ! I do thee no wrong, for didst thou not 13

Agree to work for that?   Then take up what Matt.
XX. 14
Is thine, and go thy way.   It shall thus be.
I 'll give the last the same as I give thee.
May I not with my own do what I would?   15
Is thine eye evil because I am good ?'

Thus shall the first be last, who murmur blame ;   16
And the last first, because they make no claim.
Salvation is a gift in any case ;
Were it of debt, it would not be of grace.
Many are called, but most the call refuse ;   17
Few are the chosen, for they 're few that choose."

LUKE XVII. 7-10.

Saw'st thou thy servant coming from the field? Luke
xvii. 7
Wouldst thou precédence at thy table yield?
Or say : 'Make ready thou, and on Me wait,   8
Then thou shalt eat?'   Or wouldst thou rate   9
His lawful service as a favor?   No!
He simply did that which he ought, I trow.
So judge yourselves unprofitable, when you   10
Have only done what you were bound to do.

XIX.

RETURN TO JERUSALEM THROUGH JERICHO.

MATT. XV. 17-34; MARK X. 32-52; LUKE XVIII. 31-43; XIX. 1-44.

WHILE on their way up to Jerusalem,   Mark
    Jesus with steady step preceding them,   x. 32

Amazement fell on them, and they were made,

As Him they followed, mightily afraid.

Taking the Twelve apart, He said to them :

" Behold, we go up to Jerusalem :   33

And, lo, the Son of Man betrayed shall be

Unto the Sanhedrim, that, presently,

Shall Him consign, whom they 've condemned to die, 34

To Gentile hands to scourge and crucify.

But He on the third day shall rise again—

For not the grave can longer Him detain."

   The mother of the sons of Zebedee   35

To Jesus came, and asked, on bended knee,

He would one favor grant. He said : " Explain !   36

What wouldst thou?" She replied : " That in Thy

      Reign,   37

One of my sons may sit on Thy right hand,   Mark
x. —
The other on Thy left, in high command."
But Jesus, all forseeing, sadly said: 38
" Your fond request is ignorantly made—
Ye know not what ye ask.   Do ye then think
That ye can drink the cup that I must drink ?
And with My baptism be yourselves baptized ?"
They said : " We can do all therein comprised."   39
" These ye, indeed, shall do and undergo ;
But that, ye ask, is not Mine to bestow   40
On human grounds of personal regard—
Essential fitness governs the award."
And when the ten heard of it, every one   41
Felt indignation against James and John.

But Jesus, having called them to Him, said: 42
" Ye know the Gentiles have their princely head—
Rulers to rule and great ones to bear sway—
Not so with you.   Ye 're taught to put away,   43
As best befits meek learners in My school,
All winged ambitions and proud thoughts of rule.
Who would be great, therefore, let him be small :   44
Who would be chief, the servant be of all.
The Son of Man e'en came to serve, and give   45
His life a ransom, that the slave might live."

As Jesus entered Jericho, along   Mark
x. 46

With His disciples and a numerous throng

Blind Bartimeus by the wayside sat,

Begging.   When he was told by some one, that   47

Jesus of Nazareth was passing by,

Losing no time, he straight began to cry :

" O Lord, Thou Son of David, pity me !"

When some rebuked, and bade him silent be,   48

He only cried the more : " Have pity, Lord '

Thou Son of David, pity me afford !"

Jesus stood still and said : "Call ye him here."   49

They to the blind man said : "Be of good cheer—

He calleth thee."   His mantle thrown aside,

He sprang up quickly and to Jesus hied,   50

Who said : " What wouldst thou have Me do to

      thee ?"   51

The blind man said : " Rabboni, make me see.

" Go !" Jesus said, "thy faith hath given thee sight."52

Straightway he saw, and praised the Lord of light.

Passing through Jericho, a well known man,   Luke
xix. 1

Rich, named Zacchéus, a chief publican,   2

Sought to see Jesus, but this could not do,   3

Because the crowd His person hid from view.

He, being of low stature, ran before,   Luke xix. 4
And climbed into a spreading sycamore
Along the route, to see Him as He passed.
When Jesus reached the tree, He stopped, and cast   5
An upward look, and said, as him He spied,
" Come down, Zacchéus, for I must abide
Within thy hospitable doors to-day."
Surprised, he, coming down without delay,   6
Received Him joyfully.   The multitude   7
Beholding this, with grumblings Him pursued,
Saying : " He 's gone with one that 's under ban—
An outcast Jew, a hateful publican—
To lodge, and eat, and thus Himself defile."

But in Zacchéus there was wrought meanwhile   8
A mighty penitence.   He stood and spake :
" I, Lord, a gift of half my goods now make
Unto the poor.   If I have, heretofore,
Taken aught wrongfully, I will restore
Fourfold."   And Jesus said : " In truth I say,   9
Salvation to this house has come to-day :
For that the Son of Man, at His own cost,   10
Has come to seek and save that which is lost."

Seeing they listened, He went on to tell   11

Th' expectant multitude a Parable— Luke xix. —

Who thought, because Jerusalem was near,

He in His Kingdom straightway would appear.

" A nobleman—preparing to resort 12

To the far city of th' Imperial Court,

To take to him his kingship and return—

That their trustworthiness he so might learn, 13

Gave to ten servants all an equal sum,

One pound to each, and said : ' Use till I come.'

But hated· by the citizens, these sent 14

An embassy th' investure to prevent—

Saying, ' We will not have him for our king.'

" When he returned—in all things prospering— 15

Having all rights of royalty obtained—

That he might know what every one had gained,

He called those servants he had money given.

" Then came the first and said : ' Lord ! thanks to

Heaven, 16

Thy pound has gained ten pounds.' He said, ' Well

done, 17

Good servant ! faithful found in this small one,

Have thou a grander trust—the government

Over ten cities.' ' Lord ! the pound me lent,' 18

The second said, ' has gained five pounds.' ' Ev'n so, 19

Be o'er five cities.'   Said another : ' Lo !   Luke
xix. 20
Here is thy pound, which I with care kept laid
Up in a napkin, for I was afraid,   21
Because thou art a man austere and hard,
To rights of others paying no regard,
Exacting that which never was thine own,
And reaping that which thou hadst never sown.'

 "' I, out of thine own mouth, will thee convict,   22
Thou wicked servant.   Knowing I was strict,
Austere, exacting what was not my own,
And reaping that which I had never sown,
Why gav'st thou not my pound to one to use,   23
That I might not thereon my interest lose?'
He said to his attendants standing round :   24
' Take ye away from him his unused pound,
And give to him who has gained ten.'   But they,   25
Surprise evincing, he went on to say :
' To every one that has, and adds thereto,   26
Shall more be given : whereas the slothful, who
Has and adds naught, shall not keep that he has,
Since found unfaithful and unfit.   But as   27
For those my foes who would not have me reign,
Let them be brought and in my presence slain.' "

Having thus spoken, going on before,   Luke xix. 28

He pressed on to Jerusalem, once more,

And came to Bethany, where Lazarus dwelt,   John xii. 1

Whom He had raised to life. The chief priests felt 10

Against the current it was vain to strive,   11

While this miraculous witness was alive,

So they designed His death. Already they

Had taken means to Jesus seize and slay.

Haste, careful Martha, thy Lord's couch prepare,

For He intends this night thy house to share.

On the next day (which was five days before   12

That Passover, when should—in type once more,

Then once for all in fact and not again—

The spotless Lamb of God for us be slain)

Fulfilling prophecy—all prescient

Of what would be—He two disciples sent,   Luke xix. 29

Saying : " Go to yon village, ye shall find   30

A colt there tied, ne'er ridden yet, unbind

And bring him here. Should any one inquire,   31

' Why loose ye him ?' say 't is by My desire,

The Lord has need of him." They went and found 32

As he had said ; and, with consent, unbound   33

And brought the colt to Jesus : and this done,   34

They threw on him their garments, and thereon, Luke xix. 35
Not otherwise caparisoned, Him set.
The honored beast, though all unbroken, yet
Not needing check nor guidance, onward went,
Knowing his rider, with proud step but bent
Low reverent neck, while many in the road   36
Their garments spread; and others lopped' and
   strowed   Mark xi. 8
Branches of myrtle; fronds of palms some bore;
And those who followed, and who went before,   9
Together cried: "Hosanna to the Son   Matt. xxi. 9
Of David! Blessed be th' Anointed One!
The King of Israel, of mighty fame,
Approved and coming in Jehovah's name!
Daughter of Zion, eastward look! behold,
Thy King approaches, even as foretold,   5
Meek, sitting on an ass's colt! Long live
Messiah! peaceful be His reign! Now give   Luke xix. 38
Glory to God, glad hallelujahs sing,
In lofty celebration of our King!"

The people, who were present, witness gave   John xii. 17
They Lazarus had seen come from the grave,
And this drew many; many more beside   18

From Galilee, of Jesus testified, John xii. —
Thereby augmenting the triumphing throng,
That sang hosannas as He passed along.

The Pharisees, alarmed at what they saw, 19
Exclaim, as they in groups together draw,
" Of what avail is all we 've said and done?
Behold, the whole world after Him is gone."
Some sharply spake, as if to His behoof : Luke xix. 39
" Give thou to Thy disciples stern reproof !"
But Jesus said : " If these refused to shout, 40
The stones for shame would instantly cry out."

When He drew nigh and saw the City, He 41
Burst into tears of grief and sympathy,
And said: " O hadst thou known ere this, ev'n thou,42
The things relating to thy peace ! but now
They're hidden from thine eyes. For soon the days 43
Will come upon thee, when thy foes will raise
A bank about thee, compass thee around
In closest siege, and dash thee to the ground, 44
And in the ruins will thy children crush,
And will not leave thee in the downward rush
One stone upon another, seeing thou
Knew'st not thine opportunity was now."

Jerusalem now entered, it occurred Matt. xxi. 10

That the whole city was profoundly stirred.

When, " Who is this?" was heard on every side,

Th' attendant multitude at once replied : 11

" A Prophet this of great celebrity,

Jesus, from Nazareth of Galilee."

Alighting, He into the Temple came, 14

And, moved with pity, healed the blind and lame.

But when the chief priests and the scribes beheld 15

The wonders He performed—heard, unrepelled,

The children, crying in the Temple, say,

" Hosanna to the Son of David,"—they

Great indignation and surprise express :

" Hear'st Thou what these are saying?" He said,

      " Yes ! 16

Did ye ne'er read (when men are dumb as now)

' Out of the mouths of babes and sucklings, Thou

Defective praise hast perfected' ?" Then He 17

Went with the Twelve and lodged in Bethany.

As to the City early He returned Mark xi. 12

Next morn, a fig tree He afar discerned, 13

Leafy and fair, and promising much fruit.

But, when He came, He found there naught to suit,

Nothing but leaves. " Let no fruit grow," He said 14

"On thee henceforth!"—and straight the tree was
    dead.   Mark
                                                                                     xi. —

Going into the Temple, stern and bold,   15
He 'gan to cast out them that bought and sold,
The tables of the brokers overthrew,
And seats of traffickers in doves, anew*—   16
Saying: "My House, 't is written, shall be styled   17
The House of Prayer, but ye have it defiled,
And made the sacred place a robbers' den,
The unhallowed haunt of false and thievish men."
The scribes and chief priests having of this heard,   18
Maddened yet more, by murd'rous fury urged,
They would have seized Him, but were checked by
      fear,
For Him the people came in crowds to hear—
(He all day, teaching, in the Temple spent,
And to the Mount of Olives nightly went).   19

As He was walking in the Temple, they   27
With haughty bearing, challenged Him to say,
By what authority He dared thus do.
He said: "I will one question ask of you,   20
Which, if ye answer, honoring truth and fact,

      *See the Evangel, p. 367, for an account of the first cleansing.
 16

I 'll tell by what authority I act.   Mark
                                                            xi. —
Touching John's baptism, whence (tell if you can)   30
Was it? from Heaven? or did it come from man?"
They reasoned thus among themselves: "If we   31
Shall say, 'From Heaven,' His reply will be,
'Why did ye not believe him then?'   But if   32
We say, 'From man,' we fear the people, stiff
In the conviction and belief that John
Was certainly a prophet."   Whereupon   33
They said, "We cannot tell."   "Nor tell I you,
By what authority I these things do."

"What think you of the story here rehearsed? Matt.
                                                   xxi. 28
A man, who had two sons, said to the first:
'Go, work to-day, son, in my vineyard.'   He
Unfilially refused, but, speedily,   29
Repented of his wickedness, and went.
He bade the second, who with feigned assent   30
Replied: 'I go, sir,' but went not.   Now say,
Which of the twain his father did obey?"   31
They said, "The first."   "E'en so I say to you,
Ye promise, feign, profess, and fail to do.
Of mortal sins, no doubt, the greatest one
Is the complacent consciousness of none.

What wonder, since repentance is the door,

Harlots and publicans go in before!

For John came in the way of righteousness—

Strict, separate, austere in food and dress—

And ye believed him not, but these believed,

And full remission of their sins received:

"Hear ye another Parable: A man

Planted a vineyard on a generous plan,

Hedged it round, dug a wine-vat, built a tower,

And gave to certain husbandmen the power

To keep and till it; and then went away

To a far country a long while to stay.

And, when the season of the fruit drew near,

He sent a servant to receive his share:

And him they seized and beat and sent away

Empty.   He sent another then; and they

Him stoned, and wounded badly in the head,

And handled shamefully.   Then, in his stead,

A third was sent, and many more—this one

They beat, that killed.   He lastly sent his son,

His only son, unutterably dear,

Saying, 'My son at least they will revere.'

But they, in council met, his death conspire.

Matt.
xxi. —

32

Mark
xii. 1

2

3

4

5

6

7

'Behold,' they said, 'all is as we desire ;   Mark
xii. —

This is the heir ; let us, now he 's alone,

Him kill, and make th' inheritance our own.'

They thrust him out the vineyard, and him slew.   8

What will the lord then of the vineyard do?   Matt.
xxi. 41

He 'll come, and will these wicked men destroy,

And others give the vineyard to enjoy.

So shall God's Kingdom taken be from you,   42

And giv'n a nation yielding fruitage due."

They, when they heard it, said : " Let it not be!"

And Jesus, looking on them, spake : " Have ye   43

Never the meaning of that Scripture weighed—

' The Stone, the builders disallowed, is made

Head of the corner by the Lord all wise.

This is His work and wondrous in our eyes ' ?

Who, stumbling, falls on it, is shattered found :   44

But he, on whom it falls, to dust is ground."

Knowing the Parable 'gainst them was said,   45

They would have seized Him, but they were afraid. 46

XX.

NEARING THE END.

MATT. XXII. 15-46; MARK XII. 13-17; LUKE XX. 20-44.

O N His destruction constantly intent, Mark xii. 13
 They partizans of Herod to Him sent,
To snare Him in His words, and get some ground
On which a charge of fatal sort to found
Before the Roman governor, whose breath
Determined questions touching life and death.
Disloyalty to Cæsar could they prove,
This would one serious obstacle remove,
Which must attend a sentence, they foresaw,
Grounded on simple breach of Jewish law.
When they were come to Him, with tongue of guile,
Feigning respect, they said in wheedling style:
" Rabbi! we know, that Thou in all art true,   14
Speaking Thy thought concerning what is due,
Fearless and bold, and caring not for men,
Tell us, we pray Thee, what Thou thinkest then—

Ought we to Cæsar tribute pay, or no?" Mark xii.—

He said: "Why tempt ye Me? Your craft I know. 15

Bring Me a penny* that I it may see."

They brought it, and He said: "Will ye tell Me, 16

Whose is this image, and whose legend 's here?"

They answered, "Cæsar's." "Then your duty 's clear:

Render to Cæsar that which Cæsar's is; 17

And give to God likewise whate'er is His."

Baffled and silenced, having naught to say,

Admiring His address, they went their way.

Came Sadducees to Him on the same day— Matt xxii. 23

Deniers of the resurrection. They,

Thinking to puzzle Him, a question raise, 24

Based on Mosaic statute-law,† which says,

' That if a man die childless, then, indeed,

His brother shall his widow wed, and seed

Raise to his brother.' " Now there were," they said, 25

" With us seven brethren. Th' eldest being dead,

No children having had, his wife was left

To be his brother's. She again bereft, 26

---

* A denarius, a Roman silver coin, worth about 17 cents. Its purchasing value has been estimated at four or five times that. The *drachma* was a Greek coin of nearly the same value as the *denarius*.

† It was named the " Levirate "—from the Latin *levir*, a husband's brother, or, brother-in-law.

Was married to the third, so up to seven :　　Matt. xxii. 27

To which of these will she be wife in heaven,　　28

After the resurrection?"　Jesus said :　　29

" Ye err, not having right the Scriptures read,

Nor known the power of God ; for, when they rise, 30

They 're like th' unmarried angels in the skies.

　" Touching the resurrection of the dead,　　31

Have ye not in the book of Moses read,

How in the bush God to him spake : ' I am　　32

Thy fathers' God, the God of Abraham,

Of Isaac, and of Jacob.'　God is hence,　　33

Not in the preterite but present tense,

Their God, not as extinct, but living yet."

Ev'n foes were glad at the defeat they met.

　The Pharisees He question'd : " What think ye　41

Of the Messiah?　Whose Son should He be?"　42

They answer, " David's."　" How does this accord　43

With what he by the Spirit says : ' The Lord

Said to my Lord, Sit Thou on My right hand,　　44

In universal and supreme command,

Until Thy victory be made complete,

And all Thy foes be put beneath Thy feet.'

If David's Son, how calls he Him his Lord?"　　45

And none of them could answer Him a word.

MATT. XXIII. 1-39; MARK XII. 38-44; LUKE XX. 45-XXI. 4.

HE, in the hearing of the people, said   Luke
XX. 45

To His disciples: " Be ye not betrayed   46

By the example of the Scribes, who love—

Dressed in long flowing robes to stately move,

And greetings in the market-place respect,

And first seats in the synagogues affect,

And covet the first couches at the feasts—

But who, like hungry and ferocious beasts,

Devour defenceless widows' maintenance,

And make long frequent prayers for a pretence,

The better to entrap them and deceive.

These shall a heavier punishment receive."

He, speaking to the multitude, besides   Matt.
xxiii. 1

His own disciples, said: " Because the Scribes   2

And Pharisees now sit in Moses' seat,

And God's commandments and His laws repeat,

Whate'er they bid you, that observe and do,   3

But all their juggling falsities eschew,

For that they say, and do not—by all modes

Binding intolerable and grievous loads   4

On others' shoulders, which they 'll not so much

As with one solitary finger touch.

Woe to you, Scribes and Pharisees, who dare   Matt.
                                                            xxiii. 13

Before th' All-seeing, act a part,* and wear

A mask, and personate and play the saint,

While all your sanctity is but a feint—

So used to your disguise, ye hardly dream

That ye are otherwise than what ye seem.

Woe to you, hypocrites!   The woe to state

Is not to wish it or to imprecate.

I speak to warn you.   Ye yourselves must know

Sin is the sure progenitor of woe.

The genial flame that warms you, also hath

A dreadful potency of dreadful wrath—

Woe to the foolish hand, that wakes the ire

And retribution of the vengeful fire!

All woe and suffering, rightly understood,

Implies some false relation to the good.

A wrong position to the universe

Will turn the best of things into a curse.

The light is sweet, and pleasant to the eye

The sun's bright pomp proceeding through the sky,

But woe to eyes that turn to it inflamed!

Yet, for the anguish, shall the light be blamed?

---

* The earlier meaning of the Greek word 'Υποκριτής (Hypocrite) is "*one who plays a part* on the stage," "a player," "an actor;" whence comes the later meaning, " a dissembler," "feigner," "*hypocrite.*"

Because ye suffer, shall the sun be wrenched Matt. xxiii. —
From its bright orbit, and its beams be quenched?
Which would ye have, the suffering sense made whole?
Or palsy strike the universal soul?
Would ye abolish feeling to obtain
Exemption and relief from local pain?
' Woe to the man who sins,' all nature cries!
And, 'Woe!' the Spirit in the Word replies!
But greater woe to him, who healing grace
Keeps back from any of the human race!

   "Woe to you, Scribes and Pharisees, therefore, 13
Who keep a jealous watch, and shut the door
Of the New Kingdom, which to enter in
Is full salvation from the power of sin—
Not entering yourselves, and, those about
To enter, hindering and barring out.
Woe, for ye roam o'er sea, and land as well, 15
To make one proselyte a child of hell.

   "Blind guides! that say, 'Who by the Temple
        swear, 16
They are not bound; if by the gold that 's there
They swear, the oath holds good.' Ye fools and blind!
Which greater is, the gold, or that behind, 17
The Temple's self, which sanctifies the gold?

'Who by the Altar swears, it does not hold; Matt.
xxiii. 18

But who swears by the gift that thereon lies,

The same is bound.' Ye blind, not having eyes! 19

For is the gift more, or the altar more

That sanctifies the gift? He who, therefore, 20

Swears by the altar, swears by what it bears.

So likewise, he, who by the Temple swears, 21

Swears both by it and Him that there abides.

Who swears by Heaven, he swears by God besides. 22

 "Woe to you, Scribes and Pharisees! because, 23

While ye tithe mint, ye slight eternal laws

Requiring justice, mercy, faith: the one

Ye do, but leave the weightier undone.

Blind guides! who filter out the gnat scarce seen, 24

But gulp the camel monstrous and unclean.

Woe to you, hypocrites, because ye wish 25

To cleanse the outside of the cup and dish,

But care not they 're filled up and foul within,

From robbery, iniquity, and sin :—

Blind Pharisee! first th' inside purify, 26

For e'en the outside shall be cleansed thereby.

 "Woe to you, hypocrites! for ye are like 27

To whited sepulchres, whose seemings strike,

Outwardly fair, but, all within the stones,

Foulness unspeakable and dead men's bones: Matt.
xxiii. —

So ye seem righteous, but ye ne'ertheless   28

Are full of inward lies and rottenness.

Woe to you, hypocrites! because ye build,   29

And deck the tombs of those your fathers killed—

Prophets and righteous men—and falsely say,   30

Ye would have been less bloody than were they.   31

Fill up the measure of your fathers, see   32

Ye match their murderous malignity!

Serpents and vipers, venomous and fell,   33

How shall ye 'scape the punishment of hell!

   "Lo, I, in love and mercy, send to you   34

Prophets and teachers to instruct and woo:

Of them, some ye will kill and crucify;

Others will scourge, afflict, and cause to fly,

That so the crowning guilt may shame your head   35

Of all the righteous blood that e'er was shed.

This generation, lo, in blood and tears,   36

Shall reap the justice of four thousand years.

   "O hadst thou been inclined, Jerusalem!   37

Who kill'st the prophets, and who stonest them

Who unto thee are sent, how oft I then

Thy children would have gathered, as a hen

Gathers her chickens 'neath her sheltering wings, _{Matt.}
But ye would not, and scorned My threatenings !
Behold the time is coming and makes haste,   38
When shall your house, abandoned and laid waste,
Be turned into a desert, and its proud
Upturned foundations, like a field be ploughed.
Henceforth, ye shall not see Me, till ye say,   39
The Lord is Lord, we own his righteous sway."

THESE woes Truth thundered into guilty ears,
Then, at the close, Love melted into tears.
He spake for the last time.   How like a knell,
In the doomed Temple, sounded His farewell.
Events to come, so clearly were foreseen,
They seemed as if they had already been,
Or were transpiring now before His eyes.
He saw the ruin in dread vision rise—
Each several stone, reel in the tottering wall
Of house and temple, making haste to fall ;
Saw on the goodliest, a stain of guilt,
The blood of innocence aforetime spilt,
And therefore fated, branded and accursed,
With leanings towards perdition from the first.
With all beholding eyes, the wisdom saw

And the unchallenged justice of the law,
Whereby each generation must and should
Be heirs of previous evil and of good—
Each sin committed, since the world began,
Its curse entailing on the race of man—
The error sown a thousand years ago,
Yielding fresh harvests of unending woe.

    The causes of a nation's ruin may
Have criminal beginnings far away:
But oh! the mounting horror of the time,
When topples down the edifice of crime!
If founded on the weakness of a lie,
Unstable were the pillars of the sky.

    Weary He sat—just ready to withdraw—   Mark xii. 41
Over against the Treasury, and saw
Rich men cast in their gifts. Among the rest   42
Came a poor widow, who threw in the chest
Two mites which make a farthing. Jesus saith   43
To His disciples: " This poor widow hath
Cast more into the Treasury, than such
As of their superfluity gave much."   44

    Certain Greek proselytes, as He passed through   John xii.20
The Outer Court, desired an interview.   21

With thoughts of His near death preoccupied, John xii. 23
He said, "The hour, when must be glorified
The Son of Man, is come. Till seed is thrown [24]
Into the ground and dies, it bides alone;
But, dying, bears much fruit. So when I die,
I, like the corn, My life will multiply.
Who loves his selfish life and keeps it sole, [25]
Shall rot unsown, and perish as a whole.
Who holds his temporal life, for my sake, cheap,
He unto life eternal shall it keep.
Would a man serve Me, let him follow Me, [26]
And where I am there shall My servant be.
   "My soul is troubled now. What shall I say? [27]
'O Father, save me from this hour? But, nay!
On purpose, for this dreadful hour I came:
Even so, Father glorify Thy name!'" [28]
A Voice from heaven said, "Full oft have I
It glorified, and it will glorify
Again." Of people standing by, who heard, [29]
Some said, "It thundered." Others there averred,
"An angel spake to Him." "This word from Heaven [30]
Was not," He said, "for Mine but your sakes given.
Now shall the world be judged. I will cast out [31]
The Prince of Evil, and his armies rout;

The reign of Love I will inaugurate

John
xii. —

Upon the ruins of the throne of Hate.

And I, if I be lifted up, will draw,

32

By the magnetic force of love and law,

All men to Me—the simple and the sage,

Throughout the earth, and to the latest age."

MATT. XXIV. 1-51; XXV. 1-46; MARK XIII. 1-37; LUKE XXI. 5-36.

HE now the Temple left for the last time ;

Mark
xiii. 1

Crossed the brook Kedron, and began to climb

The Mount of Olives.   The disciples' gaze

Directed backwards, they, struck with amaze,

Cried out: "See, Master, what great stones are here !

What splendid buildings, rising tier 'bove tier !

See those nine gates, all overlaid with gold

And silver, and that other one, behold,

Of solid rich Corinthian brass !   Note

Those blocks of marble, shaped in times remote,

Twice sixteen cubits* long, ten cubits high !

Observe how rich and gorgeous to the eye

The giant clusters of that golden vine,

That round the golden doors and door-posts twine !

How beautiful, how holy to the sight,

The topmost Naos† glittering and white—

* Josephus, *De Bell. Jud.*, V., 5.   † The Sanctuary or Temple proper.

Seen from this height, beneath the sunset glow,   Mark
                                                   xiii. —
How like a glorious mountain crowned with snow!"

And Jesus said : " As for these things ye see,   2
The day will come, in which there shall not be,
From the foundation to the topmost stone,
One left upon another not o'erthrown."*

The summit reached, He sat upon the height—   3
Temple and City lay right opposite.
All that had passed since morn to memory rose
To solemnize the day's approaching close.
Peter and James and John and Andrew came—
Part of the Twelve—and speaking in their name,
Besought, that He would tell them privately,
When this would happen; what the sign would be   4
Of His next Coming ; and, moreo'er, presage
The end and consummation of the age.

---

* Gibbon, in the seventy-first chapter of his History of the Decline and Fall of the
Roman Empire, speaks of the Coliseum as " an edifice, which, had it been left to time
and nature, might have claimed an eternal duration." He quotes the proverbial saying (reported by the venerable Bede as current in his time—he dying in the year 735):
" As long as the Coliseum stands, Rome shall stand ; when the Coliseum falls, Rome
will fall ; when Rome falls, will fall the world." It is highly probable, that the disciples had entertained a like view of the Temple ; and when the Master predicted its
ruin and the destruction of Jerusalem, they associated therewith a simultaneous destruction of the world. Of this association there are intimations in Matthew ; but in
Mark and Luke we have a simple reference to the destruction of the Temple and the
City ; and the inquiry addressed to the Lord has sole reference to the time when this

17

And Jesus answering began to say:

Mark xiii. 5

" Beware, lest any man lead you astray.

Many impostors will assume my name,

6

Saying, ' I am the Christ,' and, by that claim,

Deceiving many.   When on every side,

Ye hear of wars, be ye not terrified,

7

For these must be, but not yet is the end :

should take place. A prurient and mistaken curiosity led them on this and other occasions to ask about things which did not concern them.

Not satisfied with the information that the destruction would take place, they must know the exact time. Christ has been understood as saying that He did not know Himself. But strictly taken, this would seem to be an impossible sense. While accepting His two-fold nature, divine and human, we do not believe in such a dichotomy as would rob Him of a plenary divine consciousness and knowledge of all things. His ignorance, if ignorance it could be called, would be at best only a *quasi* ignorance, official or functional, not a real one. For Him to disclose matters which men had no right to know, and which the Father chose to keep in His own power— such as precise times and seasons—were impossible. If He knew them, it was not for us He knew them. He did not know them as the ordained Organ of Revelation. It may be laid down as a universal truth, that Revelation limits its disclosures to things needful for us to know. It comports not with its dignity to minister to an idle curiosity. Prophecy is something more and something better than a vulgar fortune-telling. Life is not fatalistic, but moral and free. Well-being is contingent on well-doing. The duty and need of watchfulness are based on the uncertainties of the future. Such a prediction of future events, therefore, as should leave no doubt in regard to the time and manner of their happening, would be fatal to moral freedom.

By keeping steadily in mind the principles which govern in all such cases, not forgetting the limitation adverted to, which confines all disclosures to some gracious purpose of utility, we cannot fail to be helped in the right interpretation of these "prophecies of the Mount." Now, the destruction of Jerusalem did concern them who asked, and Christ therefore was tolerant toward their inquiry, so far as to give them information in regard to the signs which should precede and usher it in, in order that they might make provision for their safety. Even though we admit that their question had a larger scope, Our Lord in His reply would be sure, ignoring what was irrelevant or improper, to communicate only what was important for them to know ; and Mark and Luke, as before intimated, in omitting all reference to everything else, would seem to have regarded all that was special in the prophecy as having relation

Nation shall rise 'gainst nation and contend ;   Matt.
xxiv.7

Kingdom 'gainst kingdom.   Scarcity of bread,

Plagues following, great earthquakes, sights of dread,

And signs in heaven, mark but th' initial throes*   8

And warning birthpangs of forthcoming woes.

Then they 'll afflict you, and your life will take.   9

All nations will you hate for My name's sake.

Many will stumble, and will fall away

And hate will one another and betray.

to the destruction of Jerusalem. That was a particular event, which they of that generation might live to see. Some, not all. If in that event, there was a solemn and portentous Coming of the Son of Man affecting a whole people and nation ; there were other Comings, He would have them know, awful and imminent, in the case of every individual. The knife of judgment would cut between those standing nearest to each other—one would be taken and the other left. There would seem to be no need of limiting the number of His Comings. In one sense they are infinite. He is present in every event. To me and to all men as individuals, it may be said, however, that there are two special comings. First, in the proclamation of the Word, and, second, in death, when account must be rendered of its reception. Here, if we mistake not, is the key to that recurring refrain, Watch !

It would lessen the difficulties of interpretation immensely could we be content to be simple and not subtle. Surely, Christ's mission in the world was not and is not to destroy but save. His relation to the race has ever been that of a Saviour. It was so to the inhabitants of Jerusalem even amid the culminating horrors of the siege. For aught we know, He may have been so to some in fact down to the very last hour. In what respect in principle was His coming to destroy Jerusalem different from His coming to destroy anything else that was rotten, even a tree ? He is, to be sure, the Author of self-executing laws. It is true, that fire will burn. Let him, therefore, who would not be burned avoid the fire. The calamities which befell the Jews were sequent as the links of a chain ; and were essentially self-inflicted and inevitable. Divine Pity wept over them in prospect, and interposed to shorten not prolong them. Sure am I, that let there be ten thousand hells, they are all of the sinner's own kindling. God is love.

* The Greek word rendered "sorrows" in the Received Version, means primarily and specifically " the pangs or throes of labor."

Many false prophets numbers will entice.   Matt.
xxiv. 11

Because of prevalent lawlessness and vice,   12

The love of many will wax cold.   But he,   13

Who to the end continues, saved shall be.

The Gospel of the Kingdom shall be preached   14

Among all nations,* witnessing to each.

And then shall come the end I have foretold.

" When ye then shall Jerusalem behold   15

Compassed with armies, ye may understand

Its speedy désolation is at hand.

Let them, who in Judea then shall be,   16

To the Peréan mountains† straightway flee.

Let him, that 's on the housetop, not descend   17

To take aught from the house, but his way wend,

From roof to roof to the town wall, with speed,

And thus escape, so urgent is the need.

Neither let him, that 's in the field, turn back   18

To take his clothes, for foes are on his track.

Alas, for those, who in those days shall be   19

With child, or who give suck, and cannot flee !

---

* More properly "all the Gentiles."   So in verse 9, meaning the Gentiles generally,
The " end," in the next line, refers, it is thought, to the end of the Jewish polity.

† It is stated on the authority of Eusebius, that, warned by this prophecy, the Christians fled from the city, some to Pella beyond the Jordan, and others to Mount Lebanon, and that not a single one perished in the siege.

Pray your escape be not in winter, lest   Matt.
                                                       xxiv. 20

Cold storms and swollen streams your flight arrest.

Nor on the Sabbath day, lest some through fear

Delay immediate flight on grounds sincere.

   "Then shall be tribulation, greater than   21

Was ever witnessed since the world began—

Supreme, unequalled horrors will attend

The City's siege, catastrophe and end ;

So that, did mercy not curtail the date,   22

No one would scarce survive the general fate.

   "Should, in this season of distress and fear,   23

One say, 'Behold, the Christ is here, or here,'

Believe it not. For there shall then arise

False Christs, and Prophets in pretentious guise,   24

With signs and wonders fitted to mislead.

Remember, I have warned you, so take heed.   25

If they proclaim, 'He's in the desert,' be   26

Ye not deluded, go not forth to see.

Or, 'He's within shut doors,' believe it not—

For, not unknown nor limited to one spot,

Shall be the Coming of the Son of Man ;

But sudden, swift—the instant lightning* can   27

* Calvin interprets this as referring to the preaching of the Gospel by the Apostles. Whatever other fulfilments it may have, it has inevitably one at death—when there is an instantaneous transition and revelation to all mankind.

Not equal it that flames across the sky—   Matt.
                                                 xxiv. —

A dazzling presence to the opened eye,

Where is the carcass, there the eagles are:

When time is ripe, fulfilments are not far.

[They do not err, that make the firmament

The theatre of each divine event;

And see the Godhead, on that heavenly stage

Great epochs punctuate, or end the age;

Speak of His goings forth in glorious might,

Although invisible to natural sight.]

" Immediately following those days   29

Of tribulation, and supreme amaze,

The sun and moon shall darkened* be, and all

---

* Or as we would express it in occidental speech, there will follow days of darkness to individuals, and the whole Jewish people, unrelieved by a single ray of light from any quarter.

> " O dark, dark, dark, amid the blaze of noon,
> Irrevocably dark, total eclipse
> Without all hope of day !"

Their glory will have departed, and their polity have come to an end. They will be carried away captive, and scattered among the Gentiles; and Jerusalem their pride and boast will be trodden down by profaning feet. Their ruin will be complete and overwhelming. In the conceptions of oriental poetry, this quenching of the light of the soul in the human microcosm; this national wreck, utter and hopeless, are equivalent to the fall and blotting out of the great luminaries of the physical universe—the macrocosm. The same or similar imagery is employed in the foretelling of the destruction of Babylon (Isaiah xiii. 10); also of Tyre (Isaiah xxiv. 23); again in describing the slaughter of Bozrah and Idumea (Isaiah xxxiv. 4).

The constellations, like ripe fruit, shall fall

Matt. xxiv. —

From out the shaken heavens—void to the eye

The stellar glories of the Jewish sky.

Then those, who to the sword fall not a prey,

Luke xxi. 24

Into all nations shall be led away

Captive; and their demolished buried town,

Jerusalem, shall thence be trodden down,

Continuously, by hated Gentile feet,

Until the time appointed be complete.

" Lo, everywhere upon the earth shall be   25

Distress of nations* and perplexity—

Seas and waves roaring—a heart-sickening dread   26

Of something, yet more terrible, ahead.

Then shall, o'er the horizon shining clear,   27

The signals of the Son of Man appear.

Many, convinced of sin and penitent,†

Matt. xxiv. 30

---

* The perplexity, distress and misery of the time, so far as the Roman Empire is concerned, are powerfully portrayed by Tacitus in the commencement of his History. He speaks of "four emperors murdered; three civil wars, many foreign, the greater number mixed; both Gauls threatening a revolt; Italy afflicted with new slaughters, repeated; cities (Pompeii and Herculaneum) buried and swallowed up; Rome partly laid in ashes, her most venerable temples consumed, the Capitol itself fired by the hands of citizens; the sea filled with exiles," etc. He relates how " in Rome rank and riches and virtue were certain death; how nothing was sacred, and nothing safe." His description of the prevailing corruption answers to that found in the first chapter of the Epistle of Paul to the Romans.

† It is something, he trusts, akin to Christian instinct which leads the writer to reject the current interpretation, which makes the *mourning* here spoken of, other than

Shall smite their breasts and lift a loud lament,   Matt.
                                                                      xxiv. —
Till, on the darkness of their night of grief,
At once shall break the morning of belief,
And they shall see Him with enraptured eyes
In mighty pomp descending from the skies.
But terrible the aspect of that face
To those who mourn rejection of His grace.
He shall send forth His messengers to sound   31
The Gospel trump wherever man is found ;
And they shall gather from all lands and climes
Th' elect of God down to the latest times.

  " Behold the fig tree, when the leaves appear,   32
Ye know the Summer certainly is near—
So, when ye see these things, then understand
Fulfillment of My word is close at hand.
This generation shall not pass away,   34
Till all shall happen even as I say.
But of that day the knowledge is concealed,   36
The Father's secret, not to be revealed
Ev'n by the Son—sole channel of His thought,
The Speaking Word that tells but what He ought.

repentance. Mourning is the first sign of grace ; and, surely, there is nothing better
adapted to awaken it than the believing vision of the Son of Man coming in the glory
of His love and goodness to seek and save that which is lost.

" Think it not strange, I frame ambiguous speech ;

Take heed! is the great lesson I would teach. _{Matt.}

Concerning things that to the siege pertain,

'T is needful that I speak in language plain.

But of My Future Coming, 't were not fit,

That ye should know the day and hour of it.

Enough to know, it is not far away ;

That it may be to-morrow, or to-day.

What if at death, the vision shall be given

Of My Great Coming in the clouds of heaven?

So that ye watch, 't is of small consequence,

If it be now, or twenty centuries hence.

One thing is sure, whenever it shall be, 35

This generation shall be there to see.

" Take heed, lest that your hearts o'erburdened be

With sordid cares and sensuality, Luke
xxi. 34

And that day come, when you are not aware—

For it shall come on all men as a snare. 35

Watch ye and pray therefore! Like as a man, Mark
xiii. 34

Going abroad, drew out at length a plan,

By which each servant had his task assigned.

Putting in charge, of those he left behind,

His house, he told the keeper of the gate

To watch for his return, and patient wait.   Mark
                                                    xiii.—
Watch, therefore, seeing ye all knowledge lack,
When will the Master of the house come back—
At evening, midnight, crowing of the cock,
Or morning—lest He, unexpected, knock   36
And find you sleeping.   What to you I say,
I say to all, Watch evermore, and pray !

   " Ye know, that had the householder foreseen,   Matt.
                                                    xxiv. 43
What time the coming of the thief had been,
He would have watched, and with all patience too,
And not allowed his house to be broke through.
Who is that faithful and wise servant, whom   45
His Master has appointed in his room,
While absent, o'er his household to preside,
And in due season needful food provide?
Happy that servant, whom his lord shall find   46
Doing, at his return, the work assigned!
He, verily, will set him o'er the whole   47
Of his estate, and give him full control.
But if that servant in his heart shall say :   48
' My absent lord his coming doth delay,'
And shall begin outrageously to beat   49
And vex his fellow-servants, and shall eat

And drink moreo'er with drunkards, suddenly,   Matt.
                                               xxiv.

His lord shall come—at, too, an hour when he   50

Expects him not—and shall, with dreadful lash

Asunder cut* his flesh and deeply gash,   51

And him consign to dungeon glooms beneath,

Where there are weeping eyes and gnashing teeth.

" My Kingdom shall be likened in the end   xxv. 1

Unto ten virgins, sent forth to attend

The coming bridegroom on his lighted road,

With song and music to the bride's abode.

Taking their lamps, they went forth him to meet

From the bride's house into the darkened street,

But waited, meanwhile, in some dwelling near,

Till the delayed procession should appear.

And five were wise, providing against need :   2

And five were foolish, without thought or heed.

Now while the bridegroom tarried, they all slept.   5

But, lest their lamps should fail, the wise oil kept   4

In flasks, outside their lamps, a full supply.

Not so the foolish ones should theirs run dry.   3

---

*" Shall *dichotomize* or cut in two." The meaning here cannot be the severing of the
body either with a sword or saw (which was one mode of putting to death sometimes
practiced) because he is spoken of as surviving the punishment. It is probable, therefore, that it is a hyperbolical expression for scourging.

A cry at midnight rose with noise of feet :   Matt.
                                                     xxv. 6
'Behold, the bridegroom!   Him come forth to meet!'
Then they all rose and trimm'd their lamps. Dismay'd,
The foolish to the wise petition made :   8
'Give of your oil, our lamps are going out.'
'Not so,' they said, 'we have not, beyond doubt,   9
Enough for both.   Go ye to those who sell
And buy !'   While they were going, it befell   10
The bridegroom came; and those, who ready were
Went in where was the marriage to occur,
And straight the door was shut.   And, afterward,   11
The other virgins came, saying, 'Lord! Lord!
Open to us.'   But he replied, 'Too late—
I know you not.   I 'll not unclose the gate.'
Watch without ceasing !   Ready be alway !   13
For ye know not the hour, nor know the day.

   "WHEN in that glory comes the Son of Man,   31
Had with the Father ere the world began,
And all the angels with Him, He shall then
Sit on His throne of glory, judging men.
All nations* shall before Him gathered be,   32

* Olhausen understands by the expression, "all nations," not all mankind, but all
men with the exception of true believers, *that is, all unbelievers.*   True believers he
claims, do not come into judgment at all ; but, at the resurrection of the just, enter
at once into joy.   In the present Parable, if parable it may be called, they constitute
Christ's angelic retinue, or at least a part of it, and are referred to by Him as " My

The good and bad alike promiscuously ;

And He between them shall discriminate,

And shall one from the other separate—

As doth the shepherd from his sheep divide

brethren." Stier, who adopts substantially the same view, censures the old interpretation, which assumes that the General Judgment is intended, as erroneous and false. It may be that the old interpretation needs revision, but it is impossible to accept that as the true one—which makes a few acts of hospitable kindness done to the Christian brotherhood, disjoined from repentance and faith, as sufficient for salvation—without subverting the whole scheme of Christian doctrine. It would be far easier to believe as some do, that, while it is admitted, the words "all nations," or as the Revised Version gives it, "all the nations," is the Jewish equivalent for "all the Gentiles," Our Lord intended under this judicial form or similitude to convey the solemn warning, that, according to the reception given to His Gospel about to be preached in all the world, and the treatment of His messengers (Himself being identified with it and them) will men's fates be determined. It is inevitable that wherever Christ is preached men should take sides for or against Him. They pass to His right hand or His left. The division that takes place is a voluntary one, and according to character. It pertains to this life as much as to the next. All this is in perfect correspondence with His teachings elsewhere. At the first sending out of the Twelve, He said, "He that receiveth you receiveth Me, etc. * * * He that is not for Me is against Me. And whosoever shall give to drink unto one of these little ones a cup of cold water only in the name of a disciple, he shall in no wise lose his reward." And at His final sending out, He said, "Go, preach: whosoever believeth shall be saved, and whosoever believeth not shall be condemned." It would seem to matter little, whether this adjudication takes place, with the outward pomp and circumstances of a visible Coming at the End of the World, or invisibly and now.

The motive of the above commentators, in their strange exposition, does not justify it. It springs no doubt from a desire to find some direct, explicit assurance that the virtuous heathen, who have never heard the Gospel, will nevertheless be saved. While no man has the right to say that they will not be, still it is true, that Scripture is silent upon that point. So in regard to the salvation of children dying in infancy, it is nowhere said in so many words that they will be saved, but we take it for granted that they will be. "Are there few that be saved ?" is another example of that inquisitiveness which is unwilling to trust God any farther than He has given His word. "Will not the Judge of all the earth do right?" Are we more righteous than He, or more loving? To insist upon answers to questions merely speculative is impertinent and unseemly.

The mediæval view (which is likewise the prevailing modern one) was never more vividly realized than in the famous Judgment Hymn—*Dies Iræ*—of which the writer appends a Translation, one of the Thirteen which he published some years ago.

The goats—to set the sheep on His right side,   Matt.
xxv. 33

The goats set on His left.   Then shall the King,   34

Transporting words of glorious welcoming,

Smiling to them on His right hand address:

' Ye blessed of My Father, come, possess

The kingdom destined, all the ages through,

From the foundation of the world, for you.

For I was hungry and ye gave Me meat;   35

Thirsty and gave Me drink ; lay in the street,

A stranger, and, in kindness and good will,

Received Me; naked, and ye clothed Me ; ill,   36

In prison, and made haste to visit Me.'

Then shall the righteous say : ' When, Lord, saw we 37

Thee hungry and Thee fed?   With thirst opprest,

And gave Thee drink?   A stranger, lodged thee ?
        Drest   38

Thee, naked?   Or, sick, and Thee went to see?   39

Shut up in prison, and did visit Thee ?'

The King shall answer from His Judgment Seat,   40

With voice of love melodious and sweet :

' For that ye did it to the meanest one

Of these, My brethren, it to Me was done.'

Then He will say to those who trembling stand,   41

The guilty multitude on His left hand,

' Depart, ye cursèd, and abide the ire   Matt.
xxv. —

Of the eternal, all-consuming fire!

For I was hungry, and ye would not feed;   42

Was parched with thirst, and ye despised My need;

A stranger, and against Me shut the door;   43

Was naked, and gave nothing of your store;

Ill, and in prison, and came not to Me.'

Then they will answer: ' When, Lord, saw we Thee 44

Hungry, athirst, a stranger, naked, ill,

In prison, and were wanting in good will?'

Then He shall answer them with brow severe: 45

' Since to the least of these, My brethren, here,

Ye did it not, ye did it not to Me—

Deaf to the pleading voice of charity.'

" These shall depart, to bide the lopping knife*   46

Of lasting sev'rance from the Tree of Life;

---

* The lexical meanings of the Greek κόλασις=*kolasis*, rendered, "punishment," are *a pruning*, or *lopping off*, applied to trees etc. Hence *a checking, chastisement, correction, punishment*. It answers to the Latin, *Castigatio* (whence our English word, castigation) whose primary meaning, like the Greek word, is *a pruning*, then *chastisement, correction, punishment*.   Nearly all translators and expositors agree in assigning to it the meaning of punishment—a few only construing it in its primary sense of a "lopping off."   Taking it even in this sense, it is a word of fearful import, for it could not mean less than an eternal separation and alienation from the life of God, like a branch severed from the vine and condemned to the flames.   This has always appeared to the writer to be one of the strongest texts in the whole Bible in support of the doctrine of eternal punishment ; and he frankly admits, that he would like above all things, to find justification for a different rendering and a milder exegesis than the usual one.

While that the righteous, branches of a Tree   Matt.
xxv. —
Whose roots strike deep into eternity,
Shall flourish, fixed in that immortal sod,
Full of the flowing sap and life of God."

DIES IRÆ.—*Translation.*

That Day! that awful Day! the Last!
Result and sum of all the Past:
Great necessary Day of Doom,
When wrecking fires shall all consume!

What dreadful shrieks the air shall rend,
When all shall see the Judge descend,
And hear th' Archangel's echoing shout
From heavenly spaces ringing out!

The Trump of God, with quickening breath,
Shall pierce the silent realms of death;
And sound the summons in each ear,
Arise! thy Maker calls: Appear!

From east to west, from south to north,
The earth shall travail and bring forth—
As desert's sands, and ocean's waves,
Shall be the sum of empty graves.

Th' unchanging Record of the Past
Shall then be read from first to last,
And, out of things therein contained,
Shall all be judged, and fates ordained.

No lying tongue, that truth distorts,
Shall witness in that Court of Courts:
Each secret thing shall be revealed,
And every righteous sentence sealed.

Ah! who can stand when He appears?
Confront the guilt of sinful years?
What hope for me, a wretch depraved,
When scarce the righteous man is saved?

Dread Monarch of the Earth and Heaven!
For that salvation 's great, 't is given;
And, since the boon is wholly free,
O Fount of Pity, save Thou me!

Remember, Jesus, how my case
Once moved Thy pity and Thy grace,
And brought Thee down on earth to stay:
O lose me not then on that Day!

18

I seek Thee, who didst seek me first,
Weary and hungry and athirst,
Didst pay my ransom on the tree—
Let not such labor frustrate be!

Just Judge of vengeance in the end!
Now in the accepted time befriend:
My sins, O graciously remit,
Ere Thou judicially shalt sit!

Low at Thy feet I groaning lie:
With blushing cheek, and weeping eye,
And stammering lips, I urge the prayer,
O spare me, God of mercy, spare!

When Mary Thy forgiveness sought,
Wept, but articulated naught,
Thou didst forgive; didst hear the brief
Petition of the dying thief.

On grace thus great my hope is built,
That Thou wilt cancel too my guilt;
That, though my prayers are worthless breath,
Thou wilt deliver me from death.

When Thy dividing rod of might
Appointeth stations opposite,
Among Thy sheep grant me to stand,
Far from the goats, at Thy right hand.

And when despair shall seize each heart,
That hears the dreadful sound, ' Depart!'
Be mine, the heavenly lot of some,
To hear that word of welcome, ' Come !

I come to Thee with trembling trust,
And lay my forehead in the dust :
In my last hour do Thou befriend,
And not forsake me in my end.

XXI.

THE LAST SUPPER.—FAREWELL WORDS.

MATT. XXVI. 1-29 ; MARK XIV. 1-25 ; LUKE XXII. 1-20 ; JOHN XII. 2—XIII. 35.

IN deepest silence the disciples heard, Matt.
xxvi. 2
And treasured in their hearts each solemn word.

" After two days the Feast is," Jesus said
Of the Passover and Unleavened Bread,
What time the Son of Man, betrayed and tried,
Will be condemned to death and crucified."

E'en then, conspiring and consulting sat   3
Chief priests and scribes and elders, gathered at
The house of Caiaphas, how Him to take
By craft, and kill.   They, fearing an outbreak   4
Among the people, said, it were not best   5
During the Feast, Him openly t' arrest.

Being in Bethany, at the abode   6
Of Simon, long a leper, they bestowed
A loyal welcome, and a supper made, John
xii. 2

In boundless gratitude for healing aid. John
xii. —

And Martha served ; and Lazarus was there ;

And Mary, anxious to perform her share,   3

Taking a pound of spikenard, rare and sweet,

She poured it out upon His head and feet,

Then wiped them with her hair—the rich perfume

Spread through the house, pervading every room.

Some there, who knew how much the ointment cost,* 4

Thought it a pity so much should be lost ;

And Judas, most of all, made virtuous haste

To speak his disapproval of the waste :

" Why vainly throw away what would procure 5

Three hundred pence to feed the starving poor?"

This said he, caring not for them a whit,   6

But as he bore the purse could steal from it

Then Jesus said: " Let her alone ! for she   7

Has wrought a good, and pious work on Me :

Behold, the poor ye have with you alway,   8

But Me not alway ! She forestalls the day Matt.
xxvi. 12

Of My embalmment for My burial,

Now just at hand. In all the world where shall 13

Be preached My Gospel, this shall, I aver,

Be told for a memorial of her."

* The probable cost has been estimated as high as three hundred dollars, taking into account the difference in the value of silver now and then—actual value about fifty.

Then Judas—he, surnamed Iscariot—   Matt.
xxvi. 14
Went forthwith to the chief priests, saying, " What 15
Will ye me give, if I will Him betray?"
They bargained thirty shekels* him to pay.
Taking the silver, with despatch malign,   16
He sought to execute his fell design.

Now on the first day of Unleavened Bread,   17
When must the Paschal victim's blood be shed,
Came His disciples to Him, saying, " Where
Wilt Thou that we for Thee the meal prepare
To eat the Passover?"   He said to John
And Peter, " Go ye into the City, one   18
Bearing a jar of water, will meet you ;
Him follow ; where he enters enter too.
And to the householder in My name say :   Luke
xxii. 11
' Where is the guest-chamber, where the Master may
With His disciples the Passover eat?'
And he will show you, furnished and complete,   12
A spacious upper room."   All as He said
They found, and the Passover ready made.   13

Evening now come, which was He knew His last, 14

---

* Equal to eighteen dollars, the legal value of a slave if killed by a beast.   See
Zech. xi. 12.

He sat down with the Twelve to the repast,   Luke xxii.

And said : "Much have I longed to eat with you   15

This Passover before I suffer.   True

It is, that I will eat it ne'er again,   16

Till in God's Kingdom I its ends attain,

And all is finished."   He took liquid food,   17

Consisting of the crushed grapes' living blood

Pressed in the cup, and, giving thanks, said, " Take,

And of it 'mong yourselves division make !"

Strife about seats at table previously,   24

Renewed debate, which one should greatest be.

Though they had bathed, their walk since through
        the streets,

Had, unavoidably, defiled their feet.   John xiii. —

Being too proud, 't would seem, to have it known

They 'd stooped to wash their Master's or their own,

In disregard of decency, they crouch,

And soil with dirty feet their Saviour's couch.

But He, the sinner's Advocate and Friend,   1

Loving His own, still loved them to the end.

And though He knew Himself omnipotent,   3

That He came forth from God and to God went,

He rose from supper, stripping,* left the board,   4

* The "stripping" would relate to the upper garments, probably the mantle only.

And, with a towel, girt Himself, and poured   John xiii. 5

Water into a basin, and began

To wash the feet of His disciples, man

By man ; then, afterwards, to wipe them dry

With the same towel which He was girded by

Coming to Peter he objection made :   6

" Lord ! washest Thou my feet?"   The Master said :

" What I am doing thou dost know not now,   7

But thou shalt know hereafter."   He said : " Thou

Shalt never wash my feet."   " I must wash thee,   8

For, otherwise, thou hast no part with Me."

And Simon Peter answering then said :   9

" Lord ! not my feet only, but hands and head."

" He that is bathed has need to do no more   10

Than wash his feet, for then he 's clean all o'er.

And ye are clean, but not all."   This He said,

Knowing by whom Himself would be betrayed.   11

So after He had washed their feet, and ta'en   12

His garments, and at table lay again,

He said : " Know ye what I have done to you?

Ye call Me Lord and Master, and speak true,   13

For so I am.   If I do not disdain   14

To wash your feet, to leave example plain,   15

Ye ought not, when occasion shall arise,

Refuse to wash each other's feet, likewise.

The slave s not greater than his master, nor 16

Is the apostle or ambassador

Greater than he who sends him. Happy you, 17

Who know these things, provided ye them do.

" I speak not of you all : I know whom I 18

Have chosen, and him, who will verify

That Scripture, ' He that eateth bread with me,

His heel hath lifted 'gainst me treacherously.'

I tell you of this treachery before, 19

That ye, unstaggered, may believe the more."

He sadly spake again : " In truth I say, 20

The traitor 's present, that shall Me betray. 21

The Son of Man goes as of Him 't was said,

But woe to him by whom He is betrayed."

They, struck with horror, on each other gaze,

And one by one cry out in wild amaze :

" Lord is it I ?"   And Peter beckoned John, 23

Leaning his Master's loving bosom on,

To ask, " Who is it Lord ?"   And He said, " See 24

To whom I give this morsel dipped, 't is he." 25

And having dipped the morsel, He it passed 26

To Judas, who had faltered out at last,

"Lord is it I?"   To which He answered, "Yea! _{John xiii. 27}
So what thou doest, do without delay."
John understood and Peter, all beside   28
Thought He had bid him for the feast provide.   29

After the morsel had to him been given,   30
Satan him entered, and, by fury driven,
He instantly went out, and it was night—
The Paschal moon had risen full and bright.
When he was gone—though Jesus knew full well,   31
It was to consummate his purpose fell—
He said, forestalling triumph—though foreseen
Th' unutterable agonies that lay between—
" The Son of Man 's now glorified and glad
And God is glorified in Him.   Ye 're sad
With sad forebodings.   Little children, I   33
A little while am with you.   By and by,
Ye 'll seek Me and not find Me.   Where I go
Ye cannot follow while ye live below.
I give the breadth of My commandment new,   34
' Ye one another love as I 've loved you '—
To all men your discipleship ye prove,   35
By mutual helpfulness and mutual love."

And Peter said : " Lord, whither goest Thou?"   36
" Whither I go, ye cannot follow now,"

(Was still the Lord's ambiguous reply)   _{John}
                                             _{xiii. —}
" But thou shalt follow afterwards."   " But why   37
Cannot I follow now ?   I will for Thee
Lay down my life."   Then Jesus said : " All ye   _{Matt.}
                                                      _{xxvi. 31}
Shall stumbled be this night because of Me.
For 't is written, ' The Shepherd I will smite,
And all the sheep will safety seek in flight.'
But when I 'm risen, I will go before   32
You into Galilee."   Then spake once more   33
Peter : " Though all disown, yet will not I."
" Before-cock crowing thou 'lt Me thrice deny.   34
Ah! Simon, Simon, Satan would thee gain,   _{Luke}
                                              _{xxii. 31}
And toss and sift thee, as men winnow grain,
But I have prayed for thee, and answer got,   32
That though thou fall, yet shall thy faith fail not.
And when thou art converted, made more meek,
Strengthen thy brethren, who like thee are weak."
With greater vehemence did he protest,   _{Matt.}
                                            _{xxvi. 35}
He would not Him deny ; so all the rest.

Then taking bread, and giving thanks, He brake
And gave to His disciples, saying, " Take,   _{Luke}
                                               _{xxii. 19}
Eat, this My body is, that 's broke for you,
This in commemoration of Me do."

He took the cup, and blessed it to their use,   Luke
xxii. 20

Filled with the living, uncorrupted juice*

Of the crushed cluster, 'inoffensive must'—†

A thing unleavened, worthy of all trust—

And, as He gave to them the purple food,

Said: "Drink ye all of it; this is My blood   1 Cor.
xi. 23

Of the New Covenant for many shed;

Remember me in this, as in the bread.

I'll drink no more the product of the vine,   Matt.
xxvi. 29

Till in God's Kingdom I shall drink new wine.‡

JOHN XIV. 1-37: XV. 1-33—XVII. 1-26

"Be ye not troubled in undue degree,   John
xiv. 1

Belief in God demands belief in Me.

My Father's house has mansions manifold;   2

If 't were not so, I would you it have told.

I go for each a dwelling to prepare—

A house not made with hands, divinely fair,

A body like my own.‖   If I you leave,   3

---

* To symbolize a body that "did not see corruption."

† "For drink, the grape she crushes, inoffensive must."—PARADISE LOST, v. 344.
See Gen. xi. 9-11.

‡ See the Evangel, p. 233, note.

Before any one rejects this interpretation as fanciful and unauthorized, let him, if
he will, consider whether it does not suit the context; and whether it does not har-
monize with other Scripture. Christ promised His disciples, that, having gone and
prepared a place for them, He would come again and receive them to Himself, that

I will return, and to Myself receive, John xiv.

That where I am, there ye may be also.

Ye know the whither and the way I go." 4

Said Thomas: "Lord, not knowing what Thou

 know'st, 5

We neither know the way nor place Thou go'st.'

He said: "I am the True and Living Way— 6

Who goes by other roads, he goes astray.

Comes no one to the Father but by Me—

Sole means of access, gloriously free.

Had ye known Me, ye would, in fact, have known 7

My Father too, revealed in Me alone.

Henceforth, ye know ye know Him, and have seen."

 Said Philip: "Lord, without a veil between, 8

Show us the Father, and 't will us suffice:

We fain would have the witness of our eyes.'

they might be with Him. Did He come? If so, when? If He came to them at death, He came—according to Philippians iii. 21—clothed with omnipotence to fashion them a body like unto His own glorious body. Manifestly, it were not a full salvation, "without the redemption of the body.' "The house we live in" below, is the body of flesh, wonderful beyond everything we know. And we can conceive of no "mansion" that our ascended Lord could prepare for us even in heaven so desirable, as an immortal body suited to the needs of the immortal spirit. We feel quite sure that there is no substitute for it in the whole universe.

 Another thought. The Lord's Supper, just instituted, symbolizes divine assimilations. By a believing apprehension and appropriation of Christ we are changed into the same image. He is our aliment. Our springs of life are in Him. Through Him "The inner man is renewed day by day." May we not assume, that there is some reference here to the spiritual body, which is essential to the completeness of our personality as the sons of God?

" Have I with you so long time, Philip, been,   John
                                                  xiv. 9

And dost thou not Me know ?   Who hath Me seen,

Hath seen the Father—immanent is He,   10

Speaking and working evermore in Me.   11

He that believes on Me, the works I do   12

He shall do also, yea, and greater too.

Because I go unto the Father, I

Enabling might will give you from on high,

Under Truth's banners everywhere unfurled,

To conquer nations and convert the world.

Then all ye ask in My name shall be done—   14

The Father thus be honored in the Son.

" If ye love Me, ye'll My commandments keep,   15

And out of darkness, light shall upward leap ;

And I will pray the Father you to send   16

Another Helper, Advocate and Friend,

That He may be with you forever, even

The Spirit of Truth, supremest Gift of Heaven.   17

" I will not leave you orphans without home,   18

Bereaved and desolate, but to you come :

My Father will you love, and come as well,

And We will both together with you dwell.

These things I've spoken to you while I'm here :

But He, the Comforter, your hearts will cheer—

The Holy Spirit, whom the Father will   John xiv. 26

Send in My name, His office to fulfill—

To teach you, and to your remembrance bring

Of all I've said to you, each needful thing.

And now, Farewell! receive My fond adieu!

Peace I leave with you; My peace give to you.   27

Not as the world I give, words lightly spoke,

But peace immortal on your heads invoke.

Let not your heart be troubled or dismayed,

I go away, but not to stay I said.

Ye should be glad I to My Father go,   28

For He is greater than I am below.

   "I am the Vine, the heavenly and the true: John xv. 1

My Father is the Husbandman, and you

The branches are.   Each barren branch in Me   2

He lops off, and each branch that's fruitful, He,

By pruning, cleanses, so that it may bear

More fruit.   Clean through My spoken word ye are. 3

Abide in Me, and I'll in you abide.   4

For as the branch cannot its life divide

From the main vine, and of itself bear fruit,

Neither can ye, apart from Me, the Root,

Do anything.   He who is joined to Me,   5

And shares My life, bears fruit abundantly.

The branch that has that vital oneness lost,   John xv. 6

Lopped from the Vine, into the fire is tost.

Ye by much fruit the Father glorify,   8

And My disciples prove yourselves thereby.

"E'en as the Father has loved Me, I you   9

Have loved, although no love whate'er was due.

Would ye not alienate this love immense,   10

Abide in love and in obedience.

I have addressed to you these counsels plain,   11

That so My joy in you may aye remain,

And that your joy in love may be complete—

Fraternal loves and fellowships are sweet.   12

No one a greater love than this can show,

To lay down life to save a friend or foe.

    *   *   *   *   *

"I tell you truly, it is for your good   xvi. 7

That I depart—the Paraclete else would

Not come to you,   But if I go away,   8

I'll send you Him to dwell with you and stay.

And when He comes, your Heavenly Helper, He

Will mouth and wisdom and conviction be—

Convince the world of Sin—of sins the chief,   9

Th' unpardonable sin of unbelief:

Of Righteousness—of which to meet the need,   10

My finished work I'll 'fore My Father plead :   John xvi. —
Of Judgment—for earth's prince is judged—his reign [11]
O'er souls redeemed destroyed, and broke his chain.

  " I've many things to say to you, but ye   [12]
Cannot at present bear them.   But when He,   [13]
The Spirit of Truth, is come, He will you lead
Into all truth ; for His word will proceed,
Not from Himself alone, from Me apart,
But be th' unspoken utterance of My heart.
He will Me glorify, for He will take   [14]
Of Mine, and will full revelation make
Of all I said to you while with you here,
Authenticate, complete, and make all clear ;
And He to you will things to come make known—   [15]
Divine disclosures of the Eternal Throne."

———————

Come, Holy Spirit, be my Guest !
Prepare a welcome in my breast !
Unbar the portals, swing them wide,
Enter, My Maker, and abide !

Come in, there evermore to stay !
Nor let my sins drive Thee away !

19

Alas for me, should I Thee grieve,
And Thou, offended, shouldst me leave.

Alike, Thou dwellest in the height,
And hearts made humble and contrite :
Open my eyes myself to see,
And clothe me with humility !

Sweet Comforter !   Eternal Friend !
Be my companion to the end :
And work in me to will and do,
Whate'er is pleasing, good and true.

Take of the things of Christ, and show
What it concerns me most to know,
And make me victor over sin,
That I on earth may heaven begin !

———————

*   *   *   *

" A woman has in travail sorrow, yet

John
xvi. 21

A mother's joy makes her her pangs forget.
And so ye now, because I leave you, mourn,

22

But when ye see Me from the grave reborn,
Ye shall rejoice, and no one shall deprive

You of your joy, at sight of Me alive. John xvi. 23
Then all your doubts and questionings shall cease,
And ye 'll enjoy a calm believing peace.
And what ye ask the Father, in My name,
He will be sure to freely give the same.
Ye have asked naught in My name hitherto. 24
Ask, and He 'll pour His fullness out to you.

* * * * *

I speak thus, that in Me ye may have peace : 33
Though in the world, your conflict shall ne'er cease.
Be of good cheer, I 've overcome, and ye,
Likewise, shall overcome the world through Me."

Having thus spoke, He lifted up His eyes, xvii. 1
And prayed and interceded in this wise :
 " Father ! the hour is come for Me to die,
Foreseen through all the ages. Glorify
Thy Son in His humiliation, when
For the redemption of the sons of men,
Thou mak'st His soul an offering for sin,
To everlasting righteousness bring in,
That so the Son may glorify Thee too,
To whom the honor and the praise are due—
Being endowed by Thee with power afresh, 2

Right and authority, high o'er all flesh,   John
                                                             xvii. —

To give to them, whom Thou to Him hast given,

Eternal life and happiness in heaven.

   " Now this is life eternal, Thee to know,   3

And Jesus Christ, Thy Messenger below.

I have Thee glorified here from My birth,   4

And finished have Thy work upon the earth.

Now, with that glory glorify Thou Me,   5

I had with Thee from all eternity !

As I depart, and to Thy bosom go,

I pray for these bereaved ones left below.   9

   " O Holy Father ! keep them in Thy name !   11

May they be one, as we are !   Save from blame !

And by Thy Truth them wholly sanctify—   17

Thy Word is truth, unmingled with a lie.

As Thou sent'st Me into the world, I send   18

Them, My Apostles, forth to the world's end.

Nor for these only is My prayer preferred,   20

But for those also, who shall through their word

Believe on Me, that so they all may be   21

In Us, as Thou in Me, and I in Thee.

Father ! I will, that all Thou Me hast given,   24

May with Me be, when throned with Thee in heaven,

That forasmuch, as they My likeness bear,
I in them being, they may with Me share
The love, wherewith Thou lovedst Me before
The world's foundations, since and evermore."

HYMN.

Ever, My Lord, with Thee,
  Ever with Thee!
Through all eternity
  Thy face to see!
I count this heaven, to be
Ever, my Lord, with Thee,
  Ever with Thee!

Fair is Jerusalem,
  All of pure gold,
Garnished with many a gem
  Of worth untold:
I only ask, to be
Ever, My Lord, with Thee,
  Ever with Thee!

River of Life there flows
 As crystal clear;
The Tree of Life there grows
 For healing near:
But this crowns all, to be
Ever, my Lord, with Thee,
 Ever with Thee!

No curse is there, no night,
 No grief, no fear;
Thy smile fills heaven with light,
 Dries every tear:
What rapture, there to be
Ever, my Lord, with Thee,
 Ever with Thee!

XXII.

BETRAYAL, TRIAL, AND SENTENCE.

MATT. XXVI. 30-68; MARK XIV. 26-65; LUKE XXII. 39-71; JOHN XVIII. 1-24.

THEY, having sung a Hymn, went out. And soon
   Under the light of the Passover moon—   Matt. xxvi. 30
Leaving the City by the eastern gate,
Not closed throughout the Feast, however late—
Passed the brook Kedron to (where used to be)
A quiet Garden, called Gethsemane,   36
Upon the wooded slope of Olivet,
Where He had oft with His disciples met,   John xviii. 2
Well known to Judas. He, addressing all   Luke xxii. 40
Of His disciples, said : " Pray, that ye fall
Not through temptation!" Going farther on,
And taking with Him Peter, James and John,   Matt. xxvi. 37
He to the others said : " Sit here, while I
Pray yonder." Then 'gan a strange agony.   38
Struck with amaze, He said, with gasping breath,
" My soul is compassed with the pangs of death.
Stay here, and watch!" Proceeding a short space, 39

A stone's throw further, He fell on His face,   Matt.
xxvi. —
And prayed : " Father, if it be possible,
Let this cup pass from Me ! but, if not, well:
Not what I will, but what Thou wilt be done—
Obedient unto death will be Thy Son."

Then He returned, and finding them asleep,   40
He said to Peter : " Simon, couldst thou keep
Not watch with Me one hour? Watch ye and pray, 41
Lest your frail hearts your tempted feet betray :
Strength to resist temptation humbly seek,
The spirit 's willing but the flesh is weak."
He went away the second time.   Again,   Luke
xxii.44
He, in an agony of grief and pain,
Prayed yet more earnestly ; and, lo, His sweat
Was like great drops of blood, that, falling, wet
Th' astonished ground.   As on the shuddering air
His pallid lips flung out the bitter prayer,
Appeared to Him a messenger from heaven ;
And to His fainting heart fresh strength was given.

Then going back once more, again He found   Matt.
xxv.42
The three all fast asleep upon the ground,
For that their eyes were heavy.   He withdrew,   43
And uttered the same doleful words anew :

"Father! if this unutterable cup Matt.
xxv. 44
May not pass from Me, I will drink it up:
Though red and full of mixture, drugged with pain,
I to the dregs will expiation drain.
I draw not back. Fulfilled be in the Son!
I mean to finish what I have begun.

He rose and His disciples now addressed : 45
"Ye need not watch. Sleep on and take your rest—
Vigils are useless. Not your drowsy eyes
Can more avail to guard against surprise.
The hour is come, and cannot be delayed.
The Son of Man, already, is betrayed
Into the hands of sinners. Let us go! 46
I am prepared to meet th' approaching foe."

While He yet spake, was seen a numerous band 47
With lanterns, swords, and staves, now close at hand,
From the chief priests and scribes and elders sent,
Guided by Judas, who before them went,
Having a sign them given, saying: "See 48
Whom I shall kiss, Him seize; the same is He."
As he draws near Him, he, advancing, saith : 49
"Hail Master!" and Him kisses with vile breath.
And Jesus says, "Friend! Judas! how is this? 50
The Son of Man betray'st thou with a kiss?" Luke
xii. 48

He, knowing all things that before Him lay— _{John xviii. 4}
All signs of His late struggle passed away—
Steps calmly forth. Exposed to view He stands—
The God-like One—and with firm voice demands,
" Whom seek ye?" They give faltering reply: 5
" Jesus of Nazareth." He answers, " I
Am He." They, struck with awe profound,   6
Go backward, and in heaps fall to the ground.
Recovered soon, and risen to their feet,
Again He asks: " Whom seek ye?" They repeat: 7
" Jesus of Nazareth." " I said, I 'm He.   8
Therefore, if Me ye seek, let these* go free."

Him, having seized, they bound fast with a cord. _{Matt. xxvi. 50}
Impetuous Peter drew at once a sword,   51
And smote the high priest's servant standing near,
And, as it happened, cut off his right ear.
Then Jesus said to him: " Put up thy sword!   52
Back to its scabbard let it be restored!
Who takes shall perish by it. Thinkest thou,   53
I cannot pray unto My Father now,
And He will of His angels forthwith send
More than twelve legions Me here to defend?

*How touching, this mindfulness of His disciples!

But how should then (if I My rescue willed) Matt. xxvi. 54
Th' imperatives of Scripture be fulfilled,
That say, it must thus be?   Back shall I shrink, John xviii. 11
And not the cup My Father gives Me drink?"
And Jesus touched the wounded ear, and said: Luke xxii. 51
" Suffer thus far!" and restoration made.
Then to the chief priests and the elders—who 52
Had joined the forces of the Temple to
The Roman cohort, to remove all doubt
About th' arrest—He said: " Are ye come out,
As 'gainst a robber, with a dread array
Of swords and clubs? I, teaching, day by day, 53
Sat in the Temple.   This, your hour of might,
And domination of the powers of night,
Is a permitted triumph, to fulfil
The Scriptures that declare Jehovah's will." Matt. xxvi. 56
Then all th' Eleven Him forsook and fled.

They, to the high priest's house, their captive led, 57
Where all the chief priests, scribes and elders were
Assembled, in night session, to confer,
By what pretence of crime 'gainst Cæsar, they
His death could compass on the coming day—
Resolved, that innocence should be no bar.

Peter and John had followed Him afar. John xviii. 15

Admittance unto John was not denied,

He being known, but Peter stood outside: 16

Wherefore, John spake to her who kept the port,

And brought in Peter to the inner Court,

Where all rooms opened. Looking through a door,

He could see Jesus. As he sat before Mark xiv. 54

The fire, among the servants, being cold,

A maid of the high priest, him eyeing, told 66

Him threat'ningly: "Thou, also, wast with this 67

Jesus of Nazareth." He said: "I wis 68

Not what thou sayest." And the cock then crew.

Later, another maid him charged anew, 69

Saying, "This is one of them." He denied, Matt. xxvi. 72

A second time, and with an oath beside,

Declaring, "I know not the man." About

An hour from this, one said: "Thou art, no doubt, 73

Of Galilee, and one of them: beside

I saw thee in the Garden." He denied,

The third time, and began to curse and swear:

"I know Him not, and do not for Him care."

While he was speaking, the cock crew again,

And the Lord turned, and looked on Peter. Then Luke xxii.

He called to mind His words: "Ere twice

The cock shall crow, thou wilt deny Me thrice."
And, as he thought thereon, his breast, storm swept,
Heaved like a sea, and he went forth and wept.

'T was after midnight, when they reached the gate.
While Love kept drowsy watch, unsleeping Hate
Unbroken vigils kept.   No eye was dim
Of those dark plotters of the Sanhedrim,
Informally convened—a hostile part,
All of one mind, without a wavering heart—
Sentence of death intending to report,
When should, at daybreak, meet the entire Court.
The high priest Caiaphas, in turbaned pride,
·Sat in the middle, and, on either side
The other judges in a semicirque,
Impatient to complete their bloody work,
So well begun.   It was a welcome sight,
Jesus, their dread, a prisoner that night.

Composed and calm, He stood before them then,
The Judge of judges, to be judged of men.
They could not help but feel a guilty shame,
And half allow the justice of His claim,
As, unabashed, He scanned each scowling face,
And showed of terror not the slightest trace.

E'en the high priest, a haughty Sadducee,
Was forced to own the power of purity.
But the trained worldling his misgivings masked,
And, with imperious looks, Him fiercely asked _{John}
                                   xviii. 19
Concerning His disciples, and His claims,
The nature of His doctrine, and His aims,
And what it meant, His publishing abroad
Th' immediate Coming of the Reign of God,
Calling Himself the Son of Man, and so
Hailed as Messiah a few days ago.

    Jesus him answered: "I spake, day by day,   20
Openly to the world.   I taught alway
In public places where the Jews resort,
Temple and Synagogue.   Let them report   21
Who heard Me what I said.   In secret I
Have spoken nothing."   And one standing by   22
Him forthwith struck upon the mouth, and said,
"Answerest Thou the high priest so?"   He made 23
Mild answer: "If I've spoken what's untrue,
Bear witness to th' untruth—this thou may'st do—
But if I've nothing said but what is right,
Why dost thou Me thus violently smite?"

    Left in the keeping of the Temple guard—   _{Luke}
                                                xxii.63
Fierce Jewish bigots, pitiless and hard—

With fist, with open hand, with stick and rod, _{Matt. xxvi.67}
They cuffed and smote the patient Son of God.
Buffet and blow fell on that sacred head ;
And, while blindfolded, " Prophesy " (they said,   68
In brutal mockery and cruel sport)
" Who struck Thee then." Provoked to no retort,
He gave His back to the fierce smiters there ;   Isaiah l. 6
His cheek to them that pluckéd off the hair ;
From shame and spittle did not hide His face ;
But meekly bore all outrage and disgrace.

    As soon as it was day, they Jesus brought   Luke xxii.63
Into the Council, and false witness sought   Mark xiv.:5
To bring against Him to put Him to death.
But they found none. In spite of venal breath,   56
And subornation of foul perjury,
In no case did two witnesses agree.
When two false witnesses, at last, arose,   57
They differed still, when called on to depose,   58
Concerning words which they heard Him employ—
Declaring, as one said, " I *can* destroy
This Temple "; saying, th' other witness swore,
" I *will* destroy this Temple, and restore
It without hands within three days complete."

Again they suffered failure and defeat.   Mark
xiv. —

Something was wanting to make out a case,   59

More than this proof, discordant on its face.

So the high priest, upstarting from his couch,   60

Said, angrily : " What is it these avouch

And charge against Thee? Answerest Thou naught?"

But Jesus held His peace.   To fury wrought,

He said, " I, by the Living God, adjure   Matt.
xxvi.63

Thee under oath, to tell us, and assure,

Whether Thou be the Christ, God's Son or no?"

And Jesus thus adjured, said : " I am so.   64

Hereafter, ye shall see the Son of Man,

Sitting on the right hand of Power, and scan

His dreadful coming in the clouds of heaven.

With well-feigned horror, and with vestments riven,65

The high priest said : " What further need have we

Of witnesses?   We 've heard His blasphemy.

What think ye ? "   And all gave it as their sense,   66

He 's guilty of a capital offence.

Not having power to put to death, Him they   John
xviii. 28

Led bound, and under a strong guard, away

To the Pretorium.   To enter it

Would be defilement, and make them unfit

To eat the Passover—so stayed outside.   John
xviii. —

An early audience was not denied.   2)

Pilate, the procurator, going out,

Began to ask th' authorities about

The man's offence. They gruffly said : " If He   30

Were not a malefactor, why should we

Deliver Him to thee?"   He, when he saw

They quibbled, said : " Take, judge Him by your

     law !"   31

They said : " He under it death meriteth,

But we've no right to put a man to death"—

The words of Jesus thus to verify,   32

Telling what kind of death He was to die.*

They charged Him then with criminal intent   Luke
xxiii. 2

To overturn the Roman Government ;

Sowing sedition ; leading minds astray ;

Bidding the people not to tribute pay

To Cæsar, claiming that Himself was King,   3

Their Christ, who would deliverance them bring.

Pilate withdrew into the Judgment Hall,   John
xviii. 33

And Jesus there, obedient to his call,

Was brought, that he might question Him, apart

* Crucifixion was a Roman punishment.

From His accusers. " So," he said ; " Thou art _{xviii. —}^{John}

King of the Jews?"   He answered : " In good faith,³⁴

Is this what *thou* say'st ? or another saith ? "

" Am I a Jew ? " replied he, scornfully,   ³⁵

" The chief priests have delivered Thee to me.

What hast Thou done?"   Spake the Supreme of

    Men :   ³⁶

" My Kingdom is not of this world, for then

I armed adherents' aid would not refuse,

To save Me from the vengeance of the Jews.

But now My Kingdom's not an earthly thing."

" Thou art then," Pilate said, " in fact a King?"   ³⁷

" Thou speakest truly—King, in fact and name—

I to this end was born, I for this came

Into the world, to reign and witness here

Unto the Truth.   All to My voice give ear

Who 're of the Truth.   My loyal subjects they,

Who hear the Truth, and hearing it obey."

" But what is Truth ?—Philosophy's despair."   ³⁸

Tossing the question on th' unanswering air,

Pilate went out again, and said : " I find   ³⁹

No fault in Him."   They then, with desperate

    mind,   _{xv. 3}^{Mark}

Charged Him with many things.   When He said
     naught—   Mark
xv. —
But as a lamb, that 's to the slaughter brought ;
A sheep, that 's dumb before her shearers, so
Not opening His mouth, in patient woe—
Knowing the uselessness of all defense,
Pilate much marvelled at His reticence.   5

When he persisted in affirming still,   Luke
xxiii. 4
" I find no fault in Him"—more fierce to kill,   5
They sought to brand Him as a dangerous pest,
Exciting insurrection without rest,
Teaching throughout all Jewry, the whole space
From Galilee, they said, unto this place.

No sooner mention did they Galilee,   6
Than Pilate caught at it, and asked, if He
A Galilean was?   And, when he found,
It Herod's jurisdiction was and ground   7
To which He properly belonged, he sent
Jesus to Herod, who, by accident,
Was also at Jerusalem just then—
Come to attend the Passover.   And when
He Jesus saw, he was exceeding glad ;   8
Because, for a long season, he had had

A great desire to see Him, having heard   _{Luke}
Luke
xxiii. —

A great desire to see Him, having heard
Of many things accomplished by His word,
And hoped to see some miracle now wrought.
In vain he questioned Him, He answered naught.   9
The chief priests and the scribes, with might and
    main,   10
Renewed, and pressed their calumnies again.

But Herod, too astute to be betrayed
Into th' acceptance of their wild tirade—
Knowing that what they vehemently averred
Was mostly false, malicious and absurd;
Himself acquainted with Him, by report,
And marvellings of men of his own court ;*
Not fearing Him, as dangerous to the State,
But well advised His following was great ;
Taught by experience, in the case of John
Whom he beheaded, there were risks to run—
Though flattered by the compliment him paid,
Whereby with Pilate he was friendly made,   12
True to his foxy nature, took good care
That he was caught not in the Roman's snare.

* Herod had heard of His miracles (Matt. xiv. 1); Manaen (Acts xiii. 1) his foster
brother, was one of the prophets and teachers in the church of Antioch , and Johanna,
the wife of Chuza, Herod's steward (Luke viii. 3) was one of those devoted women
who ministered to Jesus of their substance.

Though he cared not the innocent should bleed, _{Luke xxiii.} --

He 'd shun the needless odium of the deed.

While making ready Jesus back to send,   11

Supposing it would better him commend

To the fierce priesthood (strange such monsters are),

He laughing part took with his men of war

In making vulgar sport—like cruel boys,

Paying mock homage, with grimace and noise,

As to a king, what time they tricked Him out

With a white robe to wear upon the route.

Pilate, disposed to save Him if he could,   13

Let his ' I dare not' wait upon ' I would,'

Unjust demands unable to refuse.

Th' authorities and people of the Jews

Again he summons, and again affirms   14

His innocence, in most emphatic terms:

" You charge Him with exciting to revolt;

Touching this crime, I find Him without fault.

And Herod, too, to whom I you referred,   15

Has in this judgment tacitly concurred.

Having chastised Him, He shall be released,   16

Custom requiring, I should at this Feast   17

Surrender you a prisoner. Do you choose,   _{Mark xv. 9}

That I release to you King of the Jews?—"
He knowing very well the Sanhedrim
Out of sheer envy had delivered Him.

They said, with cries and shouts that did not cease,
" Away with this man ! and to us release   Luke
                                                  xxiii.18
Barabbas ! "   Now, Barabbas lay fast bound   19
For murder and sedition—dangerous found,
A restless zealot, born of troublous times,
Of bad repute because of other crimes.
" What shall I do, since you Barabbas choose,   Mark
                                                    xv. 12
With Him ye designate King of the Jews ? "
And they cried out again : " Him crucify ! "   13
Once more th' unwilling governor said, " Why ?
What evil has He done ?   I have not found   14
Just cause of death on which to sentence ground."

Outside of the Pretorium, or Hall   Matt.
                                                    xxvii. 19
Of Judgment, was a place they used to call
The Pavement, but in Hebrew Gabbatha,
Where, in the open air and light of day,
Trials might be conducted.   Pilate there
For judgment sat, in his high curule chair,
When his wife Procla warning whisper sent,
An unjust condemnation to prevent.

Saying : " Yield not! stand firm ! have naught to do

With that just man ! lest my day's dream come true."

But bulls of Bashan, the priest-goaded crowd,   Psalms xxii 12

Ceased not their bellowings—with voices loud,

And urgent clamor growing more and more,

The chief priests leading in the wild uproar,   Matt. xxvii. 20

They shouted the demand in Pilate's ear :

" Him crucify ! Him crucify !" until in fear,

He weakly but reluctantly complied,   24

And sentence gave He should be crucified.

Washing his hands before the multiude,

He told them : " I am guiltless of the blood

Of this just man.   See ye to it."   They said :   25

" His blood be on ours and our children's head."

So he released to them Barabbas.   When   26

His soldiers had scourged Jesus, they again

Led Him inside of the Pretorium,   27

And, when their whole band had together come,

Stripped Him ;   clothed Him with purple ;   platted

   now   28

A thorny crown to mock His bleeding brow ;   29

A reed put in His hand ; in mimicry

Of worship paid to sovereigns, bowed the knee ;

Saluting Him, said: " Hail, King of the Jews!" Matt.
xxvii. —
Then spat on Him ; and took the reed to use 30
In smiting Him upon the head and face,
And heaped on Him all manner of disgrace.

Pilate went forth again, and said to them : John
xix. 4
" I bring Him forth I without cause condemn."

Pale, haggard, bleeding, tottering and forlorn, 5
Wearing the purple robe and wreathing thorn,
Jesus came forth—the warm blood shuddering ran,
While Pilate, pointing, said: " Behold the Man!"
Chief priests and underlings, a barking crowd, 6
Th' assembly of the wicked, yelping loud,
At sight of Him sent up the th' impatient cry,
Unceasing, " Crucify! Him Crucify!"
Then Pilate said : " Since ye refuse to halt,
Ye take and crucify, for I no fault
Have found in Him against the Roman laws."
The Jews replied : " Under our law, because 7
He made Himself the Son of God, have we
Doomed Him to death for guilt of blasphemy."
When Pilate heard this, he was more afraid. 8
The superhuman patience He displayed,
His more than mortal majesty of mien,

Transcending all that he had ever seen, John xix. —
Filled him with dread misgivings, fortified
By his wife's dream and warning words beside.
Who is He? this mysterious silent One,
Claiming the awful title of God's Son.
He feared the Jews, but then to brave the curse
And wrath of the immortal gods were worse.

    So, going back to the Pretorium,   9
He said to Jesus: "Whence art Thou?"   When
       dumb,
Yielding no answer, Pilate said: "Dost Thou   10
Not speak to me? Dost Thou not know, that now
I 've power to crucify Thee or set free?"
He said: "Thou couldst no power have over Me   11
Unless Heaven-given. Who did this wrong begin,
And Me delivered, has the greater sin."

    Pilate sought thenceforth to release Him. "No!" 12
The Jews cried out. "If thou let this Man go
Thou art not Cæsar's friend. Who claims to be
A King, he strikes at his authority."

    When Pilate heard these words, not sure about John xix. 13
His own position, he brought Jesus out.
The hour was nine. Intending it to sting,   14
He said unto the Jews, "Behold your King!"

" Away with Him ! away with Him ! " they cry—

" Him crucify ! "   He said : " What ! crucify

Your King ? "   " We have no King," chief priests
         replied,

" But Cæsar."   He the doom then ratified.

MOTIVES, that Judas moved, soon spent their force,

When followed an intolerable remorse.   Matt.
                                                   xxvii. 3

No sooner had the dreadful deed been done,

Than, like the utter quenching of the Sun,

The blackness of a darkness round him fell

Out of the bottom of profoundest hell.

Not power of fire, nor yet the moon's clear light,

The stars' bright flames, could lighten that dread
         night—

An earnest of the darkness that shall bind

With chains perpetual the guilty mind.

When Conscience wakens who can with her strive ?

Terrors and troubles from a sick soul drive ?

Naught so unpitying as the ire of sin,

The inappeas'ble Nemesis within.

O thought of horror ! since twelve hours ago,

He had pulled down eternities of woe.

The dream of avarice was at an end.

He had betrayed his loving Lord and Friend. Matt.
xxvii.—
Lost to all hope, by all the furies driven,
He heard behind him close the gates of Heaven.
The world seemed different. A bodeful sound
Rose from the shuddering, accusing ground.
Traitor and murderer, the conscious skies
Looked down with wrathful and reproving eyes.
By some strange sorcery, all things appeared
Eldritch, possessed, unnatural and weird.
Was it a demon's, or his own soul's hiss
That filled his ears? so like that mortal kiss
By which he stung his Lord with serpent mouth.
He felt the burning of a dreadful drouth,
That dried up all the moisture of the throat—
Scarce able to articulate a note,
As in the clutches of a strong despair
He tried to shape his guilty lips to prayer.

He saw Him scourged, mocked, spit upon, contemned,
And as a felon to the Cross condemned.   3
And was all this his work? What should he do?
He to the chief priests and the elders flew,
And throwing down the price, he wildly said :
"Lo I have sinned, in that I have betrayed   4
The Innocent. I your base bribe return."

They said : "What's that to us ? That's your concern."
Leaving behind Him the accursèd pelf Matt. xxvii. 5
He in a frenzy went and hanged himself.

Being the price of blood, the chief priests thought 6
It would defile the treasury, so bought
The potter's field to bury strangers in 7
With the nefarious reward of sin.
Wherefore the field was called Aceldama, 8
The Field of Blood, and is so to this day.

XXIII.

THE CRUCIFIXION.

Matt. xxvii. 31-66; Mark xv. 20-47; Luke xxiii. 33-56; John xix. 28-42.

TIRED of the sport, their cruel mockings o'er,
    They doff His robes, and His own clothes restore.
Then lead away, weighed down with His own cross,
Jesus to crucifixion. Faint with loss   John xix. 17
Of blood, and His long agony, He fell
Beneath the load. They, thereupon, compel   Luke xxiii. 26
One Simon, a Cyrenian, to bear
His cross behind Him, while close followed there   27
A crowd of people and of women, who
With wailings loud His painful steps pursue.
He, turning round, said to them tenderly :   28
" Ye daughters of Jerusalem weep not for Me.
Weep for yourselves, and for your children. Yea,
The time is coming in which they will say,   29
' Happy the barren wombs that never bore,
And breasts that ne'er gave suck ;' and will implore 30
The mountains to fall on them, and the hills

To cover them from unexampled ills.   Luke
                                                   xxiii. —

Your rulers are triumphant and elate,

That they have slain the object of their hate.

But to reject their promised Christ and King,

Then slay Him is a dark and dreadful thing.

The wickedness that did this sin contrive,   31

Is green and flourishing, and, while alive,

Will grow each year to more and more, until

The bound is reached and limit of God's will;

Then the tree 's dry and bending boughs shall rain

O'er the doomed land full recompense of pain."

By the same band to execution led   32

Two malefactors Him accompanied.

Come to the place called Golgotha, a Skull,   Mark
                                                   xv. 22

Outside the gate, they first, His pains to dull,

Gave Him to drink wine, drugged with myrrh*—

        but He   23

Preferred to bear th' unsoftened agony.

---

*As myrrh does not of itself possess any anodyne properties, it may have been used as a mere flavorer to disguise the taste of some other drug—possibly, *Mandragora* which is said to have been employed by the ancients as an anæsthetic in surgical operations—in the same way as Chloroform, and other like agents are now. Mandragora (Mandrake) is allied to Belladonna, botanically and medicinally, and is said to be even more powerfully narcotic. Its root, which is large, is divided into two or three forks, giving it some resemblance to the human body ; whence rose, probably, the superstition, that it was endowed with animal feelings ; and the fabulous stories of its

'T was the third hour when He was crucified, Mark
xv. 25

The two thieves with Him placed on either side, 27

Fulfilling Scripture, which had in the past 28

Foretold He with transgressors should be classed.

They pierced His hands and feet with cruel steel, Luke
xxiii. 34

That had been only used to bless and heal.

And Jesus said, as they the nails drove through,

"Father, forgive! They know not what they do."

Taking the outer garments Jesus wore, John
xix. 23

These the four soldiers parted into four;

But for one tunic, seamless and entire, 24

uttering shrieks when torn from the earth. Shakespeare, in several places, alludes to this plant. As when Banquo in *Macbeth*, says:

> "Or have we eaten of the insane root
> That takes the reason prisoner."

Again in *Anthony and Cleopatra*:

> "Give me to drink mandragora."

Also in *Othello:*

> "Not poppy, nor mandragora,
> Nor all the drowsy syrups of the world
> Shall ever medicine thee to that sweet sleep
> Which thou ow'dst yesterday."

In *Romeo and Juliet*, there is an allusion to it in another aspect:

> "And shrieks like mandrakes torn out of the earth
> That living mortals hearing them run mad."

It was potent in all kinds of enchantment, and is supposed to have been the same as the magical herb *Boaras*, said to cure demoniacs; and was procured at great risk by the death of the dog employed to pull it up. Josephus, B. J. vii. 6, § 3. That it might have been found curative in cases of Epilepsy, mistaken for demoniacal possession, is rendered probable by the fact, that Belladonna has been regarded by some as a specific in Epilepsy.

They all cast lots, as they did not desire   John
xix. —

To tear it.   Scripture thus was verified,

' My garments they among them did divide ;

They cast lots on My vesture.'   Pilate wrote   19

A title o'er His head, so all might note :

' THIS JESUS IS, KING OF THE JEWS '—displayed

In Hebrew, Greek, and Latin.   Murmuring, said   20

The chief priests then to Pilate : " Rather use   21

The words, He said I King am of the Jews,

Not that He is."   But Pilate answered, " No!   22

What I have written I have written.   Go ! "

The people stood beholding.   Passing by,   Matt.
xxvii. 39

Some rail and wag their heads, and, taunting, cry,   40

" Thou Who the Temple dost destroy, and dost,

In three days, it rebuild, make good thy boast !

Now save Thyself, and come down from the cross."

The rulers, likewise, stooped their gibes to toss :   41

" Let Christ, the King of Israel, descend !

He claimed He others saved, but, in the end,   42

He cannot save Himself.   God's will be done !   43

Let God deliver, if He will, His Son."

One of the malefactors blasphemed thus :   Luke
xxiii. 39

" If Thou be Christ, now save Thyself and us ! "

The other him rebuked: " Hast thou no fear   Luke xxiii. 40
Of God, before whom thou wilt soon appear,
Since thou in the same condemnation art?
We suffer justly, merited the smart,   41
The due reward of our misdeeds; but this,
The murdered Christ, has nothing done amiss."
He spake to Jesus: " Lord! remember me,   42
When in Thy Kingdom Thou enthroned shalt be.'
" Thou shalt to-day," He from the cross replies,   43
" Be verily with Me in Paradise."
His mother and His mother's sister stood   John xix. 25
With Mary Magdalene beside the wood
On which He hung.   When Jesus saw, therefore,   26
His mother desolate and weeping sore,
And, standing by, His loved disciple John,
He said unto her: " Woman! see thy son."
Then said to him: " Thy mother see!"   And they   27
Maintained that dear relation from that day.

'T was night at noonday.   Over all the land   Matt. xxvii. 45
Brooded a darkness, none could understand,
Hiding His person with a decorous shroud
From the coarse vision of the scoffing crowd.
The sun was darkened, but without eclipse,
A frown of Nature hushing impious lips—

21

A preternatural, Egyptian gloom,   Matt.
                                                    xxvii. —

Prophetic of the day of final doom.

After three hours, or the ninth hour about,   46

From Jesus' lips the anguished cry rang out:

" Eli! Eli! lama sabacthani!"

My God! Oh why hast thou forsaken Me?

Some said: " He for Elijah calls.   Let be,   47

Whether he 'll come to save Him we will see."

And Jesus spake again: "I thirst."   Straightway,   48

One wet a sponge with vinegar, and lay

It on His lips, which opening now to speak,

Cried: " It is finished!" followed by a shriek   John
                                                    xix. 30

As His heart broke,* and, through the fatal rent, Luke
                                                   xxiii. 46

The spirting life blood found unnatural vent.

---

* The opinion that the immediate physical cause of death in our Lord was Rupture
of the Heart, derives much support from the facts of the case so far as recorded. The
cry or shriek which immediately preceded His "giving up the ghost" may have been
due to a violent spasm of the organ, causing the rupture. The Heart is enclosed in a
shut sac, called the Pericardium, which is sometimes the seat of a dropsical effusion,
filling it up and distending it to that degree that the Heart has no room to act. In case
of Rupture of the Heart, the contraction which should drive the blood into the arteries,
forces it into the Pericardium, filling and distending it, and if the rent is large death
follows immediately. The retained blood undergoes the familiar change which everybody must have observed, when blood is drawn in a basin—*i. e.*, its separation into a
soft coagulum or clot which is red, and serum which is nearly colorless like water.
Should the containing sac be punctured under such circumstances, there would necessarily be an escape of gore and serum, popularly described as blood and water. It
is difficult to understand how blood and water in any considerable quantity should
have followed from a spear-thrust in any other way. The Heart itself after death is
found entirely empty, except in rare cases, when there is a clot, called heart-clot, regarded as abnormal. It is singular that the great painters make the mistake of pic-
turing the wound on the right side instead of the left.

Out of the lifting darkness, there was heard
His final, loud, and lamentable word:
" Reproach My heart has broken—now 's the end.
Father! My spirit I to Thee commend." Psalm
lxix 20

   At the dread moment He gave up the ghost,
A new amazement seized the heavenly host.
The great veil of the Temple, sacred screen, Matt.
xxvii. 51
From top to bottom rent by hands unseen,
Allowed th' excluded day beyond to shine,
To show a vacant and abandoned shrine.
And the earth trembled, and the rocks were rent,
Tombs opened, and from riven monument, 52
After His resurrection, saints, who slept,
Divinely quickened and raised up, forth stepped, 53
And went into the City, and appeared
To many. All the guard of soldiers feared 54
Exceedingly, with the centurion,
When they the earthquake saw, and wonders done.
" This was," they all instinctively cried out,
" A righteous man, the Son of God no doubt."
All His acquaintance, and the women who 55
Waited on Him, and other women too
From Galilee, far off with streaming eyes
Beheld these things, and filled the air with cries.

Wicked hands, how sad the story !
Crucified the Lord of Glory,
　Nailed Him to the accursèd tree :
In Thy side the spear did bury,
Son of God ! and Son of Mary !
　Murdered One of Calvary !

Was there ever known such malice ?
Gall of hatred in the chalice
　For Thy lips of love wrung out :
Priests, with scribes and elders, mocking,
As they pass, O sight most shocking !
　Wag their heads, revile and flout.

Was there, Thine own words to borrow,
Ever sorrow like Thy sorrow,
　When our sins were on Thee laid ?
Sorrow, which that cry could waken,
" Why, My God, am I forsaken ? "
　Never was since worlds were made.

Never, after such dear fashion,
Was there witnessed such compassion ;
　Publish ye, who know the grace !
Make commanded proclamation
Of the Gospel of Salvation,
　To each creature of the race !

For 't was the Preparation,* the next day   John xix. 31

Being the Paschal Sabbath, to let stay

The bodies on the cross beyond the hour

When holy time began, were trespass sour.

The Jews, therefore, prayed Pilate to direct

Their bones be broken, thereby to effect

Their speedy death, so they could be removed.

The soldiers broke the other two's, who proved   32

To be still living, but, when they perceived   33

Jesus was dead already, they believed

It needless in His case, His legs to break:

But with a spear a soldier (death to make   34

Most sure) the heart-sac pierced, with blood distent,

Filled from the bursting heart's own fatal rent.

And John, from the wide wound, saw forthwith pour

Water and blood, pale serum and red gore,   35

These Scriptures to fulfil, "Of Him a bone   36

Shall not be broken." "They shall look on One

Whom they have pierced."   37

           That eve, to Pilate came   Mark xv. 42

A man of Arimathéa, whose name   43

Was Joseph, rich, a good man and a just,

---

* Sabbath-eve, which was the latter half of the afternoon of Friday, was called the Preparation or *Parasceve*, that being the time set apart by the Jews to *prepare* for the Sabbath. Jesus was crucified at or between 9 a. m. and 12 m.; expired at 3 p. m.

One of the Sanhedrim, who, with disgust Mark xv. —

And open disapproval, had beheld

The furious prejudice which had impelled

His fellow-judges wickedly to lie,

And on false charges Jesus crucify.

Although convinced, by all he saw and knew,

His august claims authentic were and true,

He had not dared to openly avow

His faith and his discipleship; but now,

He, boldly, knowing well what shame he braved,

His body of the procurator craved.

Pilate, surprised He 'd died so soon, inquired 44

Of the centurion when He expired.

And, having learned, he gave the asked for leave. 45

Joseph the body hastened to receive ;

And found, awaiting him, most welcome aid John xix. 39

In Nicodemus (once like him afraid,

But now no longer), who brought ample store,

Aloes and myrrh a hundred pounds or more,

For his embalming—Joseph, with like thought, Mark xv. 46

Having supply of finest linen brought.

Now in the place, where He was crucified, John xix. 41

He had a garden ; in it on one side

There was a tomb, rock-hewn and newly-made,

In which, as yet, no man was ever laid.   John
xix. —

Lifting the lifeless form with tender care,   4²

They thither it most reverently bear.

And, having washed from all defiling stains

The mangled, bruised, thrice sacred, dear remains,

They take the spices and the linen bands,   4³

And swathe the body with soft loving hands,

Then place it in the tomb, and close the door

Of entrance with a stone they roll before.

The sun was setting when the task was done,

And as they left the Sabbath had begun.

Next day, chief priests and Pharisees combined

To say to Pilate, " We recall to mind,   Matt.
xxvii. 6²

That that deceiver said while yet alive.   6³

' After three days I will again revive.'

Command, therefore, the sepulchre be made   6⁴

Sure, till the third day, else, we are afraid,

That His disciples will Him steal away

During the night, and to the people say,

He's risen from the dead, so shall be worse,

By far, the final error, than the first."

And Pilate said : " Ye have a watch.   It make   6⁵

Sure as ye can—your own precautions take."

They set a watch, and not with this content,

They sealed the stone that closed the monument.

CHRIST CRUCIFIED.

Christ crucified! amazing theme!
  I see, beneath that mean disguise,
Th' undoubted peer of God Supreme!
  The awful Monarch of the Skies!

No malefactor He, whose gore
  Drips from the wood and dyes the sod:
Gashed, pierced, and bleeding, I adore
  The meek and patient Son of God.

O Friend Divine! I hear those groans
  The shuddering universe appall:
The pleading pity of those tones,
  Which on my head forgiveness call.

If I such matchless grace forget,
  This costly charity of heaven,
Then may I bear th' uncancelled debt,
  And die and never be forgiven.

VEXILLA REGIS PRODEUNT.— *Translation.*

I.

The Royal Ensign forth is flung,

    The blazon of the Cross unfurled,

On which incarnate Godhead hung,

    Flesh of our flesh, who made the world.

II.

Where from His wounded side, moreo'er,

    By thrust of cruel spear point keen

Flowed forthwith water mixed with gore,

    To wash from guilt and make us clean.

III.

That which the Psalmist David sung

    In faithful song, was thus made good ;

Saying, ' The Lord hath reigned among

    The subject nations from the wood.'*

IV.

Thrice beautiful, far-beaming Tree !

    Adorned with kingly purple, much

Hast thou been honored, thus to be

    Chosen His holy limbs to touch.

* In some Greek copies, and in the old Latin or Italic Version the tenth verse of the 96th Psalm is : " Tell it out among the heathen that the Lord reigneth from the Tree,"

V.

Blest thou, whose arms outstretched were made

The balance, on whose mystic beam

The ransom of the world was weighed,

Souls from perdition to redeem.

I.

Vexilla Regis prodeunt,
Fulget crucis mysterium,
Quo carne carnis conditor
Suspensus est patibulo :

II.

Quo vulneratus insuper
Mucrone diro lanceæ,
Ut nos lavaret crimine
Manavit unda et sanguine.

III.

Impleta sunt quæ concinit
David fideli carmine,
Dicens, In nationibus
Regnavit a ligno Deus :

IV.

Arbora decora et fulgida,
Ornata Regis purpura,
Electa digno stipite
Tam sancta membra tangere.

V.

Beata cujus brachiis
Pretium perpendit sæculi,
Statera facta corporis,
Tulitque praedam tartaris.

Although the words, "from the tree' had evidently been added, much stress was laid on them by Justin Martyr, Augustine and others, as containing a prophetic intimation of the manner of Christ's death.—TRENCH.

This world-famous Processional Hymn, which Daniel calls "one of the grandest in the treasury of the Latin church," was composed by *Fortunatus*—who lived in the sixth century.

XXIV.

RESURRECTION AND ASCENSION.

MATT. XXVIII. 2-20 ; MARK XVI. 1-20 ; LUKE XXIV. 1-53 ; JOHN XX. 1—XXI. 25.

THE Sabbath o'er, at early dawn was seen,   , Mark
    In the dim twilight, Mary Magdalene,   xvi. 1
And Mary who the mother was of James,
And at her side Salóme—sainted names—
Wending their way unto the Sepulchre,
Sweet spices bringing each along with her,
That the embalming which had been begun
They might complete.   They all supposed the Sun
Had not yet risen, for the East was gray,
Streaked with faint tokens of the breaking day.
They thought it early ; little did they know,
Their Sun was up an hour or more ago,
And, with His rising light, had chased the gloom,
And all the doubt and terror of the tomb.
They, at the time, had heard a rumbling sound, Matt.
                                xxviii. 2
And thought it was an earthquake.   Had they known,
That mighty hands then rolled away the stone,

From the tomb's mouth, they'd had no need to ask
Who should perform for them the friendly task: ^{Mark xvi. 3}
For, lo, an angel had come down from heaven, ^{Matt. xxviii. 3}
And ingress to an empty tomb had given.
His face like lightning was; his raiment white,
Blinding and terrible to mortal sight.
For fear of him the keepers shook, and then,   4
Swooning away, became like to dead men.

Now Mary Magdalene, with quickened pace,   ^{John xx. 1}
Reached sooner than the rest th' appointed place.
And, having seen the stone was rolled away,
She waited not, but ran, without delay,   2
To John and Peter with the heavy word:
" They have removed, we know not where, the Lord."
Peter and John both run, but John outrun,   3, 4
And reached the tomb before the other one,   5
And, stooping down, the linen clothes he saw,
But went not in, restrained by sense of awe.
Then Peter came, and, ent'ring, saw inside,   6
The linen clothes, and napkin that was tied   7
About His head—each folded up with care,
And lying separate.   Then entered there   8
John too, who having seen, in part believed—

For they, as yet, had not the sense perceived   John
                                                        xx. 9
Of what the Scriptures, and Himself had said,

Touching His resurrection from the dead.

They went away, but Mary still remained.

Meanwhile,* it chanced, the other women gained

The Sepulchre soon after she had gone ;   Luke
                                                        xxiv. 2
And saw, to their surprise, the ponderous stone,

That closed the entrance, had been rolled away.

And, entering in, they found to their dismay   3

The body gone.   Perplexed in the extreme,   4

They suddenly beheld, as in a dream,

Two men stand by them in apparel bright,

Whose dazzling presence filled them with affright.

" Be not afraid ! " one said, " Ye need not fear.   Mark
                                                        xvi. 6
I know ye Jesus seek ; He is not here ;

He is already risen, as He said.

Why do ye seek the living 'mong the dead ?   Luke
                                                        xxiv. 5
Come see the place, most fragrant still and sweet,

Where lay His blessed head and where His feet.

Remember how He said to you, when He   6

Was present with you yet in Galilee :

*It is here assumed, that when the other women reached the tomb Mary Magdalene
had already gone to tell Peter and John ; and what is related as happening to them
took place during her absence. When Mary returned with Peter and John, the other
women had left.

' The Son of Man, delivered to be tried,   Luke
                                                  xxiv. 7

After mock trial must be crucified,

And then on the third day must rise again.'

Yes! they remembered, and now all was plain.   8

" Haste! " said the angel, " knowing it is true,   Mark
                                                   xvi. 7

Tell His disciples, and tell Peter too—

Unable since his fall to lift his head—

Your buried Lord is risen from the dead,

And goes before you into Galilee.

There, He has promised you, ye Him shall see."

And they departed quickly, filled with awe   Matt.
                                                  xxviii. 8

And trembling joy at all they heard and saw,

To go to the disciples.   While they yet

Were on the way, behold, them Jesus met,   · 9

And said: "All hail!"   Thrilled with that voice so
          sweet,

They prostrate fell, and held Him by His feet,

And worshipped Him—but they embrace refrained,

By mighty awe and reverence restrained.

He said : "Go, tell My brethren to repair   10

To Galilee, and I will see them there.

They went, and told th' apostles and the rest,   Luke
                                                   xxiv. 9

Who disbelief of their report expressed.   11

But, Mary Magdalene, when all had left,   John
                                                  xx. 11

Lingered behind.   Of her dear Lord bereft,

His body taken, she would not despair,

But push inquiry till she found out where.

Outside the Sepulchre she weeping stood,

And, as she wept, the thought sprung up, she would

Look in once more, and, lo! there met her sight

Two Angels seated, robed in dazzling white   12

One at the head, the other at the feet,

Where had the body lain.   With accents sweet,   13

"Woman!" they said to her, "why weepest thou?"

" Because they have, I know not where or how,

Removed my Lord."   Her head, then turning, she   14

Saw Jesus standing, but knew not 't was He.

And Jesus said : "Woman ! why dost thou weep?   15

Whom seekest thou?"   This man, employed to keep

The garden, so she thought, can end suspense,

So said : " O Sir, if thou hast borne Him hence,

Tell me where thou hast laid Him, and I will

Take Him away."   There shot a mighty thrill   16

Of wild delight and wonder through her frame,

Then when His well-known voice pronounced her
          name :

" Mary!"   She turned, and with a joyful shout

Towards Him sprang with both her arms stretched

    out,   John
xx. —

Saying: "Rabboni!" and would on His neck

Have fallen, had He, her first transports to check,

Not said: "Embrace Me not!* draw not too near. 17

Temper thy love with reverence and fear!

Worship befits thee! but the awful bond,

---

* The difficulties which beset this passage have grown, we venture to think, out of an error of punctuation, and are mostly or wholly disposed of, by simply placing a full stop after "Touch Me not." By this means the words are made to form a sentence which is complete in itself, having neither syntactical nor logical connection with anything that follows. Mary was in the act of throwing her arms around her Lord's neck. It was the fault, let us say rather the ecstasy of the moment, and she did not need to be told twice the impropriety of the freedom. Nothing seems more incredible, than that our Lord would think it necessary to offer an excuse for not permitting an embrace whose impropriety was obvious—giving as a reason, that "He had not yet ascended to His Father." This would constitute an excellent reason why she should hasten to His disciples, having in her possession a piece of information so unspeakably interesting and important; but none, so far as we can see, why she should not touch Him. Within the space of a few minutes, either immediately before or immediately after, we know that He allowed other women, not only to touch Him, but hold Him by His feet. Theirs was an act of worship. He, on that occasion, gave no signs of hurry, or impatience at detention. Indeed, we should as soon think of associating hurry with the eternities as with the Risen Lord.

Most strangely, the disciples, notwithstanding declarations the most explicit many times repeated, that He would rise again, remained in total ignorance of "what the rising from the dead should mean." That it meant that His body was to rise and come from the tomb, they had not so much as dreamed. They supposed His words were to be understood in some mystic sense, they did not know exactly what. When they saw His body taken down from the cross and laid in the sepulchre, they had no other thought than that was the end, so far as His life upon the earth was concerned. Believing that He had ascended at once to the Father, they never expected to see Him again below. It was now the third day since His death; and to be told that He was alive, and still upon the earth—that He had not ascended to the Father yet—would be news indeed. But lest they should go to the other extreme, and fall into the error of supposing that He intended to remain on the earth to set up His Kingdom in person,

Forbids familiar touch, and acts too fond.

For that I would My rising certify,

By proofs infallible and many, I

Have not ascended to My Father yet.

Go, therefore, to My brethren, now, to set

Their troubled minds at rest.   Tell them I say

I live again, but am not here to stay.

He instructed Mary to say to them, that He was about to ascend, but would see them before He did so finally, even as He had promised. Read in the light of these facts— with the corrected punctuation, which serves to isolate the words, "Touch Me Not" from everything else, as relating to an incident having nothing to do with the communication which she was to make to the disciples—all is plain and simple. In that case the message would run in this wise: "For [or forasmuch as] I am not yet ascended unto My Father, go [now] to My brethren, and say unto them, I ascend [after forty days?] unto My Father and your Father; and to My God and your God." Or some might prefer this reading, which involves no change of words, only the transposition of the last member of the sentence, putting it first: "But go to My brethren, and say unto them, I ascend unto My Father and unto your Father, and to My God and your God ; for I am not yet ascended [bodily?] to My Father.' This preserves the "but," which in the other case is rendered "now."

As it can hardly be claimed that the punctuation is inspired, this slight change— which makes easy what has been found so difficult and has led to ten thousand absurdities of interpretation—is, we think, abundantly justified. The error (if error it be, and we cannot doubt it) is undoubtedly an ancient one ; and one naturally wonders how it has happened, that so many learned and good men have allowed themselves to stumble over so small a pebble.

His actual stay upon the earth was forty days. Where He was during that time it were vain to speculate. He could not fail to be at home anywhere in the universe ; for were not all things made by Him? One of the objects of this sojourn (there may have been others) was to "shew Himself alive after His passion," and certify to His disciples the fact of His bodily resurrection, "by many infallible proofs." In order that nothing might be wanting to the completeness of the identification, He preserved to Himself the organic sameness of His original body—modified possibly in some of its accidents, but essentially unchanged—until the time of His Ascension. It may be that this "body of His humiliation," as the apostle calls it, while it was the only one suited to earthly conditions, was at the same time wholly unfitted for heavenly ; and this would constitute a reason why He should not assume "the body of His glory"

22

I, to My Father and to yours, ascend,

My God and your God, when My stay shall end.

And tell them to return to Galilee,

And that I there, hereafter, will them see."

To the disciples she the news conveyed,

How she had seen the Lord, and what He said.

The guard, into the City having gone,   Matt.
                                               xxviii. 11

Showed to the chief priests all things that were done.

At the strange tidings, startled and appalled,   12

They straight the Sanhedrim together called,

Which, after counsel, judged it best to pay

The soldiers a large sum, if they would say,

That His disciples in the night had crept   13

And stole away the body while they slept—

Pledging to shield them, to allay their fears,

until the forty days were fully expired. It was important to the proof, that no one should be able to say that His appearance were phantasmal, or even like the Theophanies and Angelophanies recorded in the Old Testament.

A little common sense is sometimes better than much learning. It is quite marvelous, how the human mind runs on in the same ever deepening rut of error through thousands of years, without putting forth an effort to get out of it. We see this illustrated in false religions; and, in a small way, we witness something like it in mistakes of interpretation. No error however slight is insignificant. A misplaced period may be the source of endless perplexity to innumerable minds. The casual omission of brackets which ought to have been inserted has been the cause not only of incalculable ink-shedding, but blood-shedding likewise. The tenth chapter of Joshua has been fruitful of endless logomachies which have not ceased in our day, arising from the failure of some ancient transcriber to preserve lines and marks of division, separating poetry from prose. See The Evangel, First Part of this Work pp. 324-332, foot-note.

In case it reached the procurator's ears.
Taking the bribe, they labored to diffuse
This false report, still current 'mong the Jews.

And Jesus next Himself to Peter showed.
That day, as two disciples on the road
To Emmaus were journeying, they talked
Of these occurences, and as they walked,
Discussing matters, He Himself drew near,
And traveled with them their discourse to hear—
Appearing, for a purpose, in such guise
As they, at first, should not Him recognize.
He said: "What mournful subject have ye had,
To make you as you walk downcast and sad?"
"Great things have happened in Jerusalem,"
They answered. "If Thou hast not heard of them
Thou art the sole sojourner that has not."
And Jesus said: "What things? Tell briefly what."
"About Jesus of Nazareth (in fact
A Prophet, powerful in word and act
Before the Lord, and all the people). Him,
Chief priests and others of the Sanhedrim
Condemned to death and crucified. But we
Trusted 't was He who would set Israel free.

Marginal references:
- Matt. xxviii. 14
- 15
- 1 Cor. xv. 5
- Luke xxiv. 13
- 14
- 15
- 16
- 17
- 18
- 19
- 20
- 21

Besides all this, this being the third day Luke xxiv. —
Since these things happened, certain women say, 22
That, going early to the Sepulchre,
They did not find the body ; and aver 23
They Angels saw, who said He was alive.
From their own eyes assurance to derive, 24
Some of our number went, and witness bare
The tomb was empty, but Him saw nowhere."

He said, in tones tinged with reproof and grief, 25
" O dull of mind, and backward of belief
Concerning what the prophets testify !
Ought not the Christ to suffer and to die 26
And pass into His glory through that door,
Death and the Grave, unbarred forevermore?"
Beginning then with Moses, he went on, 27
Until through all the prophets He had gone,
And all the Scriptures opened and explained,
Which to Himself and Kingdom appertained.
When to the destined village they drew nigh, 28
It seemed as though He purposed to pass by,
But they pressed Him to stop, saying, " Abide 29
With us, for it grows late." And He complied.
As He there lay at meat with them, He took 30

The loaf, blessed, brake, and gave it them. They look,

They scan His features now with opened eyes, Luke xxiv. 31

And all at once their Lord they recognize.

He disappeared next moment, and they said :

" In that last act, the breaking of the bread,

How could we fail the Master to discern ?

Did not our hearts, moreo'er, within us burn 32

While He talked with us all along the road,

And the deep meaning of the Scriptures showed?"

And they rose up that very hour and went 33

Back to Jerusalem, with the intent

To tell th' Eleven. These, with the rest, they found

Assembled, who them greeted with the sound :

" The Lord is risen indeed, and has been seen 34

Of Simon." Then they told, how He had been 35

With them, and how they suddenly were led

To know Him in the breaking of the bread.

While they were speaking, Jesus Himself stood, 36

Though shut and barred the solid doors of wood,

There in their midst, and said : " Peace be to you!"

The sight them into consternation threw, 37

Thinking they saw a spirit. " Why," He said, 38

" Do doubts arise ? or why are ye afraid ?

See My pierced hands and feet, and know 't is I. Luke xxiv. 39
Draw near; My body handle; test and try, 40
Till its identity each doubter owns,
Knowing a spirit has not flesh and bones."
When they, for joy and wonder, scarce could be 41
Convinced, He was a dear reality,
He said for proof: "Have ye not here some meat?"
And He before them some broiled fish did eat. 42
Then further spake: "Remember I you told, 44
While I was yet with you, that, what of old
Was in the Law and Prophets said of Me 45
And written in the Psalms, fulfilled must be,
That, in accordance with all prophecies,
Christ it behooved to suffer, and to rise, 46
And that repentance, holy change within, 47
And the remission of all forms of sin,
Should, in His name, be confidently preached
Among all nations, till each soul is reached,
Beginning at Jerusalem. Since ye 48
Are of these things the witnesses to be, 48
The Spirit, promised of the Father, I 49
Will pour on you, when I ascend on high.
And He with power will plenteously endue
Authenticating and attesting you—

Great signs shall follow them, who having heard,

Believe the proclamation in the Word.

Go ye, My Gospel preach! go everywhere !   Mark

To every creature the glad tidings bear !   xvi. 15

Who trusts and is baptized, he saved shall be :   16

Who trusts not, cannot My salvation see.

These are the terms on which, by Heaven ordained,

Men's sins remitted are, or are retained."   John
xx. 23

Thomas, one of the Twelve, called Didymus   24

Not there to see, remained incredulous,

When told by others, " We have seen the Lord!"   25

" I 'll not believe He is to life restored,"

He said, "unless I in His hands shall see -

Plainly the nail-prints, and 't is granted me

To put therein my finger, and to guide

My hand and thrust it in His wounded side."

When the disciples, after eight days' space,   26

Again were met together in one place,

And Thomas with them, Jesus came, and stood

There in their midst (shut doors could not exclude),

And said, " Peace be to you !"   Then, Thomas told : 27

" Reach hither now thy finger, and behold

My wounded hands; and hither also guide

Thy hand, and thrust it in My wounded side;   John
xx. —
And be not faithless, but believing."   He
Exclaimed, " My Lord! my God! I worship Thee: [28]
Great Vanquisher of Death! I doubt no more,
Thou art the Christ the ages waited for!"
" Because thou hast Me seen, thou dost not doubt. [29]
Happy who see not, yet believe without!"

O FILII ET FILIÆ.—*Translation.*

I.

O sons and daughters, join the lay!
The King, all heavenly powers obey,
Rose Victor from the dead to-day,
            Alleluia!

II.

Upon the first day of the week,
As dawn began the east to streak,
Disciples went the tomb to seek.
            Alleluia!

III.

Salóme, Mary Magdalene,
And James's mother—sad in mien—
Come to embalm Him, there were seen.
            Alleluia!

IV.

One clothed in white sat at the door,
Who said : " The Lord is here no more
To Galilee He goes before."
Alleluia !

V.

Th' Apostle John, with love as spur,
His feet, outrunning Peter's, were
First at the empty sepulchre.
Alleluia !

VI.

When the Disciples met, appeared
Christ in their midst, and when they feared,
Pronouncing "Peace !" their hearts He cheered.
Alleluia !

VII.

As Didymus, not there to see,
Was told that Christ had risen, he
Doubted and thought it could not be.
Alleluia !

VIII.

" Thomas, behold," the Master cried,
" My hands, my feet, my wounded side,
And be not faithless, but confide !"
Alleluia !

IX.

When Thomas did as Christ him bade,

His finger in the nail-prints laid,

"Thou art my Lord and God," he said.

Alleluia!

X.

Blessed are they who have not seen

Yet on His word securely lean—

They shall have endless life serene.

Alleluia!

I.

O filii et filiæ,
Rex cœlestis, Rex gloriæ,
Morte surrexit hodie,
Alleluia !

II.

Et mane prima Sabbati,
Ad ostium monumenti
Accesserunt discipuli.
Alleluia !

III.

Et Maria Magdalene
Et Jacobi, et Salome
Venerunt corpus ungere,
Alleluia !

IV.

In albis sedens angelus
Praedixit mulieribus,
In Galilea est Dominus.
Alleluia !

V.

Et Joannes apostolus
Concurrit Petro citius,
Monumento venit prius.
Alleluia !

VI.

Discipulis astantibus,
In medio stetit Christus
Dicens, Pax vobis omnibus,
Alleluia !

VII.

Ut intellexit Didymus,
Quia surrexerat Jesus,
Remansit fere dubius.
Alleluia !

VIII.

Vide, Thoma, vide latus,
Vide pedes, vide manus,
Noli esse incredulus.
Alleluia !

IX.

Quando Thomas vidit Christum,
Pedes, manus, latus suum,
Dixit : Tu es Deus meus ·
Alleluia !

X.

Beati qui non viderunt,
Et firmiter crediderunt,
Vitam eternam habebunt.
Alleluia.

SURREXIT CHRISTUS HODIE.— *Translation.*

I.

For human solace, Christ to-day
Rose from the dead to live alway,
    Alleluia.

II.

Who suffered death, with anguish sore,
For wretched man two days before,
    Alleluia.

III.

Women, His body to perfume,
Brought gifts of spices to the tomb.
    Alleluia.

IV.

Seeking the Lord, with sorrowing mind,
Who is the Saviour of mankind.
    Alleluia.

V.

They saw a white-robed angel there,
Who did the joyful news declare,
    Alleluia.

VI.

" Would you, O trembling women! see
The Master, go to Galilee.
Alleluia.

VII.

" To His disciples tell this thing,
That He is risen, Glory's King.'
Alleluia.

VIII.

He first appeared to Peter, then
To all of the remaining ten.
Alleluia.

IX.

Thee in this paschal joy we bless,
Who art the Lord our righteousness.
Alleluia.

X.

Glory to Thee our Sovereign Head,
Who rose triumphant from the dead.
Alleluia.

I.
Surrexit Christus hodie
Humano pro solamine,
Alleluia.

II.
Mortem qui passus pridie.
Miserrimo pro homine,
Alleluia.

III.
Mulieres ad tumulum
Dona ferunt aromatum,
Alleluia.
IV.
Quærentes Jesum Dominum,
Qui est Salvator hominum,
Alleluia.
V.
Album cernentes angelum
Annunciatum gaudium,
Alleluia.
VI.
Mulieres O tremulæ,
In Galilæam pergite,
Alleluia.

VII.
Discipulis hoc dicite,
Quod surrexit Rex gloriæ,
Alleluia.
VIII.
Petro dehinc et cæteris
Apparuit apostolis,
Alleluia.
IX.
In hoc paschali gaudio,
Benedicamus Domino,
Alleluia.
X.
Gloria tibi, Domine,
Qui surrexisti a morte,
Alleluia.

This and the foregoing Hymn, of unknown authorship, belong to the thirteenth century. The first is preëminently the Easter Hymn. Neale remarks: " It is scarcely possible for any one, not acquainted with the melody, to imagine the jubilant effect of the triumphant *Alleluia* attached to the apparently less important circumstances of the resurrection, *e. g.*, Peter's being outstripped by John. It seems to speak of the majesty of that event, the smallest portions of which are worthy to be so chronicled." The rude simplicity of the originals is preserved in the translation.

REX SEMPITERNE CŒLITUM.—*Translation.*

I.

Eternal Sovereign of the skies!

Maker of all things that are made!

Thou wast the Father's equal Son

Ere were the world's foundations laid.

II.

Thou didst, in Thine own image, make,

After Thy likeness, man at first

And to His body, formed of clay

Conjoined a noble spirit erst.

III.

And, when Satanic fraud and spite
Corrupted had the human race,
Thou, clothed with flesh, didst mould anew
The perished beauty and the grace.

IV.

Thou, who wast once from Virgin born,
Art born now from the grave likewise ;
And Thou commandest that with Thee
We buried from the dead shall rise.

V.

Nailed to the cross, Redeemer, Thou
To pay our debt didst freely pour
Thy life-blood out, the price immense,
Of our salvation evermore.

I.
Rex sempiterne cœlitum,
Rerum Creator omnium,
Æqualis ante sæcula
Semper parenti filius.

II.
Nascente mundi qui faber
Imaginem vultus tui,
Tradens Adamo nobilem,
Limo jugasti spiritum.

III.
Cum livor et fraus dæmonis,
Fœdasset humanum genus,
Tu carne amictus perditam
Formam reformes artifex.

IV.
Qui natus olim et virgine,
Nunc e sepulcro nasceris,
Tecumque nos a mortuis,
Jubes sepultos surgere.

V.
Nobis diu qui debitæ,
Redemptor affixus cruci,
Nostra dedisti prodigus,
Pretium salutis sanguinem.

Then the Eleven returned to Galilee,   Matt.
                                                        xxviii. 19
Not doubting they should there again Him see,
According to His promise.   On this wise,   John
                                                        xxi. 1
He showed Himself to their adoring eyes
Peter and Thomas and Nathanaël,   2
With James and John, and other two, as well,
Were fishing on the Lake, and had all night   3
Caught nothing.   Jesus stood at morning light   4
Upon the shore, but they knew not 't was He.
"Children, how fare ye? aught to eat have ye?"   5
They answered, "No!"   "Cast on the boat's right
         side   6
The net, and ye shall find."   When they complied,
The number of the fishes was so great
They could not draw it, baffled by the weight.
And John to Peter said: "It is the Lord!"   7
And he, forgetting all else at that word,
First girding on, with haste, his outer coat,
Leaped in the sea.   The rest came in the boat,   8
Dragging the net, some hundred yards, to shore,
Filled with thrice fifty fishes and three more—   11
And though so many yet was it entire.
When they were come to land, they saw a fire   9
Of coals; a fish there lying; and some bread.

"Bring ye the fishes ye have caught," He said. John xxi. 10

The broiling done, and everything prepared,

He said: "Come, break your fast!" But no one dared   12

To ask their Entertainer, 'Who art Thou?'

Knowing it was the Lord. He gave them now   13

The bread and fish—His Providence *seen* then,

At other times *invisible* to men.

When they had breakfasted, the Risen One   15

To Simon Peter spake: "Say, Simon, son

Of Jonas, dost thou care* for me above

All these?" "Yea, Lord, Thou knowest I Thee love."

Jesus said: "Feed My lambs!" "But, Simon, dost   16

Thou care much for Me?" " I no more dare boast

Like the vain braggart of some days ago

But that, Dear Lord, I love Thee Thou dost know."

Jesus said: "Tend My sheep!" A third time He   17

Asked: " Simon, son of Jonas, lov'st thou Me?"

---

* An imperfect attempt is here made to preserve the distinction between two Greek words, αγαπαω and φιλεω, lost in our English version, both being indifferently translated ' to love.' The first answers to the Latin *diligo*, ' to esteem highly '; the other to *amo*, ' to love.' The sentiment expressed in the last is thought to be warmer, partaking more of passion than the first. It is remarkable that our Lord in addressing Peter, the first two times, used the colder term ; and it was only in His third inquiry that he employed the more endearing form. So there are two Greek words, one meaning " to feed " properly ; the other expressing " care and tendance," but rendered into English by a common word, " to feed."

Peter was grieved because He three times said,   John xxi. —
"Lovest thou Me,"—and so appeal he made :
" Thou knowest all things, and Thou, Lord, dost know
Despite my base denial, it is so,
That my love for Thee is sincere and deep.'
And Jesus said : " To prove it, Feed My sheep !

" Is the wound tender?   Make I thee to wince,
Probing thy hurt?   Thus I My love evince—
'T is for thy good I cause thee present pain,
Lest slightly healed, the sore break out again.
The lesson of thy fall must not be lost,
Purchased by thee at such a dreadful cost—
Sad warning 'gainst self-confidence and pride :
Clothed with humility, thou shalt abide
Firm to the end.   I speak a faithful word :
When thou wast young, thou didst thy own self
        gird,   18
And, wheresoe'er thou wouldst, thou wentest—free
To come and go—but when thou old shalt be,
Thou shalt stretch forth involuntary hands,
And thee another gird, and bind with bands,
And make thee tread the path thy Master trod,
By crucifixion glorifying God."   19

23

Having thus spoken, He said, "Follow* Me,   John
                                               xxi. —

As now I walk before, My footprints see,

And plant thy feet where My own feet have been.

Hereby thy duty's symbolized and seen:

I leave thee My example: Follow on!

When Peter, turning, saw th' apostle John   20

Walking behind, in the same footmarks, too,

He, curious, said: "Lord! what shall this man do?"21

He said; "If I so will, what's that to thee,   22

That he should wait My coming?   Follow Me!"

Among the brethren a belief thereby

Grew up, that that disciple should not die.   23

After this, Jesus by appointment, showed   Matt.
                                             xxviii. 16

Himself alive, in a more public mode,

Upon a Mount He named in Galilee.

Beside th' Eleven, there present were to see

Above five hundred brethren.   When they knew   1 Cor.
                                                xv. 6

---

*Some commentators suppose, that Jesus intended only a *spiritual* following, but that, just then, being in the act of leaving them, Peter understood Him *literally* (thinking he was invited to a private conference), and followed Him accordingly. We, on the contrary, assume, that He meant to symbolize by significant bodily acts the duty of an *exact* imitation of his example in life and death. That Peter never forgot the lesson appears from 1 Peter ii. 21.

All the Apostles prior to Christ's death had been comparatively ignorant and weak. Never, probably, in the history of mankind, was there wrought so mighty a transformation as took place in them afterwards, more particularly after they had received the promised gift of the Holy Ghost. They were no longer the same men, either intellectually or morally. But, even then, how unlike their Master?

Their Risen Saviour, standing in full view,   Matt.
                                                xxviii. 17
They worshipped Him,   He said: "To Me is given
Supreme authority in earth and heaven.   18
Go ye, therefore, convert and christianize   19
All nations of the earth, and them baptize
Into the Godhead of the Father, Son,
And Holy Ghost, th' Eternal Three in One!
Teaching them to observe, and all things do   20
Which, heretofore, I have commanded you.
And, lo! I'm with you alway—still your Friend,
Helper, Upholder, even to the end."

He next was seen of James, then all th' Eleven,   1 Cor.
                                                   xv. 7
By proofs infallible and many given,   Acts
                                         I. 3
Showing Himself alive to their rapt gaze
After His Passion, during forty days,
And speaking of the things that appertain
To God's dear Kingdom and Messiah's Reign.

The day of Pentecost at hand, with them
Once more assembled at Jerusalem,
He charged them there to wait, and not to leave
Till they the Father's "Promise" should receive—
The mighty baptism of the Holy Ghost—
To be poured out in a few days at most.

Again convened, they asked Him: "Lord, wilt
Thou   Acts
                                            i. 6
Restore to Israel the kingdom now?"
He said : "Ye seek to know what is concealed,   7
The times and seasons are things unrevealed,
The Father these has put in His own power—
Divine fulfillments wait their proper hour.
But ye'll new powers receive, and functions new :   8
For when the Holy Ghost is come on you,
Ye then shall be My witnesses to them
Who were My murderers in Jerusalem,
And testify of Me in every place—
The willing Saviour of the human race."

He led them forth then, after these commands,   Luke
                                                 xxiv. 50
To Bethany; and lifting up His hands   51
He blessed them ; and, with wondering dazed eyes,
Through the still air they saw His body rise—
Not needing wings—till in th' ethereal height
A waiting cloud received Him out of sight.
He, passing through the portals of the sky,
Sat down at the right hand of God on high.

PORTAS VESTRAS ÆTERNALES.—*Translation.*

I.

Lift ye up the eternal portals,
O ye high and blest immortals!
  Heavenly doors wide open swing.
Comes the Lord of Angels straightway,
Nears the everlasting gateway,
  Lift ye up, admit your King!

II.

Joyful He, all white and ruddy,
Lo, He comes from conquest bloody,
  Bright in vestments purple dyed,
Glorious in His raiment holy,
Marching in His own strength solely,
  Many thousands by His side.

III.

All alone and unattended,
Forth from Heaven His way He wended;
  But returning, many brings—
Fruit of His divine affection,
Of His death and resurrection,
  Crop of heavenly harvestings.

IV.

Joy ye in the God of Zion!

Conquered hath His foes, the Lion,

 Seed of Abraham, triumphed hath.

Ruins earth no more shall cumber,

Heaven shall be increased in number,

 Guilty souls be saved from wrath.

V.

May He reign, the Vindicator,

Christ of men, the Liberator,

 King of Mercy, Prince of Peace,

God Most Mighty, Life-bestower,

And of death the Overthrower,

 May His praises never cease!

I.

Portas vestras æternales
Triumphales, principales,
Angeli, attollite,
Eja, tollite actutum,
Venit Dominus virtutum,
Rex æternæ gloriæ.

II.

Venit totus lætabundus,
Candidus et rubicundus,
Tinctis clarus vestibus.
Nova gloriosus stolâ
Gradiens virtute sola
Multis cinctus millibus.

III.

Solus erat in egressu
Sed ingentem regressu
Affert multitudinem.
Fructum suae passionis
Testum resurrectionis
Novam cœli segetem.

IV.

Eja, jubilate Deo,
Jacent hostes, vicit leo
Vicit semen Abrahæ.
Jam ruinæ replebuntur
Cœli civis augebuntur
Salvabuntur animæ.

V.

Regnet Christus triumphator
Hominumque liberator
Rex misericordiæ.
Princeps pacis, Deus fortis.
Vitæ dator, victor mortis,
Laus cœlestis curiæ.

ACTS II 1-38.

The day of Pentecost now fully come—   Acts ii. 1
End of the numbered weeks completed sum,
Ten days from the Ascension of our Lord—
As the disciples were with one accord
(Six score about) assembled in one place,   i. 15
Waiting in prayer before the Throne of Grace,
All suddenly a sound from Heaven there came,   ii. 2
Like a strong rushing wind, and tongues of flame   3
Divided sat on each, while everywhere
Was interfused in air a God-breathed air,   4
Filling the house, and filling all the lungs—
And they began to speak in foreign tongues.

Men from all lands astonished gathered round,   5
Attracted by the miracle of sound—
Strange pulsings of that inner atmosphere
With modulations varied to each ear,
So that each spoken word was understood
By all that polyglottous multitude.
" What meaneth this?" they said—" we hear them
          teach   7
God's wondrous doings in our native speech."   8
But others said, jocosely : " We mistrust   13

These men have drunk too freely of sweet must." *

But Peter, standing up with the Eleven,   Acts
ii. 14

With loud voice spake beneath the open heaven:

" Men of Judea ! and, all ye who dwell

Here in Jerusalem ! hearken, while I tell,

These are not drunk, as ye assume and say,   '5

Since it is but the third hour of the day.

But this is what the prophet Joel meant—   16

Being fulfillment and accomplishment

---

* The word here rendered "new wine" is in the original Greek, γλευκους = *gleu-kous*. The meaning assigned to it in the Greek Lexicon is *must*. It is so rendered in the Vulgate. These Pentecostal mockers evidently used it in that sense. To understand them otherwise were to miss the point of their sarcasm. They thought it was severely funny to ascribe (ironically, of course) impossible effects to simple grape juice. Could we have overheard their talk among themselves, it would probably have been much after this fashion: "These men are drunk; but being good men, it is not permitted us to think, that they would drink anything stronger than water, or must, at most; and so, if found intoxicated, it cannot be due to any fault of theirs, but has resulted from some unaccountable perversity in the operation of an innocent beverage"—the jibe, having its counterpart in modern slang, which imputes to excess of sweet cider, or soda water, antiphrastically, great intoxicating powers.

This would pass with them for wit, and raise a laugh, which would be sure to have been renewed, culminating in loud explosions of laughter, had any one present, with a grave face and an aspect of profound wisdom, denied the possibility of water or must making any one drunk, and had insisted, therefore, that it must have been some fermented article. They little thought, that two thousand years afterwards, learned men, through failure to appreciate their sorry joke, would feel it incumbent on them to show that "gleukos" was a *very intoxicating liquor*, causing a *peculiar kind of drunkenness*, distinguishable from every other—for unless distinguishable, how should they know that it was *gleukos* that made them drunk rather than something else. This however is only one of many illustrations of the truth of what Shakespeare says:

> " A jest's prosperity lies in the ear
> Of him that hears it, never in the tongue
> Of him that makes it."

Of the sure word of ancient prophecy,   Acts ii. —

Concerning what in the Last Days should be :   17

" I will," God said, " My Spirit pour out, then,

Upon the daughters and the sons of men,   18

And they shall prophecy—and one and all

Shall then be saved, who on the Lord shall call.   21

Ye men of Israel, to me give ear !

Jesus of Nazareth—by proofs most clear,

By miracles and signs and wonders shown,

Among you wrought, and, therefore, to you known

To be the power of God—Him up being given,   23

By the foreknowledge and the will of Heaven,

Ye wickedly did crucify and slay ;

Whom God raised from the dead on the third day—24

Loosing the bands inviolate of old—

For 't was not possible Him death should hold.

For David in His name speaks in one place :   25

' I aye the Lord beheld before My face ;

For He 's on My right hand ; My heart, therefore,

Was glad ; My tongue rejoiced. My flesh, moreo'er,26

Shall also dwell in hope, because, that Thou   27

Wilt not My soul in Hades leave, nor wilt allow

Thy Holy One to see corruption?   Let   29

Me say, that David died, and we have yet Acts
ii. —

His tomb with us.   Being a prophet, he, 30

Knowing that God hath sworn, that there should be

One from his loins to sit upon his throne,

In dignity surpassing far his own,

Spake with a foresight that the end sufficed,

Touching the resurrection of the Christ— 31

His soul was not in Hades left, nor did

His flesh corruption see, as thing forbid.

This Jesus, God raised up, whereof we are 32

All witnesses.   Being exalted, far 33

Above the highest heaven, to God's right hand,

Clothed with supreme dominion and command,

And having of the Father (all achieved)

The promise of the Holy Ghost received,

He hath poured forth this which ye see and hear.

For David further saith, with meaning clear: 34

" The Lord to my Lord said : " Sit in repose

On my right hand, until I make Thy foes 35

Thy footstool!   Let the house of Israel 36

Be certain, therefore, of the truth I tell—

This Jesus. whom ye lately crucified,

Hath God made Christ and Sovereign Lord beside."

While he was speaking, pricked in heart, there
    spread   _{Acts ii. 37}
Through the vast multitude a solemn dread;
And, at the end, from lips of pallid hue
Arose the cry: "What, brethren, shall we do?"
And Peter said: "Repent, and be baptized   38
In Jesus' name, for thus is symbolized
Remission of offences against Heaven,
So shall the Holy Ghost to you be given.   39
Then were baptized, all who the word believed,
Three thousand being on that day received.

VENI, CREATOR SPIRITUS.— *Translation.*

I.

Creator Spirit, come!
    Thy praying people wait;
Fill with Thyself and make Thy home
    In breasts Thou didst create.

II.

Thou Gift of God above!
    Our Paraclete Thou art—

The Living Fount, the Fire, the Love,
　　The Breath that sets apart.

III.

With sevenfold grace endue:
　　Finger of God here reach:
Thou, Promise of the Father, who
　　Dost throats enrich with speech.

IV.

Kindle a light within:
　　Love in our bosoms pour,   .
Strengthen our weakness, purge our sin,
　　Make steadfast evermore.

V.

The enemy drive far:
　　Give peace to every one:
Be Thou our Leader in the war,
　　That we all ill may shun.

VI.

May we the Father know,
　　And know the Son through Thee,
Believe Thou art of both, and so
　　Forevermore wilt be.

VII.

Let praise to Father, Son,

And Paraclete be said!

And may there be on everyone

The Spirit's charism* shed!

I.

Veni, Creator Spiritus,
Mentes tuorum visita,
Imple superna gratia
Quæ tu creâsti pectora.

II.

Qui Paraclitus diceris,
Altissimi donum Dei,
Fons vivus, ignis, caritas,
Et spiritalis unctio.

III.

Tu septiformis munere,
Dextræ Dei tu digitus,
Tu rite promissum Patris
Sermone ditans guttura.

IV.

Accende lumen sensibus,
Infunde amorem cordibus,
Infirma nostri corporis
Virtute firmans perpete.

V.

Hostem repellas longius,
Pacemque dones protinus,
Ductore sic te prævio
Vitemus omne noxium.

VI.

Per te sciamus, da, Patrem,
Noscamus atque Filium,
Te utriusque Spiritum
Credamus omni tempore.

VII.

Sit laus Patri cum Filio,
Sancto simul Paraclito,
Nobisque mittat Filius,
Charisma Sancto Spiritus.

*Charism (Gr. *charisma*, a gift). A miraculous gift, *e. g.*, as of healing, of tongues, etc.

VENI, CREATOR SPIRITUS.—*Paraphrased.*

I.

Creator Spirit, who didst brood
Above the watery solitude,
And shoot into abysmal night
The blessèd beams of life and light,
Whence worlds on worlds in beauty rose
To fill the void, and at the close
Didst fashion man above the rest
To make a Temple of his breast—
O come, inhabit it once more,
Its pristine purity restore!

II.

Thou, who art called the Paraclete—
Of highest God the Gift most sweet—
The Living Fount that gushes free,
Upspringing to eternity;
The Fire that warms and purifies;
The Love that antedates the skies;

The Unction and the Breath Divine
That consecrate and make us Thine,—.
Come, visit us, come, Holy Ghost!
And let us be Thy honored host.

III.

Sevenfold the gifts Thou dost dispense,
Finger of God's omnipotence!
Before the might Thou dost supply,
The unresisting demons fly,
The sick, by a swift miracle,
Thou makest in a moment well:
The Promise of the Father, sent
To make throats rich and opulent
With the divinity of speech
And power in various tongues to teach.

IV.

Light in our darkened senses dart;
Love shed abroad in every heart;
The frailties of our body aid—
By virtue strengthened and upstayed;
The enemy of souls repel;
Let peace henceforth within us dwell;

Be Thou our Leader and our Guide,
Nor suffer us to turn aside ;
Against our treacherous hearts defend,
And be our Advocate and Friend !

V.

Both from the Father and the Son
Thou dost proceed, for God is One.
Help us to apprehend through Thee
The dearness of the Trinity :
With interceding groans and cries
Let our doxologies arise,
And with a pathos all their own
Plead for us at th' Eternal Throne.
We Father, Son and Thee adore—
The Triune God forevermore.

TEXTUAL INDEX.

OLD TESTAMENT.

Chap.	Verse.	Volume.	Page.	Chap.	Verse.	Volume.	Page.
				xvi.	10	Evangel	141
	GENESIS.			xviii.	21	"	276
				xx.	2-5	"	276
				xxiv.	16	"	67
i.	26	Evangel.	13, 14				
iii	15	"	49		NUMBERS.		
vii.	11-17	"	144				
xi	9-11	L. of W.	284				
xiii.	10	Evangel.	129	vi.	2	Evangel	226-229
xiv.	3-10	"	130, 140		3	"	234
xviii.	2, 22	"	22	xiii.	16	"	65
xix.	24, 25	"	129	xxi.	21, 23	"	250, 259
	30	"	270	xxii.	1, 2-28	"	290, 310
xxii.	18	"	50	xxvii.	8, 10	"	27
xxiii.	19	"	270	xxix.	2-18	"	299-310
xxxii.	1-11	"	258, 259	xxxii.	1-26	"	250
	22, 23	"	262-264				
	24, 30	"	22		DEUTERONOMY.		
xl.	9-11	"	232				
xli.	43	"	82	ii.	12	Evangel	270
xlix.	10	"	50, 57	iii.	3-11	"	250
					4	"	105
	EXODUS.			xviii.	15	"	52
				xxxii.	13, 14	"	259
xii.	8-20	Evangel.	226		14	"	237
xiii.	2, 14-16	"	70, 71		33	"	218, 219
xviii.	13-24	"	292, 293	xxxiii.	1, 2	"	310, 298
xix.		"	298	xxxiv.	1, 5, 10	"	310, 311
xxv.		"	8				
	LEVITICUS.				JOSHUA.		
ii.	11	Evangel.	230	i	1, 5, 9	Evangel.	311
viii.	6-12	"	122, 123	ii.	1-22	"	311-312
xii.	2-8	"	71, 72	iii.	2-16	"	312, 317

24

Chap.	Verse.	Volume.	Page.	Chap.	Verse.	Volume.	Page.
iv.	1-19	Evangel.	317	x.	1, 2	Evangel.	290, 291
v.	1-15	"	315-319	xi.	1-14	"	291, 292
	13-16	"	22	xii.	1, 12, 23	"	291, 292
vi.	1-19	"	319, 321	xiii.	6	"	270
vii.	1-26	"	320-322	xv.	22, 23	"	286
viii.	1	"	322	xvi.	1, 10	"	187, 294
ix.	3-16	"	322	xix.	22	"	187-189
x.	1-43	"	322-328	xxii.	1	"	270
xi.	1-23	"	328-332	xxiii.	25	"	270
xxii.	1-6	"	332, 333	xxiv.	3	"	270
xxiv.	31	"	334				

II SAMUEL.

Chap.	Verse.	Volume.	Page.
i.	17-27	Evangel.	326
ii.	4-17	"	348, 260
iii.	1	"	348
iv.	5-12	"	348
v.	3-9	"	348, 349
vi.	2-15	"	349
vii.	2-13	"	352
xvii.	24	"	260
xviii.	9, 14, 33	"	261, 262

JUDGES.

Chap.	Verse.	Volume.	Page.
ii.	11-21	Evangel.	335, 336
iii.	5, 31	"	336, 337
iv.	1-23	"	337-340
v.	1-31	"	339, 340
	16, 17	"	259
vi.	1-32	"	264-272
	2	"	269
	20	"	326
v-xv.		"	340
viii.	1-28	"	269-272
x.	6-11	"	272, 273
xi.	1-45	"	274-282
xii.	1-16	"	288, 289
xvi.	1, 5, 6	"	343
xvii.	6	"	283
xxi.	25	"	283

I KINGS.

Chap.	Verse.	Volume.	Page.
iv.	33	Evangel	244, 245
viii.	3-39	"	352-355
x.	11, 43	"	356
	31, 33	"	361
xi.	1-43	"	355, 356
xii.	1-32	"	357, 358
xv.	29	"	361
xviii.	4-13	"	270
xix.	14-18	"	358, 359
xxii.	29-37	"	359, 360
xxvii.	6	"	361
xxviii.	1	"	362

RUTH.

Chap.	Verse.	Volume.	Page.
i.	1-21	Evangel.	343-348

I SAMUEL.

II KINGS.

Chap.	Verse.	Volume.	Page.
iv.	3-11	Evangel.	340, 341
v.	1-10	"	341, 342
vi.	1-21	"	342
xii.	1, 2	"	343
ix.	1-15	"	294
xvii.		L. of W.	20

Chap.	Verse.	Volume.	Page.	Chap.	Verse.	Volume.	Page.
I CHRONICLES.				PROVERBS.			
vi.	8-15	Evangel	260	vii.	5	L. of W.	83
				viii.	12	Evangel.	225
II CHRONICLES.					Note.	"	225
					22, 31	"	91, 92
				xx.		"	212-217
xxxvi.	17-19	Evangel.	364	xxiii.	29-35	"	212-218
				xxxiii.	4. 5	"	212-218
JOB.				ECCLESIASTES.			
xxx.	5, 6	Evangel.	270	ii.	4-6	Evangel	244
xxxi.	26-28	"	272	vi.	1, 2	"	381
xl.	23	"	129	SONG OF SOLOMON.			
PSALMS.				i.	2-6	Evangel.	238-248
				ii.	3, 10-16	"	238-248
i.	Trans.	L. of W.	96, 97	iv.	8-16	"	238-241
viii.	3	Evangel.	39, 60	v.	10-19	"	238-248
xxii.	12	"	237	vi	3	"	238-248
xxiii.		"	248, 249	viii.	8	"	238-248
xxiv.	7	"	54	ISAIAH.			
	3-8	"	351				
xxxvii.	12	"	74, 75	ii.	12-13	Evangel.	237
xliii.	1-7	"	262	vii.	14	"	5
li.	Trans.	L. of W.	116, 117	viii.	14	"	74, 75
lv.	15	Evangel.	140	ix.	4-6	"	268, 269
lix.	9	L. of W.	236	xiii.	8	"	189
lv.	6-8	"	260		10	L. of W.	262
lxii.	7-10	Evangel.	165, 167	xxiv.	23	"	262
lxviii.	15, 16	"	236	xxv.	7	Evangel.	74
	22	L. of W.	363	xxviii.	15-18	"	285
lxix	20	"	323	xxx.	33	"	140
lxxii.	12	"	311	xxxiii.	9	"	238
	17	Evangel.	51	xxxiv.	4	L. of W.	260
lxxiii.	11-14	L. of W.	265, 266	xl.	3	Evangel	363, 364
xcvi.	10	"	329	xli.	2	"	79
cv.	27	"	295-298	xliv.	23-28	"	365
cvi.	35-38	"	276	xlv.	1, 7	"	81
cix.	1-5	"	315, 316	xlvi.	2	"	79
cx.	1	Evangel.	51	l.	6	L. of W.	303
cxxxii.	1-8	L. of W.	350, 351	li.	2-11	Evangel.	363
cxxxiii.	1	Evangel.	289, 290	lii.	7	"	366
cxxxvi.		"	252-257	lx.	1, 2, 3	"	76
cxxxvii.	1	"	365				

Chap.	Verse.	Volume.	Page.	Chap.	Verse.	Volume.	Page.
		JEREMIAH.				**MICAH.**	
i.	19	Evangel.	238	v.	2-6	Evangel.	270
vii.	11	"	367		2	"	52
viii.	22	"	238	vi.	6-8	"	286, 287
xxiii.	6	"	51		5-8	"	303
xxix.	10	"	364	iv.	6, 7	L. of W.	5
xxxii.	35	"	276				
xliii.	13	"	82			**NAHUM.**	
xlix.	16	"	270				
				i.	4	Evangel	235
		EZEKIEL.					
						HABAKKUK.	
viii.	16	Evangel.	236				
xxvii.	5, 6	"	237	ii	15	Evangel.	219
xxxiv.	23, 24	"	51				
xxxix	11, 18	"	237, 238			**HAGGAI.**	
xlvii	6, 8	"	132, 138				
				ii.	7	Evangel	51
		DANIEL.			3-9	"	366
ii.	24	L. of W.	5			**ZECHARIAH.**	
vii.	13, 14	"	5				
ix.	25	"	5	vi.	12, 13	Evangel.	51
	24-27	Evangel.	51	xi.	12	L. of W.	278
		OBADIAH.				**MALACHI.**	
i.	3, 4	Evangel.	270				
				iv.	5, 6	Evangel	112
		JONAH.			5, 6	"	171
ii.	2-6	Evangel.	124, 125				

NEW TESTAMENT.

Chap.	Verse.	Volume.	Page.	Chap.	Verse.	Volume.	Page.
		MATTHEW.			3-12	L. of W.	100, 103
					58	"	34
					55	Evangel.	102, 103
i.	1-17	Evangel.	26-28	xiv.	3-12	L. of W.	100, 103
	18-25	"	42, 43		1	"	308
	21	"	65-69		6-10	Evangel	283
ii.	1-23	"	77-90		13-36	L. of W.	149-153
iii.	1-12	"	104-119	xv.	1-38	"	159-164
	13-17	"	120-141	xvi.	15, 19	Evangel.	177-181
	12	L. of W.	8		13-23	L. of W.	66, 167
iv.	1-11	Evangel.	142-169	xvii.	1-21	"	167, 170
	12-16	"	234-240	xviii.	1-35	"	172, 175
	13-22	L. of W.	38-43		8, Note.	"	162
	17	"	30		18	Evangel.	179, 181
v.	1-48	"	75-87	xix.	13-30	L. of W.	225-228
	33, 37	Evangel.	284, 285	xx.	1-16	"	228-230
vi.	5-15	"	372-385		17-34	"	231-233
	1-34	L. of W.	87-92		28	Evangel.	101, 102
vii.	23	Evangel.	120-125	xxi.	1-17	L. of W.	237-240
	1-29	L. of W.	92-96		28-46	"	242-244
viii.	29	Evangel.	187-191		29-32	Evangel.	109
	1, 5-13	L. of W.	98, 99	xxii.	41-45	"	51
	14-17	"	44-50		15-46	L. of W.	245-247
	2-4	"	50, 51	xxiii.	1-39	"	248-254
	18-34	"	135-139		35	Evangel.	83
ix.	2-8	"	51-55	xxiv.	1-51	L. of W.	256-267
	9-17	"	55-60		34, Note	"	209
	1, 18-35	"	139-149	xxv.	1-46	"	267-272
x.	1, 5-39	"	143-149		12, Note	Evangel.	120, 121
	34-36	Evangel.	75	xxvi.	1-29	L. of W.	276-284
xi.	1	L. of W.	149		17-29	Evangel.	226-228
	2-19	"	103-109		30-75	L. of W.	295-303
	25-27	Evangel.	92, 93		53	Evangel.	277, 278
	27	"	121-125	xxvii.	1-30	L. of W.	310-316
xii.	1-21	L. of W.	69, 72		31-66	"	317-327
	24-50	"	118-124		3	Evangel.	109
	46-50	Evangel.	197, 198	xxviii.	1-20	L. of W.	331-351
	Note.	"	186		19	"	
xiii.	1-52	L. of W.	128-134		18-20	Evangel.	166, 118

MARK.

Chap.	Verse.	Volume.	Page.
i.	1-8	Evangel.	104, 119
	12, 13	"	142-169
	35	"	236
	38	L. of W.	30
	16-20	"	39-43
	21-45	"	44-51
ii.	1-12	Evangel.	369-371
	16, 17	"	214
	27, 28	"	292, 293
	1-12	L. of W.	51-53
	13-28	"	55-70
iii.	31-35	Evangel.	195, 197
	Note.	,,	186
	1-12	L. of W.	70-72
	13-19	"	75
	19-35	"	118-124
iv.	1-32	"	128-132
	35-41	L. of W.	135, 136
v.	20-43	"	136-142
	3	Evangel.	270
vi.	6-13	L. of W.	143, 144
	21-27	"	100-103
	30-56	"	149-153
vii.	1-37	"	159-163
viii.	1-10	"	163, 164
	27-30	"	165, 166
ix.	2-29	"	167-170
	30, 33-50	"	172, 173
	49	"	78
x.	1	"	211
	13-52	"	225-233
xi.	1-33	"	238-242
xii.	1-44	"	242-254
xiii.	1-37	"	256-267
xiv.	1-25	"	276-284
	26-72	"	295-304
xv.	1-19	"	306-317
	20-47	"	317-327
xvi.	1-20	"	331-351
	15	"	6

LUKE.

Chap.	Verse.	Volume.	Page.
i.	5-25	Evangel.	29-35
	26-56	"	35-42
	57-80	"	44-48
	31	"	65-69
	15, N.	"	230
ii.	1-7	"	55-58
	8-20	"	58-62
	21	"	65-69
	22-29	"	71-76
	52	"	91-93
	41-51	"	94-103
	42, N.	"	2
iii.	1-18	"	104-119
	23-38	"	26-28
	23	"	140, 141
iv.	1-13	"	142-169
	15	L. of W.	30-36
	31-44	"	44-50
v.	1-11	"	43
	12-26	"	50-53
	27-39	"	55-60
vi.	1-11	"	69, 70
	12-49	"	75-96
vii.	24, 25	"	47, 48
	1-17	"	98-100
	18-35	"	103-109
	36-50	"	109-115
viii.	19-21	Evangel.	195-198
	Note.	"	186
	1-3	L. of W.	114-118
	3	"	308
	4-15	"	128, 130
	19-21	"	124
	22-56	"	135-142
ix.	23	Evangel.	216
	1-6	L. of W.	143-144
	6	"	149
	10-17	"	149-151
	28-62	"	167-176
x.	13	Evangel.	161-164
	21-23	"	92-93
	15	"	244

Chap.	Verse.	Volume.	Page.
	1, 17-20	L. of W.	175, 176
	25-42	"	182-185
xi.	27, 28	Evangel.	195-198
	Note.	"	186
	13	L. of W.	8
	14-36	"	118
	27	"	124
xii.	1	"	124, 125
	13-21	"	125
xiii.	32	Evangel.	105
	25-27, N.	"	120-123
	1-9	L. of W.	126, 127
	22-35	"	211, 212
xiv.	5-24	"	212-214
xv.	1-32	"	214-218
xvi.	1-31	"	220-223
xvii.	20, 21	"	6
	12-18	"	176, 177
xviii.	16, 17	Evangel.	92, 93
	1-8	L. of W.	224, 225
	15-30	"	231-233
xix.	46	Evangel.	367
	1-44	L. of W.	233-240
xx.	20-47	"	245-248
xxi.	20, N.	Evangel.	
	1-36	L. of W.	254-257
xxii.	31, 32, 40	Evangel.	218
	7-20	"	226
	1-20	L. of W.	276-284
	39-71	"	295-304
xxiii.	1-19	"	305-309
	33-56	"	317-327
xxiv.	1-53	"	331-356

JOHN.

Chap.	Verse.	Volume.	Page.
i.	1-18	Evangel.	13-18
	17	"	92, 93
	31-34	"	120-141
	19-51	"	170-184
	11	"	235
	13	L. of W.	7
ii.	1-11	"	185-234
	12	"	235
	17	Evangel.	366
	13-21	"	367-369
	23-25	L. of W.	1, 2
	8	"	208
iii.	3	Evangel	21
	16	"	18
	1-21	L. of W.	3-10
	3-6	"	206
	22-36	"	14-16
iv.	14	"	8
	1-42	"	19-27
	21-23	"	27, 28
	43-54	"	29, 30
v.	15-21	"	149-153
	32	"	207
	19	Evangel.	209
	1	L. of W.	2
	1-47	"	60-68
vi.	42	Evangel.	21
	5-21	L. of W.	150, 151
	22-69	"	153-157
	39, 40	"	207
vii.	5, 13	Evangel.	236
	1	L. of W.	2
	8-52	"	177-179
viii.	37	Evangel.	75
	58, N.	L. of W.	258
	1-59	"	179-181
ix.	1-41	"	185-189
x.	1-42	"	189-193
xi.	1, 38	Evangel.	372
	1-46	L. of W.	194-198
	20-25	"	199
	47-54	"	210, 211
xii.	20	"	254-256
	2	"	276
	1, 10-19	"	237-239
xiii.	1-38	"	278-283
xiv.	30	Evangel.	52
	26	"	213
	1-31	L. of W.	284-291
	2	"	209
xv.	1-27	"	284-287
xvi.	1-33	"	287-291
xvii.	1-26	"	291-293
	25	"	199

Chap.	Verse.	Volume.	Page.	Chap.	Verse.	Volume.	Page.
		ACTS.				II CORINTHIANS.	
i.	3-8	L. of W.	355, 356				
	15	"	359	v.	21	L. of W.	9
ii.	1-39	"	359-363		1, 3	"	205, 203
	37, 38	Evangel.	179-181	vii.	10	Evangel.	108
iii.	19	"	179-181				
iv.	11, 12	"	179-181			GALATIANS.	
vi.	1-3	"	292, 293				
vii.	45, 54	"	64-95	iii.	28	L. of W.	7
viii.	9-11	"	78	iv.	4, 6	Evangel.	49, 64
x.	38	"	122, 123		6-19	"	186
	34	L. of W.	7				
xi.	1	Evangel.	283			EPHESIANS·	
xiii.	6, 8	"	66, 78				
	33	"	122, 123	i.	5, 8	Evangel.	225
	1	L. of W.	308	ii.	50	"	178, 181
xvi.	24-28	"	27, 28		1-5	L. of W.	1, 68
xx.	21	"	179, 181	v.	8-10	Evangel.	78, 125
					26	"	8
		ROMANS.					
						PHILIPPIANS.	
i.	25	Evangel.	66				
ii.	5	"	107	ii.	6	Evangel.	63, 101
	4	L. of W.	113		9	L. of W.	68
vii.	13	"	113	iii.	20	"	7
viii.	19. 23, 32	"	208		21	"	202, 285
ix.	4, 5	Evangel.	23		10, 11	"	207
	5	"	234	iv.	1	"	26
x.	4	"	52				
	12	L. of W.	7			COLOSSIANS.	
xi.	29	Evangel.	108				
xv.	1	"	222	i.	15, 16	Evangel.	63
				ii.	13	L. of W.	7, 68
		I. CORINTHIANS.		iii.	3	"	201
				iv.	5, 6	"	78
ii.	9	L. of W.	9		11	"	66
iii.	11, 21, 22	Evangel.	178, 179				
v.	6-8	"	227				
	7	"	236				
vi.	10	"	225				
xi.	23	L. of W.	284				
xv.	5	"	339				
	6, 7	"	354, 355				
	36-52	"	203, 204				

Chap.	Verse.	Volume.	Page.		Chap.	Verse.	Volume.	Page.

I THESSALONIANS.

Chap.	Verse.	Volume.	Page.
ii.	19, 20	L. of W.	26
v.	6-8	Evangel.	223, 224
	23	L. of W,	198

II THESSALONIANS.

Chap.	Verse.	Volume.	Page.
ii.	8	Evangel	89

I TIMOTHY.

Chap.	Verse.	Volume.	Page.
ii.	14	Evangel.	50
iii.	2, 3	"	220-222
iv.	7	"	103
vi.	14	"	89
	20	"	19

II TIMOTHY.

Chap.	Verse.	Volume.	Page.
i.	10	Evangel.	89
ii.	17, 18	"	19
iv	1, 8	"	89
	3, 4	"	103

TITUS.

Chap.	Verse.	Volume.	Page.
ii.	13	Evangel.	90
iii.	5	L. of W.	8

HEBREWS.

Chap.	Verse.	Volume.	Page.
i.	4, 6	Evangel	63
	5, 6	"	122, 123
iv.	8	"	65
v.	5	"	122, 123
	5-10	"	120-141
vii.	14	"	56
	21	"	109
	21-27	"	52, 53
	25	"	197
x.	1-7	"	53, 54
xii.	3	"	75
	29	"	119
xiii.	8	"	197

JAMES.

Chap.	Verse.	Volume.	Page.
i.	17	Evangel	197
v.	20	L. of W.	78

I PETER.

Chap.	Verse.	Volume.	Page.
i.	23	L. of W.	5
	23	"	8
ii.	4, 5	Evangel.	177
	6	"	74, 75
	21	L. of W.	354
v.	8, 9	Evangel.	213
	8, 9	"	224, 225

II PETER

Chap.	Verse.	Volume.	Page.
ii.	1	Evangel	73

Chap.	Verse.	Volume.	Page.	Chap.	Verse.	Volume.	Page.
		I JOHN.				REVELATION.	
i.	1	Evangel.	19				
	1-6	"	16-18				
ii.	1	"	72	i.	8	Evangel.	92, 93
iii.	8	"	161-165		18	L. of W.	206
iv.	2-3	"	19	iii.	14	"	5
	16	"	18		20	"	34
v.	1	L. of W.	8	vii.	15	"	201
	6-9	Evangel.	119-141	xi.	15	"	165-167
	6-9	"	125	xxii.	15	"	66
	7	"	332				

L ATIN HYMNS WITH ORIGINAL TRANSLA-
TIONS. By ABRAHAM COLES, M. D., LL. D.
D. Appleton & Company, New York.

In Four Parts, viz.:

1—DIES IRÆ, IN THIRTEEN ORIGINAL VERSIONS. Fifth
Edition. pp. 110.

2—STABAT MATER (dolorosa). Second Edition. pp. 37.

3—STABAT MATER (speciosa). pp. 25.

4—OLD GEMS IN NEW SETTINGS. Being additional se-
lections from Mediæval Hymnology. pp. 77.

All bound together, with Biographical and Critical
Prefaces, Illustrations, etc. Crown 8vo., pp. 249.

By the Same Author,

THE MICROCOSM AND OTHER POEMS. Beautifully Illustrated. Crown 8vo., pp. 348. $2.50.

Also,

THE LIFE AND TEACHINGS OF OUR LORD,
IN VERSE. Being a complete Harmonized Expo-
sition of the Four Gospels, with Original Notes, etc.
In Two Volumes, viz.:

Vol. I., THE EVANGEL (pp. 405); Illustrated with
28 full-page "Artotype" copies of costly first-
class Engravings. Crown 8vo. $5.00.

Vol. II., THE LIGHT OF THE WORLD (pp. 395),
Illustrated with a full-page "Artotype" copy
of Munkacsy's celebrated picture of "Christ
Before Pilate." Crown 8vo. $2.50.

THE SAME, Two Volumes in One. Illustrated with Munkacsy's "Christ Before Pilate." Crown 8vo., pp.
405 + 395 = pp. 800. $2.50.

NOTICES OF THE PRESS.

" We commend the volume (DIES IRÆ, *In Thirteen Original Ver-sions*) as one of great interest, and an admirable tribute from American scholarship and poetic taste to the supreme nobility of the original poem. Dr. Coles has shown a fine appreciation of the spirit and rhythmic movement of the Hymn, as well as unusual command of language and rhyme ; and we much doubt whether any translation of the *Dies Iræ*, better than the first of the thirteen, will ever be produced in English, except perhaps by himself. . . . As to the translation of the Hymn, it is perhaps the most difficult task that could be undertaken. To render *Faust* or the *Songs of Egmont* into fitting English numbers, would be easy in comparison.—*Richard Grant White (The Albion).*

" The book is a gem both typographically and intrinsically ; beautifully printed at the ' Riverside Press,' in the loveliest antique type, on tinted paper, with liberal margins, embellished with exquisite photographs of the great masterpieces of Christian Art, and withal elegantly and solidly bound in Matthew's best style, a gentleman-like book, suggestive of Christmas and the centre-table ; and its contents worthy of their dainty envelope, amply entitling it as well to a place on the shelves of the scholar. . . . . The first two of the Thirteen Versions of the *Dies Iræ* appeared in the ' Newark Daily Advertiser' as long ago as 1847. They were extensively copied by the press, and warmly commended—particularly by the Rev. Drs. James W. Alexander and W. R. Williams, scholars whose critical acumen and literary ability are universally recognized—as being the best of the English versions in double rhyme ; and examples of singular success in a difficult undertaking, in which many, and of eminent name, had been competitors. The eleven other versions are worthy companions of those which have received such eminent endorsement. Indeed, we are not sure but that the last, which is in the same measure as Crashaw's, but in our judgment far superior, will please the general taste most of all."—*Rev. S. I. Prime, D. D. (New York Observer).*

" There are few versions of the Hymn which will bear to be compared with these ; we are surprised that they are all so well done." *William C. Bryant (N. Y. Evening Post).*

" Dr. Coles has made, we think, the most successful attempt at an English translation of the hymn that we have ever seen. . . . He has done so well that we hope he will try his hand on some of the other Latin Hymns. By rendering them in their own metres, and with so large a transfusion of their spirit as characterizes his present attempt, he will be doing a real service to the lovers of that kind of religious poetry in which neither the religion nor the poetry is left out. He has shown that he knows the worth of faithfulness."—*James Russell Lowell* (*Atlantic Monthly*).

"Of Dr. Coles' remarkable success as respects these particulars (namely, faithfulness and variety), no one competent to judge can doubt....For all that enters into a good translation, fidelity to the sense of the original, uniform conformity to its tenses, preservation of its metrical form without awkwardly inverting, inelegantly abbreviating, or violently straining the sense of the words, and the reproduction of its vital spirit—for all these qualities Dr. Coles' first translation stands, we believe, not only unsurpassed, but unequalled in the English language."—*Christian* (*Quarterly*) *Review*.

"Dr. A. Coles has long been known to the literary world as specially successful in the translation of Latin Hymns. His renderings of the *Dies Iræ* are familiar to many readers. He has now also prepared a book entitled *Old Gems in New Settings*, an exquisite volume, in which we find the *De Contemptu Mundi*, the *Veni Sancte Spiritus*, and other fine old favorites skillfully and gracefully translated. The grand hymn or poem of Bernard de Clugny, of which the extracts in this book are styled *Urbs Cælestis Syon*, is rendered in a style very nearly resembling the original, and gives the reader, who does not understand Latin, an excellent idea of the peculiar characteristics of the hymn of Bernard. Besides these, we have the *Stabat Mater*, with a complete history of the noble hymn, and a very fine translation. The lovers of old hymns owe a special debt of gratitude to Dr. Coles for the good taste and the thorough appreciation and ability which he brings to the work of placing these glorious old songs within reach of the modern world. We could wish them to become favorites in every family, and they will so become in spite of their Latin origin." —*William C. Prime* (*Journal of Commerce*).

"United with a rare command of language and facility of versification, this is the secret of the eminent success with which the Translator has reproduced the solemn litany of the Middle Ages in such a variety of forms. If not all of equal excellence, it is hard to decide as to their respective merits, so admirably do they embody the tone and sentiment of the original in vigorous and impressive verse. The essays which precede and follow the Hymn, exhibit the learning and the taste of the translator in a most favorable light, and show that an antiquary and a poet have not been lost in the study of science and the practice of a laborious profession. In addition to the Thirteen Versions of *Dies Iræ*, the volume contains translations of the *Stabat Mater*, *Urbs Cælestis Syon*, *Veni Creator Spiritus*, and other choice mediæval hymns which have been executed with equal unction and felicity.

"We have also a poem by the same author, entitled *The Microcosm*, read before the Medical Society of New Jersey at its Centenary anniversary. It is an ingenious attempt to present the principles of the animal economy in a philosophical poem, somewhat after the manner of Lucretius, and combining scientific analysis with religious senti- ment. In ordinary hands, we should not regard this as a happy, nor a safe experiment, but the dexterity with which it has been managed by Dr. Coles, illustrates his versatile talent as well as the originality of his conceptions."—*George Ripley* (*New York Tribune*).

" Dr. Coles has been too long away from a public which has already shown itself kindly to him, and we thank him, especially, for this book of his own (*The Microcosm*). . . Why should not the wonderful make of man—the might and cunning skill that are moulded in him— furnish a very choice theme for poetry ? Dr. Coles, accustomed, by his profession, to search among and study out these marvels, knowing how they are grouped together, what work they do, and how they are fitted for it, believes that here is one of the very noblest themes for such use, hitherto strangely left alone. This therefore is the occasion of his writing *The Microcosm*. . The Eustachian Tube, and Cerebellum and Œsophagus, made into poetry, must have astonished the well- informed Medical Faculty of New Jersey, much as a farmer's smoke- house and pig-sty and shed would astonish him, if made into a picture. And Dr. Coles has really made them into poetry....Tissue and organ, and channel, and duct are very skillfully and beautifully described, and made to witness to God's goodness : the skin, the nerves, the flesh, the heart, the eye, the tongue, the ear, the seeing, hearing, speech, light, tears, sleep, music, the blind, the dumb, the living mind. Whatever in man is good, and strong, and fine, and beautiful, finds place in Dr. Coles' Poem, and is so set forth that the man of science and the man who can read and feel the force of good thoughts and tuneful words, and knows nothing of anatomy and physiology, beside the cheapest axioms of food and sleep, may alike enjoy the reading. Whoever has only grovelling notions of man's nature, and knows the body only as an instrument of low pleasure and a vehicle of pain and punishment, would here learn something better of himself and worthier of the answer which he, like holier men, must make, at last. Not that all is preaching. The book is, indeed, written by a Christian man, to whom his faith in his Redeemer and relationship to God are dearer than all other things ; but the blush of maiden-love and the conscious glance of the eye ; the deep mother's love for the infant nestling in the bosom, and nursing at the breast ; the hallowed happiness of two made one, in Christ ; all these glow in his pages, with an attractive beauty beyond the common. All that imaginative and eloquent account of the brain and its great faculty, we would take, whole, if we could....If high thoughts, in glowing words, be noble, is not this which we have just read ?....One meets, continually, in this poem, such passages as the following ; and one such, even, would show the fine skill and glowing power of the writer.

" The second book whose title stands at the head of this article— the *Stabat Mater*—is a translation with very interesting comments.... Like most poets, the author of *The Microcosm* writes prose beautifully, and the reader will never find, in the prose of these volumes, anything but what is interesting. In the poem and remarks which accompany the *Stabat Mater* is the utmost justness of criticism, fullness of information, and gracefulness of expression. If as much can be learned, elsewhere, of the origin and character, and history of that hymn, we may safely say that it can nowhere be learned so pleasantly. These parts of the book, like the corresponding parts of the book on the *Dies Iræ*, we hold to be especially valuable."—*Rev. Robert Lowell, D. D. (The Church Monthly).*

"Dr. Coles has supplied a want and done a graceful work in *The Microcosm*. What the flower or babbling stream is to Wordsworth, that is the stranger, more complex, and more beautiful human frame to our author. In its organs, its powers, its aspirations, and its passions, he finds ample theme for song... Everywhere the rhythm is flowing and easy, and no scholarly man can peruse the work without a glance of wonder at the varied erudition, classical, poetical, and learned, that crowds its pages, and overflows in foot-notes. And through the whole is a devout religious tone and a purity of purpose worthy of all praise."—*Newark Daily Advertiser.*

"Dr. Coles' researches, made so lovingly and conscientiously in his special field of poetical scholarship, have given him a distinct and most enviable position among American authors. We of the younger sort learn a lesson of reverent humility from the pure enthusiasm with which he approaches and handles his noble themes. The 'tone' of all his works is perfect. He is so thoroughly in sympathy with his subjects that the lay reader instantly shares his feeling ; and there is a kind of 'white light' pervading the whole—prose and verse— which at any time tranquilizes and purifies the mind."—*Edmund C. Stedman.*

"I have finished the reading of *The Microcosm*, which has afforded me unmingled delight. It is really a remarkable poem, and has passages of great beauty and power. It cannot fail to secure the admiration of all capable of appreciating it. Its ease, its exquisite finish, its vivid yet delicate and powerful imagery, and above all its sublime religious interest, entitle it to a very high place in our literature."— *Rev. Robert Turnbull, D. D.*

"The idea of *The Microcosm* is novel and daring, but it is worked out with great skill and delicacy. *The Evangel* is a work of piety and beauty. The Proem opens with strong, vigorous yet melodious verse."—*John G. Whittier.*

"*The Evangel in Verse*, is the ripest fruit of the scholarship, taste and poetic talent of one of our accomplished students of English verse, whose translations of *Dies Iræ* and other poems have made the name of Dr. Coles familiar in the literature of our day. In the work before us he has attempted something higher and better than any former essay of his skillful pen. He has rendered the Gospel story of our Lord and Saviour into verse, with copious notes, giving the largest amount of knowledge from critical authorities to justify and explain the readings and to illuminate the sacred narrative. . . . He excludes everything fictitious, and clings to the orthodox view of the character and mission of the God-man. The illustrations are a complete pictorial anthology. Thus the poet, critic, commentator and artist has made a volume that will take its place among the rare productions of the age, as an illustration of the genius, taste, and fertile scholarship of the author."—*Rev. S. Irenæus Prime, D. D. (The New York Observer)*.

" The purpose of this volume would be usually regarded as beyond the scope of poetic composition. It aims to reproduce the scenes of the Gospel History in verse, with a strict adherence to the sacred narrative and no greater degree of imaginative coloring than would serve to present the facts in the most brilliant and impressive light. But the subject is one with which the author cherishes so profound a sympathy, as in some sense to justify the boldness of the attempt. The Oriental cast of his mind allures him to the haunts of sacred song, and produces a vital communion with the spirit of Hebrew poetry. Had he lived in the days of Isaiah or Jeremiah, he might have been one of the bards who sought inspiration 'at Siloa's brook that flowed fast by the oracle of God.' The present work is not the first fruits of his religious Muse, but he is already known to the lovers of mediæval literature by his admirable translations of the *Dies Iræ*. . . . . The volume is brought out in a style of unusual elegance, as it respects the essential requisites of paper, print and binding, while the copious illustrations will attract notice by their selection of the most celebrated works of the best masters."—*George Ripley (The New York Tribune)*.

" *The Evangel in Verse* is a feast to the eye and ear and heart. The careful exegesis, the conscientious loyalty to the statements of the Holy Story, the sympathetic reproduction of a remote and Oriental past, the sacred insight into the meaning of the Peerless Career, the homageful yet manly, unsuperstitious reverence, the rhythm as melodious as stately, the frequent notes, opulent in learning and doctrine and devotion, the illustrations deftly culled from whatever is choice in ancient and modern art, these are some of the many excellencies which give to *The Evangel in Verse* an immortal beauty and worth, adding it as another coronet for Him on whose brow are many diadems."—*Rev. Geo. D. Boardman, D. D.*

" I admire the skill which *The Evangel* displays in investing with rainbow hues the simple narrations of the Gospels. All, however, who have read Dr. Coles' versions of the *Dies Iræ* and other Latin Hymns must be prepared to receive any new productions from his pen with high expectations. In these days when even the clerical office seems in many cases insufficient to protect from the present fashionable form of scepticism, it is a great satisfaction to see a man of science and a scholar adhering so faithfully to the simple Gospel." —*Rev. Charles Hodge, D. D., LL. D.*

" Dr. Coles is plainly a man of a very religious heart and a deeply reverential mind. . . . Moreover he has so much learning in his favorite subject, and so much critical instinct and experience, that those who can relish honest thinking, and tender and most skillful and true deductions, accept his teaching and suggestion with a ready —sometimes surprised—sympathy and confidence. Add to all this, that he has the sure taste of a poet, and the warm and loving earnest-ness of a true believer in the redeeming Son of God, and the catho-lic spirit of one who knows with mind and heart that Christianity at its beginning was Christianity, and we have the man who can write such books as earnest Christian people will welcome and be thankful for. . . . . In this new book he proposes ' that *The Evangel* shall be a poetic version, and verse by verse paraphrase, so far as it goes, of the Four Gospels, anciently and properly regarded as one.' He makes an exquisite plea, in his preface, for giving leave to the glad words to rejoice at the Lord's coming in the Flesh, for which all other beings and things show their happiness. . . . . In the notes the reader will find (if he have skill for such things) a treasure-house, in which everything is worthy of its place. Where he has offered new interpretations, or set forth at large interpretations not generally re-ceived or familiar, he modestly asks only to have place given him, and gives every one free leave to differ. Everywhere there is the largest and most true-hearted charity. . . . The reader cannot open anywhere without finding in these notes, if he be not wiser or more learned than ourselves, a great deal that he never saw, or never saw so well set forth before."—*Rev. Robert Lowell, D. D. (Church Monthly)*.

" There is a kind of straightforward simplicity about the poetical paraphrases which reminds one of the homelier but still always inter-esting verses which John Bunyan sprinkles like drops of heavenly dew along the pages of the Pilgrim's Progress. The illustrations add much to the work, in the way of ornament, and aid to the imag-ination. One among them is of terrible power, as it seems to me, such as it would be hard to show the equal of in the work of any modern artist. I mean Holman Hunt's 'Scapegoat.' There is a whole Theology in that picture. It haunts me with its fearful sugges-tiveness like a nightmare. I find *The Evangel* an impressive and charming book. It does not provoke criticism—it is too devout, too sincere, too thoroughly conscientious in its elaboration to allow of fault-finding or fault-hunting."—*Dr. Oliver Wendell Holmes.*

" I have read a considerable part of *The Evangel* and with pleasure and satisfaction. The versification of the Lord's Prayer is both an expansion of the sense and a commentary. The thought has often occurred to me what a world of meaning is there wrapped up, and that meaning is admirably brought out."—*William C. Bryant.*

"The skill of Dr. Coles as an artistic poet, his reverent, religious spirit, and the exalted flight of his Muse in the regions of holy meditation are familiar to our readers. It is, therefore, superfluous for us to do more than to announce a new and elegant volume from his pen—*The Microcosm and Other Poems*. It is rich in its contents. The Microcosm is an essay in verse on the Science of the Human Body; it is literally the science of physiology condensed into 1,400 lines. The many occasional poems that follow are the efflorescence of a mind sensitive to the Beautiful and rejoicing in the True; finding God in everything, and delighting to trace the Revelation of His Love in all the works of His hand. Such a volume is not to be looked at for a moment and then laid aside. Like the great epics, it is a book for all time, and will lose none of its interest and value by the lapse of years. The publishers have given it a splendid dress, and the illustrations add greatly to the attractions of this truly elegant book."—*New York Observer*.

"The flavor of the book—*The Microcosm and Other Poems*—is most quaint, suggesting, on the religious side, George Herbert, and on the naturalistic side, the elder Darwin, who, in "The Botanic Garden," laid the seed of the revolution in science accomplished by the patient genius of his grandson. Some of the hymns for children are beautiful in their simplicity and truth."—*New York Times*.

"The long poem, *The Microcosm*, which gives its name to the present collection, has many beautiful and stately passages. Among the shorter pieces following it, is to be found some of the best devotional and patriotic poetry that has been written in this country."—*The Critic*.

"In this exquisite and brilliantly illustrated volume, the scholarly author has gathered up various children of his pen and grouped them in family unity. The Microcosm, which forms one-fifth of the volume of 350 pages, is an attempt to present, in poetical form, a compendium of the Science of the Human Body. In originality of conception and felicity of expression, it has not been approached by any work of our best modern poets. The other poems are all marked by the highest poetic taste, having passages of great beauty and power."—*Frank Leslie's Illustrated Newspaper*.

"The title-poem in this exquisitely printed and charmingly illustrated volume—*The Microcosm and Other Poems*—has been for some time before the public, and has received generous commendation for the tact and skill evinced in handling a very unpromising theme. A poetic description, minute and thorough going of the human body was a serious undertaking; but Dr. Coles delights in what is difficult and hazardous. He had already associated his name forever with the mediæval Latin Hymn, *Dies Iræ*, by publishing no less than thirteen distinct versions of it. In the volume before us he gives us three more versions. The other poems will not detract from the author's previous reputation."—*Examiner and Chronicle*.